Endorsements for *Another Country*

From the United States and Europe, to Africa, Latin America and Asia, activists and scholars alike are advancing powerful cases for the urgency of radical redress. *Another Country* is a compelling and original addition to this canon. With impressive clarity and forceful logic, Swartz argues in favor of 'social restitution', a holistic and inclusive process of 'making good' for the injustices of the past, reaching beyond purely financial or legal remedies, and beyond the restrictive cast of perpetrator or victim. This thoughtful and well-researched book is relevant to a wide audience looking for feasible strategies for moving forward better.

– Professor Jacqueline Bhabha, Professor of the Practice of Health and Human Rights, Harvard University

This is a profound book dealing with race in a new way. It questions conventional notions of restorative justice and critically examines some of the current claims of Black Consciousness.

– Professor Ben Turok, former South African member of Parliament, author of *With My Head Above the Parapet*

The dormant volcano built upon South Africa's twenty-two years of 'supposed democracy', fraught with entrenched racism and socioeconomic inequalities, has finally erupted, and South Africans are at crossroads. Swartz offers a timely, robust, uncomfortable, yet necessary dialogue for White South Africans. Read *Another Country* if you are tired of being tired, if you are interested in moving the country forward, for the benefit of all. Poignant, inconvenient and damning. No reconciliation without restitution is the leitmotif.

– Paballo Chauke, Commonwealth Scholar, University of Oxford

Another Country is a sobering exposition of how South Africans can begin to change its sociopolitical positioning. By dovetailing the experiences and beliefs of South Africans with her own personal journey towards achieving social restitution, Swartz has provided an in-depth look into how South Africa can be rehumanised.

– Kgotsi Chikane, South Africa-Washington International Programme alumnus, University of Oxford Chevening scholar

Another Country offers a vision, through critical self-reflection, dialogue and action, for a socially transformed South Africa. It provides a helpful vocabulary for readers to locate themselves in the past, present and future as they make sense of the complexity of racial injustice. It strongly asserts that we have a moral obligation to repair harm done to our personhood, and suggests concrete everyday actions to rehabilitate and restore our humanity. Read, reflect, dialogue, and do!

> – Anye Nyamnjoh, Graduate student, University of Cape Town

Our failure to achieve our post-Apartheid dreams haunts us. We have attained neither reconciliation nor socioeconomic justice. In this honest and profoundly thoughtful study Swartz offers a concept of social restitution as a tool accessible to all of us. We can learn through engagement across all our divisions to find ways of restoring dignity, providing practical and financial mechanisms of redress, and addressing the burdens of memory and pain. She reminds us 'The best time to plant a tree is 20 years ago; the next-best time is today'.

> – Dr Mary Burton, Black Sash, TRC Commissioner

Swartz's brilliant research explores the possibilities of restitution for a new or 'another country'. She weaves indepth interviews with two simple parables—producing convincing possibilities for new beginnings—with dignity for all, despite obstacles and resistance. If there is a will to admit complicity and privilege, *Another Country*, with its concluding practical applications, can be a profound means of restorative justice and racial reconciliation in South Africa and elsewhere.

> – Professor Dean Borgman, Gordon Conwell Theological

Can South Africa right the wrongs of the past? Can a divided society find common ground? Another Country marshals social science insights in the noble quest for a more peaceful, prosperous, and inclusive South Africa. It provides an optimistic, but realistic, starting point for a fresh conversation about where the country has been and where it might go. Impressive!

> – Professor Evan S. Lieberman, Total Professor of Political Science and
> Contemporary Africa, Massachusetts Institute of Technology

Race can be a divisive and emotional issue, especially in South Africa with its recent history of Apartheid where it is easy for Whites who benefited to feel defensive. Swartz has addressed these issues with insight and humanity and calls for personal commitment to contribute to redress and social justice. This beautiful piece of work made me think, question myself and inspired belief that maybe we can find a way out.

– Professor Robert Morrell, author of Changing Men in Southern

---

Swartz's *Another Country* serves as a strong antidote for our current paralysis, and clears the fog that gets in the way of honest engagement with our past. A practical and conceptual guide for taking the steps towards building a more just country.

– Marlyn Faure, Graduate student, University of Cape Town

In a world where silence and apathy are no longer options, *Another Country* is a book to live and learn by. We are shown how privilege, discrimination and inequality shape the daily lives of South Africans in insidious and devastating ways. In connecting our past with our present Swartz enlightens a future that must be achieved if we believe in a better and truly equal South Africa.

– Parusha Naidoo, Institute for Justice and Reconciliation

The last twenty years in South Africa have squeezed the life out of the term reconciliation such that it doesn't have much to offer South Africa anymore. Another Country offers new possibilities for a more sustained South African miracle that deals with the spirit of Apartheid that still infects our country. Swartz writes from a deeply informed theoretical understanding along with a life where she applies her own advice.

– Craig Stewart, CEO The Warehouse

Swartz's conceptions of restitution as messy and provocative, the weaving of multiple perspectives into a reflexive examination of how we got here, what it means, and her development of the various positionalities we can occupy are all innovative and important.

– Emma Arogundade, Graduate student, University of Cape Town

Swartz has dug deep into the minds of a cross section of South Africans and uncovered their thoughts about our Apartheid past, and about where we are now. She discusses clearly, in simple language, the need for White South Africans to make individual and collective restitution to overcome the tragic legacy of

Apartheid. The book should also be read by those holding elected office.

– Denis Goldberg, author of *A Life For Freedom*, Rivonia trialist

The poignant legacy of Apartheid remains evident in the inequality, racism, and uncertainty about how to heal South Africa. Through vivid interviews, Swartz brilliantly explores anxieties and hopes and offers richly insightful proposals for what 'restitution' could mean for all South Africa's citizens.

– Professor Helen Haste, Visiting Professor of Education, Harvard University

Genuine original thinking is combined here with comprehensive knowledge and research, as well as Swartz's special brand of humanity. This is a call to action wherever injustice has occurred.

– Dr Sarah Pickard, Contemporary British Studies, Université Sorbonne Nouvelle

Another Country speaks directly into our current moment, a moment of immense privilege and gross injustice. The student movement of the past year has placed a mirror in front of White South Africans and forced us to confront our privilege in ways never done before. What comes next? Very few have adequately tackled this question the way Swartz does and the practical lens with which she looks at racial injustice in SA is both refreshing and necessary. Restitution cannot be ignored.

– Jessica Breakey, Graduate student, Wits University

This elegantly written, commendably personalised and thoughtfully substantiated book echoes the urgent need for vital, frank and open conversations around power, privilege and racialized inequalities. *Another Country* is a bold and courageous statement on the unfinished and largely ignored imperative of 'social restitution' and a truly inclusive citizenship.

– Professor Francis B. Nyamnjoh, Professor of Social Anthropology, University of Cape Town

The notion of a 'rainbow nation' has led us to laziness and complacency, hoping that God would extend his 'miracle' to solve all our problems and challenges. Swartz offers us a way of dealing with difficult dialogues while still holding on to a seemingly impossible dream.

– Dr Llewellyn MacMaster, Stellenbosch University, and minister of the Uniting Reformed Church in Southern Africa

ANOTHER

EVERYDAY SOCIAL RESTITUTION

COUNTRY

SHARLENE SWARTZ

with a foreword by
Antjie Krog

Published by BestRed, an imprint of HSRC Press
Private Bag X9182, Cape Town, 8000, South Africa
www.bestred.co.za

First published 2016

ISBN 978-1-928246-11-4 (soft cover)

Copy-edited by Audrey Williams
Typeset by Robin Yule
Cover design by Nic Jooste
Printed by Capitil Press, Paarden Island, South Africa

Distributed in Africa by Blue Weaver
Tel: +27 (021) 701 4477; Fax Local: (021) 701 7302; Fax International: 09 +27 8 6524 2139
www.blueweaver.co.za

Distributed in Europe and the United Kingdom by Eurospan Distribution Services (EDS)
Tel: +44 (0) 17 6760 4972; Fax: +44 (0) 17 6760 1640
www.eurospanbookstore.com

Distributed in North America by River North Editions, from IPG
Call toll-free: (800) 888 4741; Fax: +1 (312) 337 5985
www.ipgbook.com

For every South African committed to 'another country' in our lifetime

There is a place for anger, things we won't forgive
And I know it's not enough to face your shame with words you'll never live
But let's begin to look within, to where the future lies
And find the strength to live beneath another country's skies
You'll walk beside me, I'll tell you no lies
And then you'll see another country in my eyes

– From 'Another Country', Mango Groove –

Table of contents

List of figures and tables

List of acronyms

AIDS	acquired immune deficiency syndrome
ANC	African National Congress
ARE	anti-racist education
AWB	Afrikaner-Weerstands Beweging (Afrikaner resistance movement)
BCM	Black Consciousness Movement
BEE	Black Economic Empowerment
BRICS	Brazil, Russia, India, China and South Africa
CBO	community-based organisation
CIA	Central Intelligence Agency (US)
CRT	Critical Race Theory
DA	Democratic Alliance
DSTV	Digital Satellite television, South Africa's pay channels
EFF	Economic Freedom Fighters
FASD	foetal alcohol spectrum disorder
FBO	faith-based organisation
HIV	human immunodeficiency virus
HRV	human rights violations
IEB	Independent Examinations Board (used by private schools mainly)
IFP	Inkatha Freedom Party
IJR	Institute for Justice and Reconciliation
ILC	International Law Commission
LGBTI	lesbian, gay, bisexual, transgender and intersex
MBA	Masters in Business Administration
MK	uMkhonto we Sizwe [the Spear of the Nation], the former armed wing of the ANC
NDP	National Development Plan
NGO	non-governmental organisation
RDP	Reconstruction and Development Programme
RLRA	Restitution of Land Rights Act
SADF	South African Defence Force (under Apartheid)
TRC	Truth and Reconciliation Commission
YRBS	Youth Risk Behaviour Survey

A note on 'race' in South Africa

Racial descriptions have always been problematic in South Africa. Race is not biologically fixed but socially constructed. In this book where I use the term 'race' I am referring to it as a social construct, albeit with real effects.

In South Africa's Apartheid classification, specifically the Population Registration Act of 1950, four categories were used to describe different 'Population Groups' which changed somewhat over time: variations of 'Black' 'African' 'Native' and 'Bantu' to denote Black African South Africans; 'Coloured' to denote those of Khoi, San, Griqua, Malay, slave and people of mixed ethnic descent; 'Indian' and 'Asian' from South Asia; and 'White' for those of European descent or able to pass for European descent through a number of arbitrary tests.

While in general I refer to 'Black' and 'White' South Africans as in the practice of those who follow the tenets of the Black Consciousness Movement, I also use Apartheid-era population group descriptors when describing individual voices, since these have historical significance.

Foreword

Thoughts on restitution

The concept of restitution presents South Africans with profound challenges. The word in English has three meanings: to restore something lost or stolen to its proper owner; to recompense or compensate for injury or loss; the restoration of something to its original state. All three of these explanations have as a central axis *that something should be done* in order to return to some *previous equilibrium*. It seems then that the first question should be: what was the previous 'equilibrium'? In order to work out *what* should be done (the direction and amount of the deeds), it is crucial to determine *where one wants to be after the restoration act.*

Exactly how difficult it is to do that, became clear during a public meeting with the first Minister of Finance. He was asked at a press conference, focusing on the reparations for victims after the Truth and Reconciliation Commission, whether there was a post-TRC plan to get from Whites what was needed to repair the past. He answered: 'Even if we take everything Whites have, it will never make up for what they did. What we need to address in inequality is a 6% growth rate.'

This was of course the truth. Nothing could ever repair the damage of three centuries. But in another way, it was also exemplary of our collective unwillingness to do some complex thinking. What was it that Black people desired after Apartheid? What were the outlines of their dreams? Whatever was negotiated and understood, misunderstood or taken for granted – was there anybody in South Africa who thought that the country materially could stay as it was with all the resources remaining in specific areas and classes?

In 1994 it would have been important for Whites to hear the conditions under which they were to be accommodated or rejected in the new South Africa: 'We don't want you here'; or: 'We want Whites, but only poor ones – or only rich ones'; or: 'We want Whites to take responsibility willingly for everything that fails'; or: 'For three centuries the country has invested its best and most powerful resources in you, so for three generations you will use your accumulated skills, knowledge and resources to eradicate for ever the

Verwoerd education system, or mend the distorted transport system, or build an appropriate health system, or perhaps even: 'Every White should report to a township school and assist with rendering services from cleaning toilets and safeguarding buildings and people, to teaching and marking as and when necessary'. However problematic, ridiculous or impractical these suggestions might sound, they would have focused all of our minds on what kind of society we wanted to live in, under whose leadership this should be achieved and what we were willing to pay for it. The clearly spelt out decision by Black people of what White people should do, would forcefully have established a new invaluable power-relationship as well as a vision towards which all South Africans could work.

Returning to the axis in the definitions, in order to execute restitution two phases are needed: the first is to agree on what the 'original state' was (and that is more complex than simply to get a bicycle back!). Do people want to return to tribal and rural life with land and chiefs? Or is it South Africa as it is today with its interconnectedness to international human rights and individualism, its cities with all the trappings of greed and consumerism? And with Whites who know their place?

Forming an opinion based on the worst in social media, there is a desire for a personal physical experience: to see Whites impoverished, humiliated and depending for their own most basic needs on the whim and mercy of Black people. At times does it seem as if there is even a wish for a French Revolution scenario: to move into the deserted houses of the rich, run through the enormous gardens, mess in the pools and experience physical revenge by spilling blood? I believe all of this is actually underpinned by an understandable basic yearning: to take over the mines, the houses, the cars, the farms, so that one would never again live the vulnerable life of dread, anxiety, poverty and oppression.

It is in many ways an impossibility to define or probably to agree on what is the original state that people want to return to, yet it has to be done, because the closer we can get to a description or vision of such a state, the sooner the country's people can begin to take steps for a massive rearrangement. If we agree that it is not only impossible but also undesirable to return to any previous state (as happened after World War 2 in Europe) we have to begin to use the concept of paying a fine or damage tax and then determine who will pay what and how that will be distributed and by whom so that everybody benefits.

For me, personally, it has to begin with space. The essence of colonialism is space – the expropriation and personal consuming of space. The colonial and Apartheid worlds were worlds divided and dividing. Therefore, decolonisation must mean the making whole, the re-creation, re-appropriation and reconfiguration of space. It means more than simply eradicating the lines of force that keep zones apart; it requires fundamental social and economic change.

But again, how is this restitution to be executed? How is the transfer to happen? Are individual farms and houses to be transferred to individual owners, or is land to be nationalised? In other words, is the choice socialist or capitalist in nature? Are we for sharing or for individual ownership?

Ten years ago, I felt that all land should be nationalised. Then one could say: the land truly belongs to all the South African people, all of us; those on farms merely have leasehold. But with the current set of leaders, it seems impossible to execute any plan demanding of clear ethical thinking, selfless motivation and moral example. The rhetoric of freedom and justice has evaporated into increasingly shabby talk about a developmental state, while the examples of leaders suggest freedom from Apartheid means freedom to shop, and especially, freedom not to be accountable. Even worse, in the financial systems of today the poor suddenly have to become entrepreneurs.

When last did we hear anybody talk about a just society, a better life for everybody, or suggest that enough is a feast? In strikes and wage bargaining one seldom hears the words: justice, fairness, empathy. And why would we, being bombarded as we are by the vulgar excesses of celebrity life and vainglorious luxury on television, billboards and magazines only acknowledging the right to consume?

Fanon warned decades ago how quickly liberation can degenerate when it lacks humanist content. Movements without it fall into undemocratic and brutal ways, especially when a ruling party, masked by the mixed rhetoric of Africanism, Ubuntu and possessive individualism, begins to focus only on sectional and ethnic interests. He suggested that in order not to create new hierarchies, we should establish 'relations of comradeship, of solidarity, of love, relations which prefigure the sort of society we struggle for.'

And it is especially in this light that Swartz's book makes sense. As requested by Steve Biko, Swartz's issue is with Whites, and those Whites who do not feel guilty or responsible for an unjust past – she hammers them with interviews, statistics and facts. But the real value in the book is probably the attempt to describe how purposefully to go about creating relationships across race and cultural barriers. She suggests personal dialogue with those who differ from you and within this engagement, it would be possible for people to articulate a sense of responsibility, guilt and restitution as well as assist one another to achieve that. One of the most insightful suggestions is that inheritance should be more widely shared.

Individual daily reparations may be good on a one-to-one basis and no doubt, a person helped is a person helped, but these actions are also as arbitrary as they are ineffective to address the weight of an unjust past. I believe big structural changes need to happen within a set time period, but in the absence of suggestions and no coherent economic vision and ethical leadership, there is always the Mugabe route: at least one sees things change. The fact that it changes for the worse for the majority is immaterial, because the majority, at last, sees that things change.

Antjie Krog
28 July 2016

Introduction

Spitting on shoes

In 1988, I went travelling in Europe, the air ticket a 21st birthday present from my parents. One of my first priorities after arriving in London was to see the film *Cry Freedom*, the story of Black Consciousness activist Steve Biko and newspaper editor Donald Woods, since it was banned in South Africa. I remember stumbling out of the cinema with tears streaming down my face and expletives tumbling from my mouth. I was angry and in complete disbelief at the horrific extent of the violence security police meted out to Black South Africans; at how Apartheid raged on legitimised by the courts; about the loss that Steve Biko's death was to our future. It took a trip to London for this to sink in.

From the UK I crossed the channel to France, and then went on to Switzerland by train. One afternoon, just before Christmas, I found myself in a small village on a mountain overlooking Zurich. I had taken a train there and had been happily wandering around for a few hours, Irish rock band U2 blasting *Sunday Bloody Sunday* through my earphones. Northern hemisphere night falls quickly in winter, so by 6 pm I was chilled to the bone and hopelessly lost. I needed to find the train station, but everywhere I looked I saw only shadows and trees. I walked bravely towards some lights, and was relieved to find a small farm house. I marched up to the door, removed my gloves and knocked loudly.

A large white-haired, bearded man with a red bulbous nose opened the door. I greeted him politely in my best Swiss German, told him I was lost, and asked whether he could point me in the direction of the train station. I was worried that he would not understand me since all I spoke was English after the initial *Guete Aabig*, but he did. Gruffly he said, 'Speak more.' I did. I can't remember what I said. He then asked, 'South African?' and I eagerly replied, 'Yes, I am South African,' expecting the usual travel banter about rugby and Table Mountain. Instead, he glared at me, yelled 'A-PART-HEID', spat on my snow-encrusted boots, and slammed the door in my face. My coldness, my lostness were suddenly nothing in comparison to the confusion and deep shame I felt at that moment. Here I was, in a village in the middle of nowhere, and a man who looked like Father Christmas refused to help me find the train station because I was a *White South African*.

That moment has given me many years of pause for thought. It was the beginning of a profound consciousness of my country: what had happened to it and what responsibility I bore for changing it. It wasn't my first awareness of race, racism, or injustice but it was the first time I realised the enormity of what it truly means to be a White South African.

South Africa in 2016

It is now 2016, a full 22 years since the end of Apartheid, yet all is not well in South Africa. We are in the midst of widespread social protests, mainly about inequality, which have been ongoing for much of the past two decades, but which reached a crescendo recently. In 2015, students from two of South Africa's largest universities began a campaign to end institutional racism and make university fees accessible to the poor. They linked their struggle to that of workers' wages. Movements such as #RhodesMustFall at the University of Cape Town began by highlighting the presence of imperialist statues on campus, focussing on that of Cecil John Rhodes. The focus soon shifted to the dearth of Black senior academics and a curriculum still steeped in colonial thinking. This was followed by #TransformWits, a movement at the University of the Witwatersrand about similar issues including the unaffordability of fees and accommodation for township students. Stellenbosch University students began #OpenStellenbosch, a movement to eradicate Afrikaans as a medium of instruction since it excludes and disadvantages Black students. By October 2015, there was a nationwide call for all university students to embark on mass action, under the banner of #FeesMustFall, to demand no increase in fees for 2016. Students at many campuses also took up the campaign to end the practice of outsourcing for vulnerable workers in cleaning, catering, security and transport (#OutSourcingMustFall). As a result of these protests, a number of universities closed before the end of the academic year, and many postponed final exams to January. The President announced that there would be no fee increases in 2016. The country was delighted, but students vowed to continue the struggle for equality and 'decolonisation' in the next year. #ThisIsOnlyTheBeginning trended on social media as the year ended.

Students' grievances highlighted for the entire country the slow pace of economic transformation. South Africa may have undergone a political transformation, but a socio-economic transformation has yet to be realised, they argued loudly. Accompanying these protests was a renewed focus on what it means to have benefited from past injustice (#WhitePrivilegeMustFall), along with a spate of public racist incidents, which made national headlines and came from both Black and White South Africans. White examples included estate agent Penny Sparrow referring to black people as 'monkeys' in a social media comment regarding their behaviour on South Africa's beaches on New Year's Day;[1] Standard Bank strategist Chris Hart accusing Black South Africans of 'entitlement' and hating minorities;[2] Radio DJ Gareth Cliff being fired from his position as a judge on the popular reality show *Idols* for intimating that hate speech should be allowed to protect 'freedom of expression'[3] (he was subsequently rehired after a court hearing); and the FW de Klerk Foundation insisting that Whites are victims of Black racism and oppression.[4] Black examples included Gauteng government employee Velaphi Khumalo who called on White people to be killed in the way Hitler killed Jews;[5] the wearing of T-shirts on university campuses with the slogan 'Kill all

---

[1] J Wicks (1 April 2016) *It's just the facts – Penny Sparrow breaks her silence.* Accessed on 15 April 2016 from http://www.news24.com/SouthAfrica/News/its-just-the-facts-penny-sparrow-breaks-her-silence20160104.

[2] C Hart (3 January 2016) *More than 25 years after Apartheid ended the victims are increasing along with a sense of entitlement and hatred towards minorities.* Accessed on 15 April 2016 from https://twitter.com/chrishartZA/status/683658092467339264.

[3] SABC News (9 January 2016) *Gareth Cliff fired from Idols after 'free speech' post.* Accessed on 15 April 2016 from http://www.sabc.co.za/news/a/17f10c004b3f38998eaaee445cadceaa/Gareth-Cliff-fired-from-Idols-after-free-speech-post.

[4] S Skweyiya (18 January 2016) *The FW de Klerk Foundation sues black South Africans for racism.* Accessed on 15 April 2016 from https://www.africanexponent.com/post/racial-battle-in-south-africa-1438).

[5] M Mduduzi (7 January 2016) *Velaphi Khumalo's racist post probe.* Accessed on 15 April 2016 from http://citizen.co.za/932519/i-want-to-cleanse-this-country-of-all-white-people-got-official/.

Whites';[6] and graffiti saying 'Fuck White people' tagged on the University of the Witwatersrand's Law building.[7]

Alongside these protests and accusations of racism has been increasing criticism levelled at the ANC-led government and South Africa's President, Jacob Zuma, especially for the many cases of corruption in which he is, or has been, implicated. A growing #ZumaMustFall movement began in 2015 and has not abated as I finish this book.

The stark reality is that 22 years into democracy, South Africa is a very unequal society, among the most unequal in the world. Comprising 80% of the total population, Black South Africans are the ones who bear the largest burden of this inequality. A few examples in connection with unemployment, poverty and low quality education illustrate this point. South Africa's current unemployment figure stands at 34% (25% if discouraged job seekers are excluded). The figure for White South Africans is a mere 8%.[8] According to South Africa's definition of poverty,[9] 60% of Black South Africans live below the poverty line, compared to 4% of White South Africans. The average household income for White South Africans is six times that of Black South Africans.[10] Furthermore, around half of privately owned land is in White hands'[11] and 75% of all directors in Johannesburg Stock Exchange-listed

6   I Pijoos (11 February 2016) *UCT: 'Kill all whites' T-shirt is hate speech.* Retrieved from http://www.sowetanlive.co.za/news/2016/02/11/uct-kill-all-whites-t-shirt-is-hate-speech.

7   M Raborife (8 February 2016) *Wits condemns, removes offensive campus graffiti.* Accessed on 15 April 2016 from http://www.news24.com/SouthAfrica/News/wits-condemns-removes-offensive-campus-graffiti-20160208.

8   Statistics South Africa (2016) Quarterly labour force survey Quarter 4 2015. Pretoria, South Africa: Stats SA.

9   Statistics South Africa defines the upper poverty level as living on below R620 per month measured in 2011.

10 R365 000 for White South Africans and R61 000 for Black South Africans according to Statistics South Africa (2011) *Census.* Pretoria, South Africa: Stats SA.

11 Statistics South Africa (2014) *2014 General household survey.* Pretoria, South Africa: StatsSA.

companies are White.[12] Just over one-third of young people who begin school, exit with a school leaver's certificate (Matric);[13] twice the proportion of White South African youth have a Matric certificate compared to Black South Africans.[14] White South African youth between 18 and 29 are seven times more likely to be enrolled at university than Black South Africans.[15] Statistics for Coloured and Indian/Asian South Africans are between that of Black and White South Africans, and reflect almost exactly the relative privileges and benefits afforded each population group under Apartheid. So not only is South Africa the most unequal country in the world, but these inequalities remain clearly differentiated by race. White South Africans still have one of the highest living standards in the world,[16] despite the formal end of institutionalised privilege for White people.

Perhaps most worrying is that while White South Africans are content to enjoy the fruits of democracy, their attitude towards redress is tepid at best.[17] When it comes to land reform, affirmative action, sports quotas and Apartheid compensation, they are least in favour of these government

---

[12] See survey done by the South African Institute of Chartered Accountants (SAICA) in 2014. Accessed on 5 April 2016 from https://www.saica.co.za/News/ NewsArticlesandPressmediareleases/tabid/695/itemid/4729/language/en-ZA/ language/en-ZA/Default.aspx.

[13] The relationship between completing school and employment (and employment and poverty) is easy to see in South Africa's national statistics: 58% of those who are currently unemployed have not completed high school; only 24% of those who have completed school live in poverty.

[14] Based on 23- to 24-year-olds, measured in 2011 by Statistics South Africa (2011) *Census*. Pretoria, South Africa: Stats SA.

[15] Statistics South Africa (2014) *2014 General household survey*. Pretoria, South Africa: Stats SA.

[16] The richest 20% in South Africa have a Human Development Index ranking 101 places above the poorest 20 per cent which places them on the same standard of living as the wealthiest countries of the Global North. See also Khaya Dlanga (2012) Why blacks still raise apartheid. *Sunday Independent*.

[17] For a report of ten years' data from the Human Sciences Research Council's *South African Social Attitudes Survey* see Benjamin Roberts (2013) Your Place or Mine? Beliefs About Inequality and Redress Preferences in South Africa. *Social Indicators Research* 118(3): 1167–1190.

actions to redistribute wealth compared to Black, Coloured and Indian South Africans. Similarly, for other forms of redress such as support for the unemployed, tertiary education opportunities for the poor, progressive taxation, and increasing social grants, of which most other South Africans are highly in favour, White South Africans lag behind considerably. The irony is that the same survey shows that White South Africans know that wealth is highly unequally distributed in South Africa, and say they are opposed to such inequalities. But while they oppose inequality, they do not want to do anything about it. What is even more disturbing is that despite these blatant inequalities, two-thirds of South Africans from all population groups are very eager to 'forget the past' and 'move on'.[18]

South Africa's past

The amnesia about the past has not always been the case. After 1994, South Africa was widely applauded for its groundbreaking Truth and Reconciliation Commission (TRC) and the amnesty process (1996 to 2001). The TRC focused on perpetrators coming forward to take responsibility for their actions and receive amnesty from prosecution, and victims experiencing closure and receiving small amounts of compensation. The final TRC report made strong recommendations for a social dynamic of rebuilding and redress from individuals, civil society and government in order to bring about complete healing and reconciliation.[19] The response from individuals and civil society has yet to emerge in the way the TRC envisaged. Numerous efforts by government, especially its programmes of Black economic empowerment and land redistribution have not made inroads into the inequality, poverty and

---

[18] Two-thirds of South Africans across all historical 'race' groups agreed with the statement 'Forget apartheid and move on' (63% Black South Africans, 69% White South Africans, 73% Indian South Africans, and 67% of Coloured South Africans). See full report, Kim Wale (2013) Confronting Exclusion: Time for Radical Reconciliation. *South Africa Reconciliation Barometer Survey 2013.* Cape Town, South Africa: Institute for Justice and Reconciliation.

[19] André du Toit (2005) Experiments with Truth and Justice in South Africa: Stockenström, Gandhi and the TRC. *Journal of Southern African Studies,* 31(2): 419–448; Desmond Tutu (1999) *No future without forgiveness.* London, UK: Rider.

racism that continue to plague South Africa. Current protests[20] and muted talk of revolution[21] coexist alongside calls for forgiveness[22] and moving on.

Many commentators blame an inept or 'failed' state,[23] and finger issues of corruption, greed, 'the arrogance of power',[24] political elites who perpetuate colonial extractive and de-industrialised practices,[25] and an absence of government leadership[26] in putting things right. Hlumelo Biko[27] and others lay the blame at the door of business, especially White capital. Biko refers to the 1994 settlement as 'the great fraud'[28] and points out the huge debt and bankrupt state the Apartheid government bequeathed to the new democratic government. He provides a fine analysis of what White business has failed to do and what might be achieved if it were encouraged into meaningful public-private partnerships in, for example, education and community upliftment. Biko's analysis shows how racial and political reconciliation was favoured over a fair socioeconomic settlement. The result in 2016, however, is that we now have neither.

---

20 Richard Ballard, Adam Habib and Imraan Valodia (2006) *Voices of protest: Social movements in post-apartheid South Africa*. Pietermaritzburg, South Africa: University of KwaZulu Natal Press; Patrick Bond and George Dor (2002) *Unsustainable South Africa: Environment, development and social protest*. Pietermaritzburg, South Africa: University of KwaZulu Natal Press.

21 Adam Habib (2013) *South Africa's suspended revolution: hopes and prospects*. Johannesburg, South Africa: Wits University Press.

22 Martha Minow (1998) *Between vengeance and forgiveness: Facing history after genocide and mass violence*. Boston, MA: Beacon Press.

23 Alex Boraine (2014) *What's gone wrong: On the brink of a failed state*. Johannesburg, South Africa: Jonathan Ball.

24 Xolela Mangcu (2014a) *Arrogance of power: Twenty years of disenchantment*. Cape Town, South Africa: Tafelberg.

25 Moeletsi Mbeki (2009) *Architects of poverty: Why African capitalism needs changing*. Johannesburg, South Africa: Picador Africa, p. 64.

26 Habib (2013).

27 Hlumelo Biko (2013) *The great African society: A plan for a nation gone astray*. Johannesburg, South Africa: Jonathan Ball.

28 Biko (2013), p. 73.

Political commentator Max du Preez,[29] debunks the idea of a failed state and demonstrates the strengths of South Africa's institutions: a free and energetic press, an active civil society, a viable economy, a strong and functional constitution and an independent judiciary.[30] Instead of blaming government for a failure to deliver, Du Preez argues that our current condition is due to a failure to realise the magnitude of the effects of Apartheid. He argues that we need to change the discourse of 'Apartheid as excuse' to 'Apartheid as explanation' for structurally embedded problems and inequalities, alongside the many unearned privileges that White South Africans still enjoy. Pumla Gobodo-Madikizela, an academic and former TRC Commissioner, has noted that we remain 'a wounded and troubled country'[31] because we have failed to address the psychological fallout of Apartheid injustice that no amount of legal redress, even if it were to be successful, is able to achieve.

What no-one seems to be talking about is what restitution is expected of White South Africans, as individuals and communities. This is the subject of *Another Country*.

Talking about restitution

I have found it helpful to use two analogies when I speak about South Africa's history of injustice and inequality. The first analogy is about a soccer game in which two teams are playing each other but the pitch is tilted at a massive angle with one team playing uphill, the other downhill. The side playing downhill is unfairly advantaged and is able to run up a massive score. At a certain point during the match, the advantaged team is forced to realise that the game is grossly unfair and that the playing field must be levelled before the game can continue. Some want the score to remain in place and think it's fair merely to carry on playing now that the field is level. Others want to

---

29 Max du Preez (2013) *A rumour of spring: South Africa after 20 years of democracy.* Cape Town, South Africa: Random House Struik.

30 As reflected in the Constitutional Court's judgement about the binding powers of the Public Protector with regard to President Jacob Zuma's excessive expenditure on upgrades to his private homestead, Nkandla, in March 2016.

31 Pumla Gobodo-Madikizela (2014) *Dare we hope? Facing our past to find a new future.* Cape Town, South Africa: Tafelberg, p. iix.

level the scores as well as the pitch and start again. Yet others want to stop the game until new rules are in place and time is given to let the team who has been playing uphill recover from their exhaustion, injuries and sense of hopelessness, before replaying the match.

The other analogy is one of two children who live next door to each other – let's call them Johnny and Jabu. Both have bicycles. One day Johnny steals Jabu's bicycle. Jabu tries hard to get it back but can't. Naturally they stop being friends. A year passes and they do not talk or even look at each other. But Johnny misses his friend and goes over to Jabu's house one day and says, 'Jabu, let's be friends again'. Jabu agrees and so they shake hands and make up. They even have a gathering where Johnny explains to their friends and family the exact circumstances of the bicycle theft: Jabu relates how it made him feel, and Johnny admits to having done wrong – then they continue with their lives. A few months later Jabu says to Johnny, 'Johnny, what about my bicycle?' to which Johnny replies, 'Look Jabu, this is about becoming friends again, not about bicycles'.[32]

Of course, neither story captures all the complexities and nuances of South Africa's history of slavery, colonialism, imperialism and Apartheid, or our transition to democracy in 1994. Neither do they address all our current issues of inequality, racial segregation, hate speech, and desire to move on. What it does do however, is allow us to speak about what might be the fair thing to do in both these circumstances before relating it to our own South African story. It forces us to ask some uncomfortable questions: How does the past continue to have an effect on the present? Who has benefited from the past? Who has been hurt? What should be done about the past, about unearned benefits and undeserved pain? Have we done enough? Who should be doing more? When will we know when we've done enough? What will happen if we do nothing further?

What this book is about

This book confronts these questions. It is the culmination of my growing up as a White South African and slipping in and out of consciousness of what was really happening in this country of mine; of reading about, and grappling

---

[32] Michael Lapsley and Stephen Karakashian (2012) *Redeeming the past: My journey from freedom fighter to healer*. Cape Town, South Africa: Struik Inspirational.

with, this hard word *restitution* as part of my academic research; and a nine-year-long involvement with a small non-governmental organisation (NGO) called the Restitution Foundation.[33] When I began writing this book in 2014, I thought it would just be about *my* ideas about restitution. I decided, however, that it would be enriched by inviting people to reflect *with me* on its meaning, the possibilities it holds and how restitution, more broadly defined, might contribute to a better country as we head for the third decade of our fragile democracy. Along with three research assistants, I recruited a group of 60 South Africans from all walks of life, and from many parts of the country. They are young and old, rich and poor, men and women, Black, Coloured and White, professional and working class. (See detailed notes on my methodology and theory in Appendix 1, as well as a list in Appendix 2 of the people referred to in the book, giving their pseudonym, age, race, and occupation.[34]) The results were far beyond my expectations. These everyday South Africans offered stories about living through South Africa's transition, some personally, others through their parents, and how they see our past and future. They talked about their experiences of the lingering damage of injustice: about Black patience, pain, anger and disbelief; White oblivion; blindness to privilege[35] and shame.[36] I believe I have captured a key moment in South Africa's history in the year when 'moving on' was the dominant discourse, and just before the tipping point of the call in 2015 that #EverythingMustFall was reached.

Frequently, as I made the final edits, I found myself wondering whether this book is perhaps not too little too late; that the time for making restitution has in fact now passed; that what we need is something more radical, more coercive. But I don't think so. Instead, I believe that a new conversation about a difficult concept holds the key to a new South Africa. This is especially true as people I

---

[33] See www.restitution.org.

[34] I also give these the first time each person appears in a chapter.

[35] Osiame Molefe (2012) *Black Anger and White Obliviousness*. Johannesburg, South Africa: Parktown Publishers.

[36] I use shame intentionally and in preference to guilt throughout this book because I believe shame is a productive emotion that can urge us to action whereas guilt often paralyses us. Of course, I am aware of the large literature distinguishing between these two emotions, such as June Tangney and Ronda Dearing (2003) *Shame and guilt* (New York, NY: Guilford Press), but leave that discussion for another occasion.

interviewed spoke of a shared vision for South Africa's future and what might happen if nothing further is done about our past (see Chapter 1: *Restitution and a shared vision for South Africa's future*). There is a need to articulate clearly why we are divided in our view of the past and our current realities, centring on different experiences of change, forgetfulness about the past, and perceptions of corruption (Chapter 2: *Ways of seeing: Why we are divided about what is needed*).

Historically and legally, the word 'restitution' has been defined as restoring matters to the state they were before an injustice occurred. This is difficult, often impossible to achieve. If, however, we take the word restitution to simply mean, pending a more thorough discussion, 'making things right' for wrongs previously committed, then restitution has numerous possibilities. I have four main thoughts that I believe will help us embark on a journey of restitution.

Injustice damages all of our humanity

The first is that injustice – whether slavery, colonialism, imperialism, Apartheid, ongoing inequality and greed – damages the humanity of all of us, of victims and perpetrators. The damage has enduring effects over time and must be understood before we can simply move on with our lives, individually and corporately. In the South African context, Apartheid's damage to the human spirit has resulted in continuing social ills such as violence, crime, addiction, joblessness, educational failure, poor physical and mental health, and a sense of social inferiority. Those in positions of privilege have also suffered harm. While it cannot be compared in scope and severity, aspects of these include racism, indifference, the normalisation of inequality, blindness and numbness towards need, and an innate feeling of superiority that makes normal human relationships almost impossible. These effects of the past on the present are considered in Chapter 3: *Black pain and the outrage of racism*, Chapter 4: *Apartheid's costs: Education, opportunities, assets and wellbeing* and Chapter 5: *White privilege and responses to South Africa's past*. They are all stories that need to be heard on a journey towards restitution.

Restitution is broader than a legal issue and extends beyond victims and perpetrators

The second idea is that a broader understanding of restitution – beyond the legal usage, and beyond application only to land – is a helpful tool to bring about change. Along with widening the definition we also need new language and more categories beyond the labels of 'victim' and 'perpetrator' to talk about our roles in the past. Some of these new labels might include terms such as 'beneficiary' and 'resister', and might differentiate between an 'architect' or 'implementer' of injustice and of resistance to injustice, for instance. We may add new descriptions to 'victim', such as someone dishonoured by injustice, and explain the category 'bystander' by adding the more colloquial term 'ostrich'. These terms may also serve to help us understand how roles become complicated over time, but show that we all have a part to play in a conversation about restitution: young and old, guilty and blameless, Black and White. This idea will be considered in Chapter 6: *Restitution: A new conversation* and Chapter 7: *Locating yourself in the conversation.*

Restitution has the potential to restore our humanity

The third idea is that restitution must aim at restoring our humanity, or sense of personhood. Drawing on an African understanding, I describe personhood as including dignity, opportunity, belonging and memory, and so include symbolic, practical and financial acts and attitudes in a quest for restitution. Strategies for restoring personhood include restoring land and homes and ensuring a decent standard of living for those deliberately excluded from South Africa's development as well as enabling people to take advantage of available opportunities. An enormous array of ideas needs to be discussed and implemented. These ideas may include dialogues to remember past injustices; developing a shared vision of what it means to be a South African; implementing projects to promote physical and psychological flourishing; building friendships across former lines of hatred; transferring skills; mentoring across our usual divides; discussions about forgiveness; and disrupting the perpetuation of wealth passing from generation to generation through inheritance. These ideas will be covered in Chapter 8: *Restoring our humanity* and Chapter 9: *Everyday actions for individuals and groups.*

There is something for everyone to do in restitution

The final idea, is that when it comes to restitution, there is something for everyone to do: individuals and communities, governments and institutions. In order that we do not merely repeat the past, with one group dominating the other, the best way to decide on what actions should be taken is to decide together, in dialogue, with people different to us. So while government and legal programmes such as penalty payments, land redistribution, and affirmative action (acts of restitution with which we are most familiar) are important in bringing about social transformation after conflict and injustice, it is the participation of civil society, communities and individuals that are vital in fulfilling restitution's wider aims. I call individual and communities' involvement in restitution, social restitution, and contrast it to government-led or institutional restitution. While this final idea is to be found throughout the book, I summarise it in Chapter 10: *Critical active social restitution* and offer, in summary, ten criteria by which to measure and evaluate our efforts at social restitution. These criteria are readily translatable into ten steps that groups of people could embark upon in a journey of restitution. Appendix 3: *10-10-10 Restitution Dialogues* provides a guide for such a journey.

Who this book is for

Deciding who the intended reader is has been the hardest part of writing this book. The data collected and the historical-contemporary analysis make it a scholarly work. But the language in which it is written, I hope, makes it accessible to all South Africans who want another kind of country, a country where, in the words of Alan Paton,[37] the author of *Cry, The Beloved Country,*

> the weak are protected, and none go hungry or poor;
> the riches of creation are shared, and everyone can enjoy them;
> different races and cultures live in harmony and mutual respect;
> peace is built with justice, and justice is guided by love.

Another Country is written for the 19-year-old White male economics student at the University of Cape Town (UCT) who says, 'But I wasn't there – stop making me feel guilty about the past.' For his father who says, 'But I've worked hard for what I have – I don't owe anyone anything.' For the White dinner party grumblers who cannot see beyond the current corruption (and who too easily forget the past corruption of the Apartheid government), and who use corruption as the reason to be only for themselves and for their close family. It is for the many White South Africans for whom consciousness about the

---

[37] Commonly attributed to Alan Paton.

effects of the past has not sunk in (and who have never been spat upon for being a White South African); who retreat too easily behind high suburban walls, inherited wealth, secure jobs and multiple options for emigrating.

It is for the 30-something-year-old White chef who tells me employment equity is 'reverse racism' and that he is now 'a victim of Apartheid'. For the young White businessman who publicly tells racist jokes but is privately frustrated at the reality of not having Black people in his social circle. It's for him and his brother, both business owners, who want to do the right thing about Black economic empowerment, but are tempted to 'front' because the legislation is difficult and cumbersome. It is for the White woman who stands to inherit a few million rand from parents who by luck of birth own a house on the Atlantic seaboard and who would like help in deciding how to share this wealth. It is for these good people who want justice and change, but who forget the un-deservedness of their inherited wealth that was made possible by job reservation, privileged education, and the diabolical land ownership laws of the past.

It is also for the young Coloured woman from a small apple growing community outside Cape Town, who says we should just 'forgive and forget' while speaking of the painful, racist ways in which her children are treated. It's for the young Black man who went from pushing trolleys to being a floor manager at an upmarket supermarket, and the young Black woman with a commerce degree who works at a prestigious financial services institution who both say, 'Let's stop blaming the past and just get on with it'. It's for the middle generation Black professionals who are losing hope for real change and who are developing thick skins about the way they are treated by White people. It is also for the many young Black South Africans in their twenties and thirties who are so very disappointed, angry and frustrated, and of whom this book asks yet more: to hold up mirrors to White South Africans about unearned privilege and the amnesia about the past. It asks them to talk to White people despite their anger at the current situation, and their reluctance to damage relationships, as Welile, a 23-year-old Black man and sales representative, so eloquently described:

> **Welile:** Maybe if you had told me this is what we were going to talk about I wouldn't have come [laughs]. Because this is one of those conversations that we try and avoid. We are kind of afraid that what you're going to say is going to hurt other people.

There are a lot of things that haven't been said ... there's still a lot of anger.

***

We forget about these things. It's a wound that you just want to let heal, but at the end of the day it's what separates us. This was a good platform for me to say how I really feel about what is going on out there. We don't get this chance ... A lot of people will open up. They've got a lot to say, but we don't have the right platforms. That's why you still have a lot of racist fights.

It invites Black South Africans to tell the truth, to help White people come to see how the past will remain a part of our present until we take intentional steps to overcome it, and to work with White South Africans to make restitution. Not to make White South Africans *feel* better, but to help them *do* better in creating this other kind of country we all long for. In the words of *Mango Groove's* fabulous song of the early nineties:

There is a place for anger, things we won't forgive
And I know it's not enough to face your shame with words you'll
    never live
But let's begin to look within, to where the future lies
And find the strength to live beneath another country's skies
You'll walk beside me, I'll tell you no lies
And then you'll see another country in my eyes.[38]

My hope for this book is that it will fuel practical and productive conversations about restitution in the suburbs of Sandton, the sports fields of Strandfontein, the backyard shacks of Soweto, but more especially on university campuses, workplaces, and in school classrooms where we are less divided than in the places where we live. Here, conversations with those different to you, across racial and class divides, are at least possible.

---

[38] 'Another Country': Words and music by John Leyden/Alan Lazar (Mango Groove). Copyright 1992 by Gallo Music Publishers.

I am not expecting Black or White South Africans who hold radical views about violent revolution, or who harbour White supremacist views to want to engage in the project that this book sets out. This book is not for them. It is merely my effort to help middle-of-the-road South Africans, those who live with an unease about the current state of affairs in our beloved country, and who are willing to look within and at each other, instead of only at government for answers.

I am sure that this book will be discomforting for many. Like Sizwe (23, Black man, graduate student), you are likely to feel that 'you've opened a can of worms'. Perhaps, like 78-year-old Michael (White man, retired architect), you might start out defensively, 'It seems that you are expecting me to be going out of my way in an apologetic manner to rectify the sins perpetrated by oppressive White people on the disadvantaged,' but conclude, as Sandy (38, White woman, music teacher) does: '[Restitution] is a messy subject ... and White people don't like to engage with it ... [but] it's been a very positive experience to try and communicate what you really feel, and I think it would be beneficial for everybody to do this'.

As 38-year-old development worker Heather reported to me a few weeks after her interview:

> **Heather:** You'll also be pleased to hear that this has started an active ongoing dialogue between my dad and I regarding what should have been done, what was done and what should now be done, based on the African proverb, 'When is the best time to plant a tree? 20 years ago. When is the second best time to plant a tree: Today'.

Heather encapsulates both the thesis and hope of the book. It may have been the best time to plant a tree 20 years ago, but we did not, to our shame. Let's opt for the second best time to plant a tree: Today. It's time to talk about restitution, to plant a tree for tomorrow, and build another kind of country in our lifetime.

PART 1

A TIME TO SEE

1 Restitution and a shared vision for South Africa's future

During the years that followed my backpacking trip to Europe, I have become more conscious of my continuing privilege as a White South African, of injustice in South Africa, and what ought to be done about it. Having your shoes spat upon can prove to be a sobering experience. But I am aware that not everyone has had such an epiphany. I wish that during the dark years of Apartheid there had been more people who spat on our shoes. Perhaps one of Apartheid's most cunning ploys was to keep White South Africans isolated from outside opinions, whether through media censorship, or limited opportunities for travel.

In 1989, I returned to South Africa to pursue a career as a youth worker, mainly in churches and schools; I worked alongside young people to help them tackle the practical issues of their lives, including the new scourge of AIDS and the ongoing one of racism. Fourteen years later in 2003 I returned to the UK. This time to do a PhD. The first book I read as I started my studies was Antjie Krog's *Country of My Skull*,[1] her reflections on the TRC (Truth and Reconciliation Commission). It was a powerful exposé and once again, like my trip in 1988, I discovered things about my country I never knew, or had slipped from my consciousness. Things such as the physical brutality of Apartheid; the suffering of those who were left uncertain about the fate of their children and partners; the way in which Black South Africans were doubly victimised by the oppression of Apartheid. They were under-educated and exploited and then blamed for not rising above their circumstances. When I returned to South Africa in 2004 to conduct field research for my PhD, I was compelled by Antjie's account to immerse myself in the lives of young people living in adversity in South Africa's townships. I asked them how they understood their lives now – ten years into South Africa's democracy.

---

[1]   Antjie Krog (1998) *Country of my skull: Guilt, sorrow, and the limits of forgiveness in the new South Africa.* Johannesburg: Random House.

More than ever before, I was moved to the depths of my being when I learnt how these youths experienced poverty, poor standards of education, joblessness, fear and tragedy. My thesis showed starkly how Apartheid injustice still affected their lives, and that despite their excruciating circumstances, their sense of self, hope and agency could not be extinguished. I also realised that I was among only a very few White South Africans who spent time in the townships and who could tell other Whites, who were by now fully in the 'let's move on' club, about Apartheid's lingering effects. Again my own deep complicity in South Africa's past emerged. Young people tried to put on a brave face about the injustices of Apartheid, speaking frequently of the hope and dreams they had for the future in our new 'freedom world'. Two young people's accounts[2] of life in the new South Africa broke my heart. Nineteen-year-old Vuma from Nyanga told me about a factory close to his home where surplus bread was distributed, and of seeing '20 to 50 mothers running for bread'. He commented: 'I thought like in South Africa it has changed, but it didn't change that much ... How are their children? ... How do they take them to school when [their employers] give them so little money – and they have to run for bread?'

Another time I got into a long discussion with Vathiswa, a 19-year-old young woman from Khayelitsha, about why she lived in a shack on a sand dune and I lived alone in a very nice two-bedroomed flat in Rondebosch. Her reply was insistent: 'Because my mother has no money to buy and live in the other house ... she's not working ... [for] Black people it's not easy to find a job ... because long ago – they, the Black people, are not getting a better education.' As hard as I tried I could not get Vathiswa to blame Apartheid for her mom's lack of education, unemployment and dire living circumstances. I wrote in my field notes that day, 'I, as a White South African, had been a beneficiary of the Apartheid that robbed Vathiswa and her mom of her future. The least she could do was see it – and be angry about it and blame me or Apartheid.' But she did not. Instead, she caused me even further shame by telling me of her plans to finish school, get a job and help her mom buy a better house.

In the accounts of Vathiswa and Vuma I realised how Black South Africans were generously letting White people off the hook for the past, and probably many of my fellow White South African were unconscious of these facts: both

---

[2]   Sharlene Swartz (2009) *Ikasi: The moral ecology of South Africa's township youth.* Johannesburg, South Africa: Wits University Press.

the incredible hardships of Black South Africans and their overwhelming generosity. My study ultimately led me to ask what place restitution ought to have in South Africa's future. I gathered my thoughts and spoke about restitution at a prominent Anglican church in Cape Town before returning to the UK in 2005 to complete my thesis. The talk was met with great enthusiasm from young White South Africans, but generally disapproval or silence from the older generation. In late 2007, I returned to South Africa after completing my studies, and, in the intervening years have made an effort to build an academic and activist career focused on the two interrelated themes of youth development in adversity and restitution.

Why the word restitution?

I am fully aware that restitution is a difficult word. It is confrontational. It speaks about the past, actively deciding what needs to be done, or given up in order to address the past and ensure a better future. 'Why not talk about upliftment or development or charity or even reconciliation and social justice instead?' many ask. The answer is because only restitution can address the current viewpoints in our society that include the following: 'Let's forget the past and move on.' 'I worked for what I have. Don't blame me for something I had no part in.' 'Stop making this about race. It's about poverty and education.' 'Until the corruption stops, I'm not lifting a finger.' 'We want our land back. Full stop.' 'White people hide behind their wealth and privilege.' 'Nothing has changed. You can't eat freedom.' 'This country is going downhill fast. There's no hope.' And, 'If nothing is done, this country will burn.'

These statements are the very reason why we need to discuss and use the word 'restitution', and why no other word will do. Restitution addresses the very heart of what it means to deal with the past. Unapologetically then, this is a book about restitution. About the actions and attitudes needed to make something right. Restitution is not a neutral word. You can't just ignore it and pretend it was not said. Or, add it to the list of good things to do when you have a chance. No, this word provokes emotion, response, and hopefully action. It is a blow-to-the-gut kind of word, a noisy and restless word, which is why it should be used and examined and discussed. It is also an ideal rejoinder to the very many excuses, reasons, and objections people offer to defend doing nothing, or doing very little, or only doing things as an act of largesse or pity for others, rather than out of a sense of moral obligation.

An exchange with Sandy (White woman, 38, part-time music teacher) illustrates how useful speaking about the word restitution is. It was clear that Sandy was working things out as we spoke, but it turned the conversation into a deep engagement from the outset:

> **Sandy:** People ... don't want to let go of the past. There are a lot of angry people ... I understand why they're angry and that some of them want to get revenge, want to get stuff ... I understand how they feel, but swinging the pendulum the other way, I don't think is going to help either.
>
> **Interviewer:** Where are you seeing people wanting revenge?
>
> **Sandy:** The people in the media. The people that I know, like the lady who works in our home, she doesn't want revenge, she doesn't want stuff. She just wants peace ... to be able to work, get an income, her family to be happy and taken care of. So I don't come into contact with those people [who want revenge] except in the media and on the streets ... people who are begging, you can see they're angry.
>
> **Interviewer:** Where else?
>
> **Sandy:** In the media, leaders like Julius Malema – those kind of guys. They clearly want revenge. It comes across like they want to put White people in the same position as they were put and make them marginalised. It's just like a feeling I get. And also watching movies like the Mandela movie. I would want revenge if I was a Black person, to be completely honest. I would. It's completely unjust, it's completely inhumane and I would find it hard to let go with no recompense. I don't know, if every Black person got a million rand, would that make it okay? Or is it more of a human interaction and a human reconciling that people actually want?

I suspect there are many others like Sandy, who have not had an opportunity to work out what it is they feel about the past, to understand and discover what others feel about the past, and to act on the change they would like to see. The word restitution provokes these kinds of conversations that, until recently, have been infrequent in South Africa.

South Africa, place of hope and despair

In order to start a conversation about restitution, I began interviews by asking participants what made them hopeful or despairing about South Africa. It proved to be an easy way to begin the conversation, and people generally had similar amounts to say about both topics. Thirty-four-year-old Dylan, a White PhD student in a serious romantic relationship with a Black woman, humorously sketched out a range of changes he had seen in South Africa since 1994 that brought him hope: 'I'm going to have cinnamon-coloured children and forty years ago I would have been in prison for having a Black partner. That's a story of hope'. He continued:

> **Dylan:** White whinging people don't realise that since '94 over 90% of South Africans now have electricity. Over 95% of South Africans go to school until the age of 16 ... What they learn [at school] is another story of despair. But I think that life in a material sense has undoubtedly improved since the transformation due to the ANC's governance. I don't think a lot of White South Africans acknowledge that.

Two Black finance professionals, spoke of their hope stemming from the fact that South Africa had a 'peaceful change over of government' (Portia, 26) and of South Africa being 'a model African country that the world has embraced broadly' (Vukani, 34). A 34-year-old Black woman business executive, Mayaya, like Dylan, made it personal when she said that what gave her hope was her ability now to achieve beyond the circumstances of her grandmother:

> **Mayaya:** What gives me hope is where I come from. Look, I grew up taking care of my grandmother and she had a mud house. And we would clean up her house with cow dung ... and get water from the river using buckets ... [But] I've also worked for some of the biggest corporates in South Africa in top positions and I live a comfortable life. So it gives me hope that where I come from has not stopped me from achieving what I've achieved.

Sizwe, a 23-year-old Black graduate student, spoke of the hope that government policies and programmes aimed at improving people's lives gave him, while 38-year-old White small business owner Peter had hope because South Africa is 'a country of great opportunity for the future, particularly for people who are prepared to work hard'. For Welile, a recent Black graduate and sales representative, hope comes from seeing 'a new generation being educated'. Haley (a 42-year-old Coloured woman and priest) spoke of the huge hope she has from seeing young people no longer restrained by their race, background or gender, which was always the case under Apartheid. She told of a young Coloured teenager who aspires to become a professional golfer – an unthinkable career for a Coloured person, let alone a Coloured woman under Apartheid. 'They no longer think of themselves as being limited by the colour of their skin … or limited by the experiences of their parents and generations before. Huge hope here!' Haley exclaimed.

Across race divides people's stories of hope were both personal and corporate. There was a sense of pride in how much South Africa has achieved towards breaking down former divisions, and standing together, especially in things like large international sports events, defending people's human rights and enjoying relationships and friendships previously against the law. 'I have so many friends now who are White and Coloured' said 25-year-old Andiswa, a Black woman who works as a call centre assistant for a political party. 38-year-old Heather (White woman, in a non-profit organisation) described how visiting her friends in a Black township used to be viewed as 'abnormal' but has slowly changed over the past few years. Heather continued, 'Hope? I live with an overwhelming sense of having been forgiven and accepted by millions of people from whom I did not deserve such grace and mercy'. Echoing this, Johan (White man, 48, non-profit organisation director) spoke of 'people that have been hurt so much [and who] still see the humanity in White South Africans. That gives me a lot of hope.'

When asked about what brought them despair, those interviewed mentioned a range of topics mainly around the fact that few people were experiencing the fruits of freedom, that wealth was not being adequately redistributed, and raising the issues of corruption and inefficiencies in government:

> **Lwethu (Black woman, 24, retail merchandiser):** Even though we fought the Apartheid system and won … what is happening in South Africa currently is not what our parents fought for and went to prison for … The freedom we currently have only benefits a few.

> **Sindiswa (Black woman, 25, client services):** How rural schools and rural hospitals have never actually benefited from the change in government … that causes quite a bit of despair.

Nobuntu (Black woman, 34, business executive): I see so much scraping by and of living in horrible conditions in the townships.

Others spoke about 'ongoing bribery', 'nepotism' and the 'selfishness and greed' of 'people in charge'. Peter placed the blame on current leadership, saying they are 'only interested in their own wellbeing'. Zethu (Black woman, 40, business executive) summed up by saying 'It is these corrupt practices that deplete the hope that this country can have.'

More glaring is the legacy of racism and inferiority that many spoke of as still being present today. Statements included, 'There's fierce segregation and clear resentment', 'I'm not under the illusion that race is no longer an issue, it is an issue,' and most jarringly, 'The young Black kid still feels that he can't speak to a White person.' Leo (White man, 46, non-profit organisation director) spoke of his despondency regarding White people's failure to take collective responsibility for the past along with the 'the level of concealed anger and unacknowledged woundedness' that, in his opinion, Black people feel. Commenting on this, he said 'Let me be clear that the anger is justifiable, and it's not the anger per se that makes me despair … it's the ticking bomb.'

It is not stretching a point to conclude that South Africans, across age and race are ambivalent about South Africa. That there is hope is undeniable, but despair is its close companion. How does this ambivalence affect the kind of country we hope for?

What kind of country do we want?

To answer this question, I asked participants to reflect on how we would know when we'd done enough to address our past. The answers were profoundly moving and deeply similar – no matter where people stood in relation to the past – young, old, Black, White, wealthy, poor, educated or not. The most striking part of people's answers was the fresh and hopeful perspective they brought to thinking about the future. Only a very few were pessimistic, and said we would never be able to do enough. A few others acknowledged it would continue to be a very difficult, slow and painful process, as it has been, to change South Africa. On the whole, the answers of participants described a common vision for a shared future: A South Africa in which race no longer dominates; where there is equal access to opportunities; where there is social and geographical integration, where we know people who are different to us and have them as neighbours, and we live in a country in which poverty and inequality are a dim memory of the past. A few of these responses are illustrated under each category.

When race is no longer the chief determinant of our lives

Vukani spoke of a future environment 'where Black, White, Indian, Coloured feel that they can have a dream and achieve it without fear of someone holding you back based on your colour, creed or culture'. Thamsanqa, a 32-year-old Black man and graduate student, spoke of a future where you don't have to change who you are to fit in. For many others being able to enjoy romantic relationships and friendships across colour lines were a key gauge of a future where the past has been addressed. For Sizwe it was about knowing 'you are my friend because you are a person, not because of your Blackness or your Whiteness'. For 21-year-old White student Hillary, we will know 'when no one blinks when you see a mixed race couple walking down the road'. Peter spoke of friendships and relationships being based on 'similar interests and not colour'. Less positively, numerous people spoke of the absence of racist slurs as a key indicator: 'When someone calls you "a bad driver" rather than "a White bitch" when you drive stupidly.' (Angela, 37, White woman, graduate student), or as Lwethu puts it: 'When you no longer hear a Coloured child calling you a "kaffir" when you walk through the streets of Bonteheuwel to get to Langa.'

When we are all truly equal

Experiencing and seeing equality was the second way in which participants said we would know we have done enough about the past. This ranged from jobs, education and where people lived, to deeper issues of psychological equality. Mbali, a 28-year-old Black woman and financial administrator summed up how we would measure this equality: 'You will no longer be able to say a Black person will be a cleaner and a White person will be the CEO', while for Thomas (White man, 23, recent graduate) it would be, 'When people are hired on the quality of their work … rather than by race or because of legislation.' For 48-year-old Manny, a Coloured man and university administrator, it will be 'when the township schools resemble something where decent education happens' and for Lekho (Black woman, 26, government human resources practitioner), 'when schools are fully integrated across the different racial groups'.

Many spoke of living in truly integrated spaces as being the measure of when we would have done enough about the past; when there would no longer be a huge difference between sprawling, impoverished townships, such as Khayelitsha, and the elite Cape coastal suburb of Camps Bay. 'Twenty years down the line that's still not the case and the minority still own the most or have the most privileges in this country', Hillary lamented. Others spoke of some suburbs being more racially mixed, and of townships having a range of people living in them, rather than only people who could not afford to live in the suburbs. Olivia, a 41-year-old Coloured woman who has a doctorate and works with youth, spoke of true change being observed 'when there are 80% Black people in a restaurant in the suburbs, because that's the true demographic of our country.' For Dylan, equality would be realised 'when White people spoke isiZulu and isiXhosa as well as they spoke English or Afrikaans.' Nontembiso (Black woman, 48, domestic worker) put it more spiritedly: 'When I get an RDP[3] house, it should be located in Constantia.[4] Then I would know that we have real freedom.'

In connection with psychological equality, Black, White and Coloured respondents all agreed that when people lost inferiority and superiority complexes we would know that we had done enough about the past. Candice (Coloured woman, 29, graduate student) captured the sentiment of many: 'I think the psychological problem is more difficult than the tangible stuff. Yes, there are policies in place, but somehow if you still feel inferior, how do you fix that?' Sandy added: 'I think we will have done enough when everybody feels heard as people.'

When poverty is a thing of the past

Overall, people wanted to see an end to the grinding poverty and 'huge imbalances in the community' that still characterises much of South Africa. For Siphosethu (Black man, 29, former trolley pusher now retail floor coordinator) it would be 'when unemployment is low, when we have reached

---

3 RDP stands for Reconstruction and Development Programme. It was one of the earliest programmes of the newly democratic South African government from 1994. Amongst its first projects were the free rudimentary houses (known as RDP houses) for Black South Africans frequently erected away from existing shantytowns, but also away from people's workplaces.

4 An affluent Cape Town suburb.

equality and the end of poverty, and people are eating proper food, and have a safe comfortable home to live in.'

Many spoke of an even distribution of wealth and privilege across colour lines. By this participants meant, as Mbali explained: 'When there are Black and White people who are poor, and Black and White people who are rich. We need to change being Black as being synonymous with being poor and vice versa.' For Palesa (Black woman, 22, financial administrator), it would be 'when for the majority of the people ... poverty is not due to Apartheid.' A number of people also spoke of when a person was able to 'rise out of poverty through hard work and talent', rather than through social connections on the one hand, or affirmative action legislation on the other.

What have we already done about the past?

Because I know how difficult it was for me to remember the many injustices of Apartheid, it is useful to remind ourselves of the extent of the legislation enacted through South Africa's Parliament that legally entrenched Apartheid. Appendix 4 summarises some of this legislation, along with a brief description. The key message from this list is that no White South African can ever say, 'I worked for what I have.' You may have worked hard, but you were ensured a head start in school and university education, protection through job reservation when it came to employment, and unrivalled entitlement when it came to land ownership. This applies to those of us who were White children who lived under Apartheid, or White children born since its end. The education, jobs and homes of White parents and of their children are a direct benefit of the enacted privilege Apartheid legislation provided.

In the run-up to South Africa's first democratic election in 1994, many progressive and anti-Apartheid groups worked on programmes to repeal unjust laws and write a new Constitution that aimed to:

> Heal the divisions of the past and establish a society based on
> democratic values, social justice and fundamental human rights;
> Lay the foundations for a democratic and open society in which
> government is based on the will of the people and every citizen
> is equally protected by law; Improve the quality of life of all
> citizens and free the potential of each person; and Build a united

and democratic South Africa able to take its rightful place as a sovereign state in the family of nations.[5]

The South African government has also put in place restitutive legislation that deals with the restitution of land, economic opportunities and the recognition of past human rights violations along racial lines. Appendix 4 also provides a list of this legislation, some of the details of which are important to understand more fully the limits of government-led restitution.

Land redistribution

During Apartheid, racially discriminatory legislation significantly affected property ownership. Approximately 17 000 different statutory measures were issued before 1991 to control land issues and settlement along racial lines.[6] In the four former 'national states', six 'self-governing territories' (known collectively as 'Homelands' or 'Bantustans') and four former provincial governments, there were 14 different land control systems.[7] The government of the new democratic South Africa was therefore faced with the task of rationalising these different systems and harmonising laws across the country.

One of the most important mandates for reworking land legislation in South Africa came from the property rights outlined in Section 25 of the Constitution,[8] particularly sections 25(5–7) that state:

> (5) The state must take reasonable legislative and other measures, *within its available resources*, to foster conditions, which enable citizens to gain access to land on an equitable basis.

> (6) A person or community whose tenure of land is legally insecure as a result of past racially discriminatory laws or practices is entitled, to the extent provided by an Act of Parliament, either to *tenure which is legally secure* or to comparable redress.

---

5   Parliament of the Republic of South Africa (1996) The Constitution of the Republic of South Africa. Pretoria, South Africa: Government Printer, Preamble.
6   P Badenhorst, J Pienaar and H Mostert (2006) *Silberberg and Schoeman's: The Law of Property 5th edition*. Durban: LexisNexis Butterworths, p. 594.
7   Badenhorst et al. (2006).
8   Parliament of the Republic of South Africa (1996).

> (7) A person or community dispossessed of property *after 19 June 1913* as a result of past racially discriminatory laws or practices is entitled, to the extent provided by an Act of Parliament, either to restitution of that property or to equitable redress.

(Italics are author's emphasis)

The legal framework that was established had three interconnected land reform programmes: land restitution, land tenure reform, and land redistribution.

Land restitution through the Restitution of Land Rights Act aimed 'to restore land and provide other restitutionary remedies to people dispossessed by racially discriminatory legislation.'[9] This has been done through the Commission for the Restitution of Land Rights and the Land Claims Court. Formal land restitution means either restoration of land originally owned or 'equitable redress', i.e. alternative land, or the payment of compensation for the land.

Land tenure reform extends beyond the concept of restitution but still falls within the scope of reparatory justice legislation. One of the important pieces of legislation in securing land tenure for Black people is the Communal Property Associations Act that allows the legal means 'by which a group or community as a legal entity can acquire land and other property'.[10] The Communal Land Rights Act also addresses land tenure by allowing for the transfer of tribal land in full ownership to the groups concerned.[11] These pieces of legislation are impressive, but I do not know how successfully they have been implemented.

Section 25(7) of the Constitution specifically addresses 'dispossession on the basis of a racial law passed after 19 June, 1913'. The land distribution programme is thus aimed at providing the landless with land on which to reside and produce livelihoods.[12] Targeted beneficiaries of the legislation include 'rural poor, farm workers, labour tenants and emergent farmers.'[13]

---

9 David Carey-Miller and Anne Pope (2000) South African Land Reform. *Journal of African Law* 44(2):167–194.

10 Carey-Miller and Pope (2000), p. 175.

11 Badenhorst et al. (2006).

12 Badenhorst et al. (2006).

13 Badenhorst et al. (2006), p. 594.

Since only certain people[14] stood to benefit in terms of this restitution process, it was envisaged that many others could benefit from the group development projects under the Development Facilitation Project Act, communal property ownership, or provision of a housing subsidy. These group development projects are one way of redistributing land to the landless.

This somewhat technical explanation of land restitution will be illustrated through the narratives of participants later, but it is important to note that land restitution has not resulted in the equitable redistribution of land after the periods of colonialism and Apartheid that this legislation envisaged. The problem up to now is that land restitution has been slow,[15] and when claims have been paid, they do not reflect the current value of the land of which people have been dispossessed. The State has neither the resources nor the administrative capability to fully realise this key restitutionary goal. Furthermore, while it is almost impossible to obtain accurate figures regarding land ownership, 22 years after the fall of Apartheid, White South Africans, who make up 8.5% of the population, probably own 47% of the privately owned land in South Africa.[16] The State does not have the resources to expropriate this land at market-related rates in order to redistribute it.

Black South Africans are acutely aware of the failure, so far, of satisfactory land restitution. The aboriginal Khoikhoi and San people campaign strenuously for land restitution. Abahlali baseMjondolo, the Shack Dwellers Movement, have long been an advocate of land tenure for those who live precariously in shanty towns. In 2014, when former ANC Youth League President, Julius Malema, established the Economic Freedom Fighters, land restitution was and remains a key focus of the party's aims. Former EFF member, Andile Mngxitama

---

[14] Those who held title deeds to their land before 1913. This notably excludes many of South Africa's indigenous groups like the Khoikhoi and San peoples.

[15] By 2005, out of an estimated 3 million forced removals, the land claims court had processed 869 506 claims. See *South Africa Yearbook 2005/6*. Pretoria, South Africa: Government Communication and Information Services, p. 103. Since the deadline for claims has now been extended to June 2019, a further 57 300 claims have been received to date.

[16] These estimates are based on the Statistics South Africa *2014 General household survey*. Pretoria: Stats SA. Land audits to date have not produced national nor reliable data.

founded a civil society organisation called Black First Land First in 2015 to agitate for land restitution. He has been amongst many Black South Africans to call for radical land restitution ('the only way to break the back of White supremacy is to give back the land').[17]

Economic opportunities

The Employment Equity Act is one of the primary pieces of legislation enacted to address the impact of Apartheid law affecting employment and labour practice. The purpose of the Act is to achieve equity in the workplace through the promotion of equal opportunity and fair treatment in employment by eliminating unfair discrimination. In addition, it also aims through the implementation of affirmative action measures, to redress the disadvantages in employment experienced by designated groups in the past. This is meant to ensure their equitable representation in all occupational categories and levels in the work place, and includes the rights to organise and mobilise, rights that were denied under Apartheid.

The Broad-based Black Economic Empowerment Act (BBBEE) aims to promote economic transformation by enabling meaningful participation of Black people in the economy as well as promoting access to finance for Black business ownership. In addition, there is emphasis on increasing the extent to which communities, workers' cooperatives and other collectively-owned and managed enterprises have increased access to skills training. The Act is supported by various Codes that set standards of compliance for different industries and professions. According to these Codes, businesses may receive an 'empowerment score' calculated with reference to seven 'pillars', each with a relative weighting according to direct empowerment (equity ownership and management) and indirect empowerment (skills development, employment equity, preferential procurement). A BBBEE Amendment Bill was passed in 2015 which has made several amendments to the above criteria and the relative weightings – although these are likely to be revised again due to stakeholders' responses. Although the State's economic restitution legislation is sophisticated and praiseworthy,

---

17 A Mngxitama. Penny Sparrow: Racism's sacrificial lamb, *Mail and Guardian*, 8 January 2016. Accessed 10 April 2016, http://mg.co.za/article/2016-01-07-penny-sparrow-racisms-sacrificial-lamb.

it has basically created a wealthy Black middle class, comprising 10% of South Africa's Black population, without significantly affecting the 60% of Black South Africans who still live under the poverty threshold.

Reconciliation and limited reparations

The most well-known reconciliation initiative in South Africa was the Truth and Reconciliation Commission. It was mandated in terms of the Promotion of Reconciliation and National Unity Act (otherwise, known as the 'TRC Act'). The TRC grabbed public attention for years and created high hopes for substantial redress. However, its final report received a lukewarm reception from the ANC government under the leadership of President Thabo Mbeki, and its recommendations were left to gather dust. These recommendations remain relevant for the discussion of restitution. Section 26 of the TRC Act provided for the establishment of a Committee on Reparation and Rehabilitation. The purpose of this Committee was to consider applications from victims of gross human rights violations for (monetary) reparations to 'restore the[ir] human and civil dignity' (Section 26(3)). It was also meant to make recommendations regarding the basis and conditions for reparations.

The TRC Act established the President's Fund as the vehicle through which reparations would be administered. Recommendations for how this should be done have been approved by Parliament and arranged under four headings: symbols and monuments, rehabilitation of communities, medical benefits and other forms of social assistance, and final reparations. Regulations providing for one-off reparations payments were provided. There were also draft regulations which were released in 2011 regarding the provision of basic education, higher education and training of victims and medical benefits for victims.[18] The President's Fund has been criticised for being too limited. Immediately at the conclusion of the TRC, 22 000 victims were compensated with R30 000 each. This was meant to have been an initial and symbolic payment, but no further compensation has since been made. There have been a number of lawsuits against multinationals initiated by the Khulumani Support Group (on behalf of victims of Apartheid human rights violations),

---

[18] See South African Department of Justice and Constitutional Development website www.justice.gov.za.

but these were ultimately defeated.[19] In 2015, the issue of symbols and monuments came under the spotlight when students protested against various colonial and Apartheid era statues. Forty-six per cent of South Africans favour the removal of these statues, while 38% believe they should be left alone, and 16% don't care what happens to them.[20] No action has been taken so far on the removal of statues from public spaces.

The hope of Archbishop Emeritus Desmond Tutu that the 'emerging truth [of the TRC] unleashes a social dynamic that includes redressing the suffering of victims'[21] has not been realised. When Nelson Mandela died in December 2013, there was a renewed call by civil society and political parties for substantial socioeconomic transformation and an end to a focus on reconciliation and a 'rainbow nation'. Similarly, as Apartheid-era criminals become eligible for parole, grumblings abound regarding the failure of the 'reconciliation without restitution' project.

What would happen if nothing more were done about the past?

Together the participants in this study described a wonderful vision of what the future might look like for a South Africa that had dealt with its past: people would no longer be judged, rewarded or employed based on the colour of their skin; poverty, where it still existed, would be evenly spread regardless of skin colour and so would opportunity; and all those who lived within South Africa's borders would be equally valued and respected. Sadly, this same group

---

[19] See Narnia Bohler-Muller (2012) Apartheid victims group scores symbolic victory against multinationals, *HSRC Review* 10(3): 22–23, for an explanation of the lawsuits, which were ultimately defeated on an issue of jurisdiction – that a US court could not rule on matters related to US business practices in South Africa.

[20] See the HSRC *South African Social Attitudes Survey, 2015*. Opinion is sharply divided along racial lines and political lines, with twice as many Black people wanting statues removed as White people, and twice as many Democratic Alliance-affiliated respondents wanting them to be left alone compared to African National Congress and Economic Freedom Fighters affiliates.

[21] Truth and Reconciliation Commission (1999a) *Truth and Reconciliation Commission of South Africa Report (Vol. 1)*. London: Macmillan, p. 131.

of people were also in agreement about what would happen in the future if we stopped trying to address the past; if, in fact, we did nothing further than what has already been done. Here, everyone, regardless of race, education or age, offered the same answer, 'our country would burn.' There would be 'increasing inequality', 'we would lose the gains we have made', and 'we would have nothing to look forward to, but a disastrous future.'

A number of participants, mainly, but not exclusively, younger Black participants, spoke about being 'stuck' where we currently are, in continuing 'oppression', 'vicious cycles' and 'imbalances'. Many repeated the familiar phrase, 'The rich would keep getting richer, the poor would stay poor.' Palesa put it very strongly when she lamented: 'The people that have stolen so much from us keep getting rich and keep looking down on people. Not even helping them get to a point where they can be their equals.'

Candice spoke of how a future with no further restitution would strip us of our 'humanity' and send us backwards: 'We'll probably go back to what we had before, if not worse ... we'll end up being doubly suspicious of each other.' Sandy had similar views, but she described this loss of humanity as resulting in increasing 'aggression' and increasing 'corruption'. Twenty-six-year-old Max (Black man, financial administrator) exclaimed passionately, 'If you do nothing about the past, ha, back to the past!' Mbali, amongst many others, explained what was meant by 'going backwards': 'Having a lot of Black people being unemployed and being uneducated'.

By far, most people spoke of an apocalyptic future; a future filled with revolution, xenophobic uprisings and bloodshed. 'I promise you there will be war again', said Fundiswa, a 26-year-old Black woman precariously employed as a contract cleaner. 'The unemployed in the townships will go and destroy the houses and it will be war again.' Fundiswa was not alone in speaking clearly and directly of 'war' and 'revolution'. Sizwe, Portia, Hillary, Heather and Rebecca (a White sales administrator) all joined her, while Ayanda, Thamsanqa, and Sizwe described more chillingly:

> **Thamsanqa:** South Africa would remain unequal ... It will just keep pretending that Camps Bay and Khayelitsha are in one country. [laughs] ... We would come to blows. There will be a revolution and that's just the sad truth.

Sizwe: It will explode. It will implode … If you give your brothers to the wolves and they devour them, one day the wolves will not have anyone to devour but you.

Naledi (Black woman, 21, unemployed): I think we would have an uprising of very angry poor people that feel completely ignored, and they would want to make someone listen to their story and to change their story.

A number of participants spoke about individual factors that will lead to a revolution: for Olivia it was poorly educated youth; for Manny, masses of unemployed people; and for Ricky (66, Coloured man, small business owner), increasing poverty and the growing inability of people to feed their families. Sixty-year-old teacher, Patrice, from the former Transkei, said doing nothing to address the past would have the result that 'people would attack the other groups like we have seen in the past when the people of South Africa attacked the foreigners.' A number spoke of the possibility of experiencing the same land grabs as Zimbabwe, while Mayaya and Noah (White man, 21, student) anticipated that doing nothing further will enable more 'radical political parties, such as the Economic Freedom Fighters' to come into power. For Dylan it will produce a society with 'increasingly enclaved guarded communities … where people protect their privilege'. For Leo, the impact of 'unaddressed accumulated injustices and wounding' would result in 'a meltdown of our society before it can be rebuilt.'

Finally, the conclusion was that doing nothing further to address the past was not an option for those interviewed. Their apocalyptic vision of the future – across race groups, ages and social classes drowned out both the more moderate voices of 'we will go backwards', and 'we will experience increasing inequality.' Clearly, doing nothing more will not result in the country we want.

2 Ways of seeing: Why we are divided about what is needed

South Africans share a common vision of the future. However, they also have a complicated and varying relationship with the past, and are divided about how to address it. The Institute for Justice and Reconciliation's (IJR) South African Reconciliation Barometer[1] reported that two-thirds of South Africans across all race groups agreed with the statement, 'Forget Apartheid and move on' – a view held almost equally by Black (63%) and White (69%) South Africans. Furthermore, White South Africans are less likely than other groups to admit the lasting effects of the legacy of Apartheid on the current levels of poverty among Black South Africans. Only 33% of White South Africans agreed with the statement, 'Many Black South Africans are poor today as a result of Apartheid's legacy' compared to 77% of Black South Africans, 67% of Indian South Africans and 59% of Coloured South Africans.[2]

These two findings alone illustrate the danger of what we may lose if we forget too soon. Apartheid is an explanation for the current inequality and poverty still being experienced in South Africa. Such amnesia may also deter us from ensuring that the necessary acts and attitudes of restitution are carried out in our country, where clearly we have not yet done enough. In this chapter, I show how a group of South Africans, who participated in the study, relate to the past, who they blame for the past and therefore who they think is responsible for fixing the present. Also shown are why the participants' ways of seeing what needs to be done about the past vary as they do.

---

1   Kim Wale (2013) Confronting exclusion: Time for radical reconciliation. *South Africa Reconciliation Barometer Survey*. Cape Town, South Africa: Institute for Justice and Reconciliation.
2   Wale (2013), p. 37.

A complicated relationship with the past

The answers the respondents gave to the questions about how the past had affected their lives, clearly showed what can only be described as the different 'holds' the past had on people's lives. For some, the past was 'everything'; for others it was 'nothing but an excuse'. Many had conflicting feelings about the past, and a few had something positive to conclude about the effect of South Africa's past history on the present.

The past has made us stronger

Three Black South Africans and one White South African spoke of the positive effects of the past. For Andiswa, a 21-year-old Black woman who works at a political party call centre, the past had shown her how 'Black people are brilliant ... because Apartheid happened, it was hard. We stood up, we fought against it and we won.' For Max, a 26-year-old Black man with a degree in finance from UCT, the past made him 'the person I am ... a strong individual who has a will, who is driven and who knows that nobody will do and will give you anything.' For Jane, a 21-year-old White UCT undergraduate involved in student politics on campus, the past has resulted in 'a strong constitution and institutions like the constitutional court, and gender equality ... compared to places that don't have the South African experience.' Nevertheless, the pain displayed by the majority of responses was heart-rending.

The past is everywhere and affects everything

Several Black participants spoke of the past being everywhere and affecting everything. They offered long list of examples of how the past affects the present. Nobuntu (Black woman, 34, business executive) related the effect on people's dignity due to 'overcrowding' and 'poorly planned urban areas'. Zethu (Black woman, 40, business executive) spoke of the past 'catch[ing] you at a psycho-social level' and leaving 'emotional scars [that] are the worst because people don't see them.' Portia (Black woman, 26, finance administrator) spoke of the past 'still lurking in our hearts' affecting how we relate to each other. Max recounted how poverty, illiteracy, racism, and unemployment are legacies of the past that continue 'to keep the Black and the White folk not on the same scale'. More despairingly, Mzwakhe (Black man, 29, government human resources officer) said the past has produced 'frustrations, depression, hopelessness and powerlessness preventing any chance for Black people to live a normal life like other people'. Lyanda (Black woman, 48, contract cleaner) and Nontembiso (Black woman, 48, domestic worker) summed it up graphically:

> **Lyanda:** The past still affects my life … If I was White I would have had a house by now. … Apartheid made me feel like I was not a human being.

> **Nontembiso:** Black people are still down there cleaning the tiles while a White person walks on them then turns around and tells the Black cleaner it's still dirty … keep cleaning.

Similarly, most of the White respondents also spoke of the effects of the past on the present for Black people in terms of education, employment and 'denigration', as 74-year-old Ann put it. Graham (White man, 29, retail marketer) spoke about having been a beneficiary of the past at the expense of others, of having had 'greater opportunities to education and jobs which allowed me to stay in a good suburb, go to a good school … and come out as an educated individual with now greater opportunities to live well in South Africa'. Angela (White woman, 37, PhD student) said: 'Where people live, who we mingle with, what language we speak, what resources we have access to … all of these are still impacted by the past'. Cara, White 21-year-old student, speaking of her university experience said emphatically:

> **Cara:** The past defines our stories more than affects them … [At university] all the students arriving on campus by bus are Black … those on financial aid and in education development programmes are Black … students that are financially excluded from university are Black … I don't think that these things are affected by Apartheid, I think they're defined by it.

David, a 43-year-old White doctor captured many people's responses when he said slowly and carefully: 'We have a past with a very long shadow over the future.'

Conflicted about the past

No one said that the past had little or no effect on them, with the exception of retired White business executive 63-year-old Harry who spoke of being 'protected from the realities of that time' and of 'living in a bubble'. But most spoke of the conflict they experienced when relating to 'not yet achieving [since] 20 years is not enough to basically change whatever happened then.'

Naledi (Black woman, 21, unemployed) captured her own conflict and the experiences of others. She spoke of how the past had indirectly affected her generation:

> **Naledi:** Directly Apartheid didn't affect me ... It did affect me through my parents because if it hadn't been for Apartheid my mother wouldn't be a domestic worker and I wouldn't be living in a shack instead of a proper house.

The clearest experience of conflict was exhibited by Lekho. She is a 26-year-old Black woman, who has a Bachelor's degree from Cape Province University of Technology and a government job in human resources. She began talking about how Apartheid had restricted her mother's opportunities in terms of education, where she could live ('stuck in their rural areas'), and the kind of work she could get. Later on, though she seemed to change her mind when she said, 'I wouldn't lie and say that Apartheid has affected me because ... I was privileged to go and study, getting money from a White person ... [so] I don't see any effect that's negative.' I prompted her further, asking if she thought her life would be better if Apartheid had not happened to which she simply replied 'I wouldn't say so.' Lekho's mom had died of an AIDS-related condition a few years earlier, and so I asked whether Apartheid had an effect on her mother's quality of life and health. She again said she didn't think so. Lekho did not make the link between Apartheid's intentional strategies of inferior education, health care, job reservation and 'Homelands' policy with how her life had turned out; with how she had to struggle to access higher education, to pay fees, and find a job. Neither did she connect her mother's death from AIDS with the migrant labour system, poverty and the squalor of township life under Apartheid, and its effects beyond.

Later on in the interview, when I asked Lekho how Apartheid had affected our sense of humanity, she related a painful incident about swimming at a Cape Town beach in 2006 and overhearing a five-year-old White child say, 'Don't swim next to that Black girl.' She went on to explain, 'It can be so painful sometimes when you see White people being racist towards Black people.' Still later, Lekho spoke about how the past had 'affected a lot of people and their way of thinking'. She described her experiences at work, and how, in her opinion, Black people limit themselves by not pursuing promotions because 'We don't see ourselves up there.' She then went on to describe, with tears in her eyes, how she felt discriminated against at work, since Coloured people in her office without university degrees were getting higher grade jobs than Black graduates. Lekho's complicated relationship with the past was clearly evident.

Who is to blame for the past?

I never asked a direct question about who is to be blamed for the past, yet invariably the topic came up for discussion. Participants held three views: we need to hold ourselves responsible; we need to hold government responsible; we need to hold White people responsible. For many Black and Coloured participants, placing the blame on themselves for their situation was the default position – and hence also it was their responsibility to get themselves out of the situation. Almost half of the Black respondents were reluctant to blame the past for their present circumstances. Instead, Luxolo (Black woman, 29, unemployed), Nollie (Black woman, 32, help desk assistant with a Matric) and Ricky (Coloured man, 66, a struggling small business owner), blamed their current situation on a lack of education. Ricky pointed out that while it was true he lacked role models in his life because those close to him were 'truck drivers, bakery drivers, postmen', ultimately it was his choice to drop out of school in Grade 11. Luxolo blamed herself for being unemployed because of her drinking habits and also because she dropped out of school. Later she reluctantly conceded, 'Ya, it's not what it might have been. If it weren't for Apartheid it wasn't going to be like this.' Nollie was reluctant to blame Apartheid due to a lack of awareness of its actual effects: 'The only time I learned about what happened in our country is when I came to Cape Town from Transkei in 1992.' She continued:

> **Nollie:** It doesn't help us being stereotyped and stuck in the past, and go on about how Apartheid this and this … I believe we need to just move on with our lives, and be something. There are many doors open for us now, that only we can get ourselves to, and not be lazy or stuck in the past.

Haley (Coloured woman, 42, priest) tells me that she frequently hears Coloured and Black South Africans say, about those who are protesting for better working conditions, that 'They must stop striking and do some work for a change … stop just sitting around and expecting everything to be given to them.'

Blaming yourself for your lot when there is clear evidence of external factors that have caused it is known in the sociological literature as symbolic violence.[3] People internalise the view of the oppressor ('you are inferior and therefore you are the cause of your own problems'). Haley also reflects the meritocracy argument, in which people believe that it is always possible 'that by hard work and personal responsibility a person is able to achieve what has eluded others'[4] without acknowledging the impediments in the system that might prevent you from doing so.

A large proportion of those interviewed held the present government responsible – almost all the White participants and about half the Black and Coloured participants. Rose (White woman, 36, part-time lecturer) summarises precisely why this happens: 'Blaming government – saying it's their job to do restitution – therefore it's not my job … it's a way out of personal responsibility.'

Very few participants[5] blamed White people for their current predicament, although a few White participants spoke of their own culpability. Ted (White man, 67, leadership non-profit) described his journey:

> **Ted:** White people need to take responsibility as a group and as individuals for group wrong … It was only later that I realised that I need to take responsibility for my group … My English forebears were the colonisers – and the imperialism they brought to Africa. I suddenly realised that I couldn't be proud of Cecil John Rhodes. I needed to be ashamed of him.

Johan (White man, 48, peacebuilding non-profit) blamed White people for not insisting on greater redistribution of wealth at the end of Apartheid:

---

3   Sharlene Swartz, James Hamilton Harding, and Ariane De Lannoy (2012) Ikasi style and the quiet violence of dreams: A critique of youth belonging in post-Apartheid South Africa. *Comparative Education* 48(1): 27–40.

4   Sharlene Swartz (2009) *Ikasi: The moral ecology of South Africa's township youth.* Johannesburg, South Africa: Wits University Press, p. 100.

5   As I conclude this book, I am sure that this might no longer be the case in 2016 compared to 2014, when interviews were done. The protests of the past two years have resulted in many more Black South Africans being outspoken about White privilege and White people's failure to make restitution.

'White people could have done a lot more by saying [to government], 'Listen, this redistribution of wealth is not happening fast enough … it might be good in the short term but in our long-term interest, it's not good at all.'

The danger of forgetting

What I noticed over the course of interviews was the disconnect between assigning blame to Apartheid for the current effects people experience, and understanding the deep effects of the past on the present. Apartheid is not an excuse for current crime, the lack of motivation people feel after unsuccessfully looking for employment, the ways in which people self-medicate using alcohol and drugs for the pain and frustration of being excluded from the economy, and for the high levels of violence in our society today, but it is a good explanation for all of this.

The danger with disconnecting responsibility for the past from its effects in the present is that we then fail to deal with these problems in a way that addresses its causes not just the outcomes. While only a few respondents ultimately, after their interviews, insisted we should 'forget the past and move on' (unlike the two-thirds that the *Reconciliation Barometer* records), their assessments are still worth addressing.

Twenty-nine-year-old Siphosethu is a Black man steadily climbing the ladder at a premier South African retailer, from trolley handler to till operator to his current position as a floor coordinator. For him the reason to forget the past is in order to succeed:

> **Siphosethu:** People still use the past as an excuse on why we are not successful in our lives. People not going out there to look for jobs, they are still using our past as a way to paint themselves as victims … hiding behind the whole Apartheid situation. What happened, happened.
>
> ***
>
> If we let go of the past we can finally focus on our goals and achieving them as an individual as well as a country … We can finally be free and move forward and succeed. Nothing wastes time like holding on to the past because your whole focus is on the past and looking to blame someone.

Siphosethu might find this a good narrative to live by, and one useful for motivating himself, but for others forgetting the past is in fact de-motivating. For example, blaming oneself, instead of structural impediments, for not being able to get a job is a key contributor to depression, frustration and anger. As 38-year-old White non-profit worker, Heather, when speaking of those who want to simply forget the past, asked incredulously: 'When I hear young "born-frees" of all races comment on how we must not dwell on the past ... I wonder why they do not wonder where all the hopelessness, anger and exhaustion is coming from?'

Why is it that we have such conflicting views about what is needed?

By the end of their interviews only three respondents stuck to their view that we really should 'just move on' – forget about the past and think only of the future. For most respondents, forgetting the past was not an option, not in the face of the evidence of the effects of the past in the present, and without further attention, the future as well. People were agreed that forgetting was no longer an option – many had come to see this during the course of the interview. This forgetting and moving on, however, is a strong part of our national discourse – or at least had been until 2014. It remains one of the key reasons why we can't agree about what should be done about South Africa's history of injustice. To my mind, the geographical and social separation between Black and White, rich and poor, which we still experience in South Africa, is the key to why we are divided about restitution. It is therefore critically important that we understand the reasons for our ambivalent and inaccurate view of the past, since it affects our motivation to embark on a journey of restitution.

Different experiences of change since 1994

One of the questions I asked respondents was how had their lives changed since the advent of democracy in 1994. The answers fell into three categories: everything had changed, nothing had changed, and not enough had changed.

For those who said *everything has changed*, they referred mostly to the fact that Black people now have 'freedom', 'equality' and 'power'. Nollie and Mzwakhe spoke of the freedom to 'move ... without a pass book and without 'being questioned', respectively. Zethu spoke of the 'political power' that Black people now have, although for most there is still no 'economic power'. Lyanda spoke of racial equality:

> **Lyanda:** Life is better now … Previously we had so many restrictions … That was dehumanising and degrading being restricted in your own country. In 1983 I went to Adelaide in the Eastern Cape for a holiday. One day I went to town and was looking at clothes. I was chucked out of the shop and was told to go outside to look at the sign which said 'No Blacks'.

Haley spoke of the end of fear and powerlessness, along with less violence in society:

> **Haley:** I don't have to be afraid of the police anymore. That's a big one, because you can't explain how powerless it feels when you can't go to the police … I think there's less violence in this country than there was in the '80s. Some people think it's not so … people who were not affected by violence at all.

On the subject of equality, while Black respondents saw clearly that more needed to be done beyond political equality, they noted changes that had taken place in the job market, wealth for some, the end of inferior Bantu education, access to university and job reservation. For Thamsanqa (32, postgraduate male student), 1994 marked the beginning of 'New options for university … the world was just becoming bigger, and bigger and bigger.' Like Thamsanqa, Candice, a 29-year-old Coloured woman and graduate student said, 'This new democracy gave me the opportunity to break out.' Clearly, the opportunities afforded to Black people since 1994 are more significant than many White South Africans can begin to understand. These opportunities go beyond employment and studying. Sipho, a Black 56-year-old struggle veteran from Langa (now working as a gardener) spoke about his experience of change:

> **Sipho:** I remember the time I stayed in a hostel … with a single room that was shared by 20 people. I used to sleep on the floor in front of a fire place, but today I have an RDP house … and the elderly has a pension and children get social grants … So that is why I say there has been a change since 1994.

Beyond material changes are social changes – simple interactions that are now possible that 20 years ago were not. Thomas (a 23 year-old recent graduate) explained, 'I have friends who in the past I wouldn't be allowed to be friends with.' Donovan (Coloured man, 30, retail manager) and Rebecca (White woman, 30, sales administrator) spoke of how these changes have made it possible to have a relationship and get married. Rebecca explained that when she and Donovan met her parents were completely opposed to 'interracial relationships'. Beyond romantic relationships and friendships, she also referred to the 'Change in chatting between strangers [of different races] standing in a supermarket while buying their bread and milk.' Donovan expressed his enthusiasm concerning change candidly: 'I can really discover the beauty in people. I love the fact that we, South Africans, are not considered to be the worst people in the world anymore.'

For others, *not enough has changed*. Naledi drew attention to issues of racism, ineffective affirmative action and the way wealth remains largely in White hands in South Africa:

> **Naledi:** I feel like we haven't reached the level of freedom as other countries have. We still get incidents of racism where a White person has called a Black person the 'K-word'. I don't think racism will ever end because even today you get companies that don't hire Blacks as much as they should because they still want White domination.

For Olivia, a Coloured woman who has a PhD, the lack of change is clear when she finds herself in a suburban restaurant as 'the only Coloured person here ... In the suburbs [of Cape Town] the only Black people in restaurants are those working there'.

Nollie spoke of the geographical separation that hasn't changed enough, and that also illustrates how poverty and wealth remains distributed along racial lines:

> **Nollie:** The only thing that has changed is that we are free. We are not under Apartheid and we can do whatever we want to do. There's still so much that needs to change. A lot of people still stay in shacks. They stay in houses that a human being is not supposed to be living in ... Back then you had Whites living in these posh areas and Blacks staying in other areas. That hasn't changed. Government hasn't really done anything to correct the past ... We were suffering back then. We're still suffering even now.

Portia (a 26-year-old) started by saying, 'I have not experienced any major direct changes' then added 'I did experience us getting electricity at home.' For Black South Africans, although much has changed, they recognise it has not been enough. Thirty-seven-year-old graduate student Angela summed up the changes for her as a White South African as being 'spiritual, emotional, and intellectual, but not material':

> **Angela:** Materially I have not suffered in any way … For me it's about this new awareness, about race-based inequality as our legacy … I am more aware of the contradictions and problems of being White and privileged in a country which is both materially and racially divided.

A few people from both ends of South Africa's spectrum of wealth said *nothing has changed*. So although 48-year-old contract cleaner Lyanda said that in terms of equality and racism, everything has changed for her, a little later in the interview, she told me that nothing has changed economically:

> **Lyanda:** My life has not changed since 1994 … I voted so that there could be better work opportunities for our children, for houses and a better life. My daughter matriculated in 2006 and has not had a bursary, she could not study further. I live in a backyard shack.

A number of White South Africans, of all ages and political viewpoints, were candid and clear when they said that in terms of their own privilege and wealth, nothing has changed:

> **Noah (21, student):** Having grown up in a free South Africa, I have to say that not too much has changed in socio-economic terms for me. I still live in a mostly White society and experience White privilege on a daily basis.

> **Angela (37, PhD student):** I am not greatly affected in the material sense, as my life now is much as it was previously.

> **Anne (74, retired salaries clerk):** It can't change because I've had the education. I've had the jobs. I've got retirement money. So I'm still privileged.

Clearly, South Africans have different experiences of change. These experiences are worth noting because they are likely to affect people's responses to the notion of restitution, to making things right for the past. Those for whom everything has changed are hardly likely to demand restitution. For the many others who see that not enough, or nothing, has changed (whether poor and Black, or rich and White) restitution offers a way to rectify this.

Our perception of what the government has accomplished is different

It is ironic that most people when asked about who should be responsible for bringing about changes, speak primarily of the current government. The irony is that this government did not create the problems of the past, and is now expected to fix them – and all parts of society are critical of its efforts. In 1993, the Apartheid state was heavily indebted, probably bankrupt[6] and had intractable problems. The country had catered for 10% of its population and the roads, housing, jobs, education, the economy and infrastructure all reflected this. Furthermore, there was no option of simply starting over; instead the 'brutal inheritances'[7] of the past first had to be undone, then rebuilt. The result is that 20 years into democracy, the refrain is frequently heard that 'government is useless in providing the services that people need.' But what does a closer review of the government's track record since 1994 reveal?

The *Twenty Year Review*[8] provides documented evidence of some of these achievements, and a frank assessment of failures and gaps. An entire system of governance, consisting of balkanised institutions operating in a fragmented and racialised structure, had to be dismantled and re-established. This had to be done off a low-skills base because of the previous intentional effort to ensure that Black South Africans were only educated for servitude. This

---

6 The newly elected democratic government inherited a debt of R86.7 billion that took seven years to repay. See *The Economist*, 22 April 1999. South Africa's debt: Unforgivable. Accessed on 5 March 2016, http://www.economist.com/node/321289.

7 Pumla Dineo Gqola (2008) Brutal inheritances: Echoes, negrophobia and masculinist violence. In *Go home or die here: Violence, xenophobia and the reinvention of difference in South Africa*, Shireen Hassim, Tawana Kupe, and Eric Worby (eds). Johannesburg, South Africa: Wits University Press, pp. 209–223.

8 The Presidency of the Republic of South Africa (2014) *Twenty Year South African Review, 1994–2014*. Pretoria, South Africa: The Pesidency of the Republic of South Africa.

undoing and redoing meant the establishment of one unified system from the several Bantustan administrations and racialised government departments that were in existence in 1993. Basic services have now been extended to most communities, although not at the same level as the privileged White 10% of the population have enjoyed.

The review records that within the first two decades of democracy, the government built roughly 2.8 million houses and delivered 876 774 serviced sites (water, electricity, sanitation) for those who had been forced to live in the previous Bantustans. This provided roughly 12.5 million people access to housing and a fixed asset.[9] In 1994, just over 50% of South Africans had access to basic sanitation; this improved to 83% by 2012. Access to water improved from 60% of households in 1994, to 95% by 2012.[10] Electricity supply (despite current challenges) has improved from 50% to 86%. These are not the achievements of a 'useless government'.

In connection with education, it was necessary to replace a fragmented system of 19 different departments of education along with an equitable funding model. Under Apartheid, as measured in 1975, the state spent nearly ten times as much on White children's education than on Black children.[11] The backlog has been enormous and should not be underestimated. It took 70 years to fine-tune an Apartheid education system, and after 20 years the government is only beginning to make inroads into this travesty of justice. There is now a common curriculum that theoretically offers children equal opportunities, rather than destining one group for menial labour. Government now spends the same amount of money on every child in the system, with a pro-poor policy in place to develop infrastructure. However, not all children enter the system on an equal footing, and nor do they have the same social and family support structures through the course of their education. This is a legacy of Apartheid that no amount of government service delivery can fix. It has resulted in ongoing issues of poor educational outcomes and skewed success rates for children still largely determined by race.

---

9   The Presidency of the Republic of South Africa (2014), p. 86.
10 The Presidency of the Republic of South Africa (2014), p. 86.
11 Sampie Terreblanche (2002) *A history of inequality in South Africa, 1652–2002.* Pietermaritzburg, South Africa: University of KwaZulu Natal Press.

Some of the respondents in the study understood this, but many do not. As 36-year-old White businessman, Luke commented:

> **Luke:** If I try to put myself into the shoes of a Black rural South African, I can see that everything at the moment is better under Black rule than it ever was under White rule. So from that perspective I can completely understand how voting is going in our country ... opposition political parties are only picking up votes from educated people ... the wealthy, urban, middle class citizens.

The problem is that for most White South Africans and most middle class South Africans of whatever colour, these changes go unseen. For most Black and Coloured South Africans in the study, life today is infinitely better than how it used to be under Apartheid.

Haley's comment earlier about not being 'afraid of the police anymore' also dispels another perception, that government has done nothing about crime. The problem with this belief is that people fail to acknowledge how criminal in itself Apartheid was, including the practices of police brutality and authoritarian fear it maintained.[12] In addition, efforts to fight crime were solely directed at White areas resulting in very few resources being dedicated to the protection of the Black population on whom criminals also preyed. Coupled with the violent nature of police brutality and the response of violent struggle by those that resisted, there is evidence that during the period 1983–1992, murder, robbery and rape increased exponentially. The current government has adopted a new approach to crime fighting. Security is viewed as a social issue, and for example, community policing forums have been started. This resulted in a reduction in crime rates after 2004,[13] although lethal crime still remains high when compared to other countries.

Throughout these interviews it was abundantly clear that South Africans experienced change and government's role in bringing it about differently. On the one hand, there is little recognition of what a gargantuan effort it has taken by many diligent and committed civil servants to bring about the changes we currently experience. On the other, when Black people see the luxury and privilege that White South Africans and some Black South Africans enjoy,

---

[12] The Presidency of the Republic of South Africa (2014), p. 136.
[13] The Presidency of the Republic of South Africa (2014), p. 136.

they can be forgiven for saying that nothing has changed. Ted offered a reason for why this is so:

> **Ted:** Government is not doing a very good job of making us aware of what they are doing. Every now and again I will read on the 4th or 5th page of a newspaper about ... various initiatives of empowerment and upliftment of people ... There is a lot of publicity being given to the things that government isn't doing ... The things that they have done need more credit.

Furthermore, why should government be held solely responsible for bringing about change? Why do Nollie and many others blame government? ('Government hasn't really done anything to correct the past.') Why are Black South Africans so generous in their approach to White South Africans when White South Africans continue to enjoy the benefits of the policies of the previous White government that caused the poverty and inequality in the first place?

Clearly, South Africans have different perceptions of what government has accomplished in terms of redress for the past, and different expectations of what the government ought to be doing. These perceptions and expectations are worth exploring, especially since they affect people's responses to the notion of restitution. The questions to be asked are: who should drive restitution, and should the failure of government allow individuals to escape from the responsibility of playing a part in making restitution? The next aspect to be considered is the problem of corruption and the role of the media in shaping perceptions about corruption in South Africa.

The perception of corruption in South Africa is centre stage, but short-sighted

In South Africa, blaming government's failure to address past issues has become a national sport. An oft repeated sentiment is that 'This country is going downhill fast. There's no hope,' followed by, 'The government is corrupt.' That corruption occurs is not in question. The perception of the extent of government corruption needs to be examined, as well as the unintended consequences of a relentless focus on corruption, and also to be examined should be why such a focus is short-sighted.

Most of the White and Coloured participants interviewed spoke of corruption, along with around half of all Black participants. These comments were made mostly in response to the question about what made the participants despair about South Africa. Many were incredulous that politicians and civil servants only seemed to think about enriching themselves, when all around people were suffering. For many others it was not surprising that those in power were taking 'their turn' to accumulate benefits having been denied them for so long under Apartheid. For many, the clearest example of corruption was evident in the controversy surrounding the upgrading of President Jacob Zuma's personal home in Nkandla, as Naledi explained:

> **Naledi:** Take Jacob Zuma for example – he has a mansion in the rural areas whereas his neighbours are still living in poverty. What does that tell you about South Africa? It shows that people in power are selfish … They were starved of power in the past, so they are taking advantage of it now.

Luke and Thamsanqa were scathing in their criticisms of the ANC government for both participating in corrupt practices and allowing them to thrive:

> **Luke:** I've lost all hope in the ANC being the representation of … a hopeful future. So the tips of the corruption iceberg that we see in the media leave me feeling as though we are losing control from a government perspective … We seem to have a bunch of incompetent politicians running our country and fleecing us blind … I would put most of the ANC cabinet in that bucket … I want to see evidence of … selfless, servant-hearted leadership in public administration.

> **Thamsanqa:** They're not the ANC I grew up knowing. They've changed … It's power – having come from the history of the struggle, feeling that they've sacrificed a lot for their families, their professional development, and now they feel like they need to make up for that.

It has been estimated[14] that South Africa has lost R30 billion a year to corruption since 1994. Putting this in perspective – without corruption we

---

14 No actual figure exists. These estimates have been repeated as fact since an initial address given by the Institute of Internal Auditors South Africa, quoting corruption as costing a proportion of GDP or a proportion of the Government's procurement budget. Retrieved on 1 March 2016 from https://africacheck.org/reports/has-sa-lost-r700-billion-to-corruption-since-1994-why-the-calculation-is-wrong/.

would have had an extra 5% each year to spend on education, health and social protection. This is not negligible, but neither is it the 'wholesale flushing our country down the toilet' as some argue. In addition, government has key programmes and task groups that attempt to minimise corruption and prosecute those who are found out.

In connection with corruption, in 2015 South Africa was ranked 61st on a perceptions of corruption index (a shared position with Italy, Lesotho, Montenegro and Senegal), where one is least corrupt, 167 most corrupt. This is 75 positions better than our continental competitor, Nigeria, that is ranked 136th. South Africa's BRICS partners Brazil (76th), India (76th), China (83rd), and Russia (119th) are all ranked far worse than South Africa.[15]

There are three main implications of this relentless focus on corruption in South Africa. The first is that it weakens civic participation amongst both Black and White South Africans. Fewer people bother to vote; many who do, vote for opposition parties who focus on corruption without offering other platforms for improving the country. Lwethu (Black woman, 24, retail merchandiser) explained that voting would not bring any change to her life. Most telling was that she felt her 'voice is not heard in South Africa, they do whatever they please even though my vote is what gave them power.' For her, corruption has resulted in 'South Africa is no longer a "we nation" but an "I nation".' Graham expressed his disillusionment with corruption by voting for the opposition: 'I looked for a party that actually cared about the future of our country with equality for all.' Lekho explained: 'I'm not going to vote because of those fights, arguments that I always see in the news ... about corruption and all those stuff.'

Concentrating on the incidence of corruption insidiously fuels the racist discourse. Gina (White woman, 69, retired retail manager), is scathing as she told me, 'Every second Black [government] minister now is a millionaire.' Sixty-three-year-old Harry expanded: 'There are those in my age group who are continuously critical of the new government ... and probably don't believe that these people will ever be capable of running anything properly.' Such perceptions are only one step away from the prejudice that paints corruption as having a Black face. Connie (White woman, 71, retired non-profit administrator) exhibited this prejudice when she harshly asked:

---

[15] Transparency International (2015) *Corruption Perceptions Index 2015.*

> **Connie:** How can we live with a government that is totally corrupt ... My question is: Do the Blacks, when they grow up as children, learn about honesty in their culture? Because every day you read about fraud here, fraud there, fraud everywhere.

It follows then that how South Africans understand and speak about corruption will also affect their understanding of restitution. People are reluctant to offer support and money to restitution projects when they perceive the money they already contribute through the tax system is squandered.

Moreover, most South Africans are unaware of the amount of corruption that took place pre-1994. The fact that we know about the current corruption, and see it being dealt with by the courts, is a triumph for democracy. Under the Apartheid government the state and press colluded to hide issues of corruption, and opposition parties had little access to government records as is now the case. Hennie Van Vuuren's[16] report on the myriad corruption scandals during the Apartheid years, apart from Apartheid rule itself, is sobering. The South African Defence Force (SADF) smuggling ivory to pay for its Border War; the information scandal of the 1970s in which money was used to bribe international newspapers to run stories favourable to South Africa; sanctions busting and illegal purchases of oil; Swiss bank accounts for Apartheid ministers; insider trading deals of the Afrikaner Broederbond; the wholesale destruction of state documents and the extensive transfer of public land into private hands just before the end of Apartheid; the corrupt administration of the Bantustans that lined the pockets of government ministers; secret funds; kickbacks in procurement; tax avoidance; foreign exchange fraud; the role of the South African Reserve Bank in various scandals; mafia links in the Ciskei; and grand corruption in hotel magnate Sol Kerzner's colossal amassing of wealth. The difference between then and now is that because we lived in a totalitarian state, we never heard about the corruption.

Vukani (Black man, 34, finance executive) explained the short-sightedness of the current fixation with corruption:

> **Vukani:** So we focus a lot on Zuma's corruption but White South Africa benefited from a country which focused on benefiting

---

16 H Van Vuuren (2006) *Apartheid grand corruption: Assessing the scale of crimes of profit from 1976 to 1994.* Cape Town, South Africa: Institute for Security Studies.

them solely. It was totally corrupt, yet they got wonderful roads, tree-lined streets and facilities that worked ... We're allowing the corruption focus to derail us from real progress in the country.

Vukani also identified White South Africans' obliviousness of what has been achieved, 'If we think what has Jacob Zuma done, and what has Thabo Mbeki done, what has Nelson Mandela done? They've achieved immensely great things.'

Corruption weakens civic participation and, as mentioned, it fuels racist discourse. It causes people to disengage from nation building and the media sees to it that we are fully informed about corruption. The problem is that we do not hear the other good side of the story. Dylan (White man, 34, PhD student) provided a succinct analysis:

> **Dylan:** My perspective is mainly informed ... by my partner who works in government. I see how hard she works ... the way that she speaks about how desperately a lot of people in government are working to make the lives of South Africans better ... Whinging White people are not party to a lot of South African life that goes on in government ... [White people tend to work] in the private sector ... so they don't actually know what goes on.

A focus on corruption Zethu concludes, keeps us from 'engaging in the real stuff'. Clearly, South Africans have short-sighted and ahistorical views on corruption. These views are worth challenging, especially since they are likely to affect people's response to restitution. This is summarised by the frequently heard comment: 'Until the corruption stops, I'm not lifting a finger.'

The media's role in fuelling ambivalence and despair

The role of newspapers, radio, social media, television and online news channels shape our views of our country as well as our views of each other as fellow South Africans. Freedom of the press has resulted in a media that is largely critical of government. We have very little 'sunshine media' in South Africa. This was not the case under Apartheid, where due to draconian censorship laws, very little media critical of government was permitted. In contemporary South Africa, Dylan offered an analysis of what role the media plays:

> **Dylan:** The media needs to sell stories ... And what sells newspapers is sensation. It's not 'Bob goes to work in the office in

the Department of Home Affairs and does his job efficiently' and
so on. So I think that tales of corruption and doom, and scandal
sell … I think that we don't get the other stories enough for people
to have a better view.

Whatever you think of the South African media – overly critical, one-sided,
or just right – at the core is the question of whose voices are being heard and
documented. Nontembiso (Black woman, 48, domestic worker), Rose and
Sibu (Black woman, 27, social worker) all spoke of the way in which the media
sifts the news we receive and how it shapes our perceptions:

> **Nontembiso:** In the news there's always a government official who
> misused funds for his or her personal use that was allocated for
> some upliftment project.

> **Rose:** The media skews things and makes certain things public and
> not others.

> **Sibu:** The bad news … every week you hear your President has
> done this, so-and-so has done this … and Marikana – and it starts
> to overwhelm you.

Remember too Lekho's struggle to vote ('I'm not going to vote') and Luke's
fierce criticism of the ANC ('I've lost all hope in the ANC'). They both told me
this was because of what they had heard in the news. More telling was when
Sandy (White woman, 38, part-time teacher) said, associating restitution with
revenge, it is the people she sees 'in the media' who make her believe Black
people want revenge, rather than the Black people she knows. This fuelling
of fear and anger was called into question by Michael when he pointedly
commented: 'Haven't you noticed, in spite of the media … how incredibly
transformed South African society is? So there is a huge amount of humanity.
The average person in the street gets on incredibly well.'

Why do the media choose to tell a predominantly critical story? Certainly,
our current President has given them much material with which to paint the
picture they do. But when a new President is elected, will we hear all about his
or her skeletons and transgressions too? Perhaps these are the stories we want
to hear. Although South Africa's newspapers are no longer predominantly
White-owned or run, there is an element of what I can only call hegemonic or
dominant reporting that happens – a morbid focus on Black short-comings

rather than Black excellence.[17] I am making a more sinister claim, rather than the one we usually hear about how 'sensationalism, drama and lot of bad news sells' (Ted). In order to counter this overwhelmingly negative media discourse we urgently need 'spaces ... for real conversations that don't often happen in this country' (Dylan).

Ways of seeing

We are not divided about the future we want – this is clear. Neither are we divided about what will happen in the future if nothing further is done about our past. We also have, as South Africans, a complicated relationship with the past – we do not like to blame the past, we generally want to move on, to look to ourselves and our own abilities to bring about change, and to criticise government for slow delivery. The problem with these ways of seeing is that they are unlikely to bring about the kinds of change we long to see – one in which race is no longer the chief determinant of our lives, when we are all truly equal and when poverty is a thing of the past. But how do we get there? I strongly believe that we will not be able to get there until we fully realise the effects of past injustice on our present everyday lives; until the magnitude of the effects of Apartheid and colonialism are fully understood, and do not continue to slip from our consciousness.

Without this consciousness, a project of restitution has no motivating power. As I analysed interviews and returned time and again to the respondents' anecdotes and struggles, it became evident that people could be roughly divided into four categories: those who saw the effects of the past clearly and what needed to be done; those who came to see its effects over the course of the interview; those who sometimes saw, sometimes did not see – and often saw in distorted ways; and those who did not care to see, or who refused to see the ongoing effects of past injustice.

Those who *saw clearly*, knew South Africa's history intimately, located themselves in it precisely, and understood the transition and what had been

---

17 This is alluded to by academic Stuart Hall when he speaks about how representation maintains racial stereotypes. Stuart Hall (2001) The spectacle of the other. In M Wetherell, S Taylor and S Yates (eds) *Discourse Theory and Practice: A Reader.* London, UK: Sage, pp. 324–344.

achieved, and where weaknesses existed. They were critical of some efforts at redress and applauded others. They spoke confidently about their emotional responses as well as their own actions or failures to act.

There were plenty of respondents who I could easily categorise as *coming to see* over the course of the interview. They started out hesitantly, sometimes prickly, sometimes just overwhelmed by the subject. Slowly as they spoke and the interview became more of a dialogue, they spoke of making connections they had never previously discussed. These interviews provided opportunities for reflecting and questioning. In doing so, they came to see how the word restitution may in fact be a very helpful concept around which to explore their unease, dissatisfaction and sense of rage, shame and fear.

For those I categorised as *not caring to see* or *refusing to see* I was struck more by their desire to stick their heads in the sand in the hope that our problems would go away, rather than disagreeing with the need for restitution. Frequently older people across all race groups fell into this category, but by no means *only* older people.

Many more I categorised as *seeing through a distorted lens*, a view tainted by their own silence in the past, or their exile in a former Bantustan, or their current positive personal experience of affirmative action and social mobility. These engagements often blinded participants to the lived realities and suffering of others, or their complicity in the past. This category comprised people across race groups and of all ages.

I describe these four categories not as strict and watertight compartments, but as a helpful tool to distinguish varying strategies for engaging with each perspective. Often I couldn't make up my mind between categorising someone as coming to see and seeing in distorted ways; other times, people saw very clearly one aspect of restitution, but refused to see on others. In an effort to help us to fully realise the effects of past injustices on our current lives, the next three chapters relate stories of pain, rage, shame and ignorance that still characterise our lives as Black and White South Africans. This is done so that more of us may clearly see the effects of the past on the present. Each story has the potential to act as spitting on the shoes of all those who want another country. It is now time to begin truly to see the past in the present.

PART 2

THE PAST IN THE PRESENT

3 Black pain and the outrage of racism

In 2013, a few months after the death of Nelson Mandela, the following racist incidents made headlines in Cape Town. Cynthia Joni, a Black domestic worker, was assaulted by a White cyclist and told to 'get off my street'.[1] The cyclist, Tim Osrin, said he mistook her for a sex worker. A Coloured gardener in Claremont, Mohammed Makungua, was sjambokked[2] by a White man in a BMW who said he 'mistook him for a thief'.[3] A White student urinated from a nightclub balcony on Michelle Nomgcana, a Black taxi driver in Claremont. The student yelled, 'You're Black, I'm White, you're poor, I'm rich.'[4] These are extreme examples and I was not surprised that the press had a field day describing them. Nevertheless, having grown up in a White community, I am aware that these incidents are representative of a pervasive racism that circulates as jokes, expresses itself as attitudes and eventually spurts forth its toxicity in incidents such as these. Many more have occurred and made the headlines since.

What lasting impact has this racism and injustice had on the lives of those who were part of it – both Black and White? Furthermore, while we know of some of the brutal treatment meted out to Black South Africans by Apartheid security police (including to children)[5] how is racism, and the effects of racism

[1] S Segar (25 October 2014). *More trouble for Kenilworth 'Klapper'*. Accessed on 3 April 2016 from http://www.iol.co.za/news/crime-courts/more-trouble-for-kenilworth-klapper-1770599.

[2] Whipped. A sjambok is a whip made of rubber or rawhide.

[3] C Greach (12 November 2014). *Man held for allegedly whipping gardener*. Accessed on 3 April 2016 from http://www.iol.co.za/news/crime-courts/man-held-for-allegedly-whipping-gardener-1778813.

[4] A De Klerk & P Nombembe (19 November 2014). *Student who urinated on taxi driver not a racist says black friend*. Accessed on 3 April 2016 from http://www.timeslive.co.za/local/2014/12/19/student-who-urinated-on-taxi-driver-not-a-racist-says-black-friend.

[5] See Pamela Reynolds (2012) *War in Worcester: Youth and the Apartheid state*. Bronx, NY: Fordham University Press.

experienced today? This is a key question this book seeks to answer, partly because there is a lack of White consciousness on the topic, but also because of the worrying sentiment that the past should be buried and forgotten. It has not been an easy task to decide how to go about addressing such a question. What gives me the right, as a White South African, to speak on behalf of those who experience these effects? Teaching an undergraduate class on race at the University of Cape Town (UCT) helped me to decide what to do.

Who gets to speak?

It was a sociology class, called Race, Class and Gender. In 2013, there were 250 students in the class; two-thirds South Africans, the remainder equally divided between other African countries, and 'semester abroad' students from Europe, China and the United States (US). About half way through the course, we watched the film *Cry Freedom,* which I had first seen in London as a 21-year-old. The film is about Steve Biko, the Black Consciousness activist, and his friendship with Donald Woods, the White newspaper editor. I set the class a task based on readings from Biko's work. They were to divide themselves into two groups, as described by Biko, either 'Black' or 'Not Black',[6] and to reflect on the effects of racism and what should be done about it using Biko's definitions and principles.

The class slowly straggled to the left and right of the lecture hall with many milling around in the centre, arms folded, or hands raised wanting to object to having to classify themselves. White students were reluctant because, 'It felt awkward' they said, while Coloured, Indian, Asian and international students found it hard to decide which group to join. Some said, 'I don't consider myself Black but feel awkward congregating with White students.' Others said, 'I am Black by Biko's definition but haven't really experienced oppression.' All the international students vacillated a little, before reluctantly joining a group.

Unsurprisingly, the 'Black' group quickly came up with a long list of the ways in which South Africa's past had affected them as individuals and as a group, and were soon deep in discussion about how racist actions might be stopped and their effects overcome. The 'Not Black' group came up with a similar

---

6   Biko's definition of 'Black' is commensurate with 'oppressed' and paid no regard to Apartheid's categorisations of African, White, Coloured and Indian.

list, how South Africa's racist past had affected Black people and what Black people should do about it. I called attention to Biko's basic principle that in order to deal with racism, Black people need to reflect on 'the cause of their oppression – the Blackness of their skin – and to operate as a group to rid themselves of the shackles that bind them to perpetual servitude'.[7] White people, on the other hand, should reflect on their acts of racism (individual and institutional), and on the privileges that racism confers on them, and come up with ways to cease their practices and relinquish these privileges in order to build an equal society.[8] Only when that has happened can Black and White meet together and build a non-racial society and 'a true humanity'[9] on equal terms 'without encroaching on or being thwarted by another'.[10]

Biko's point is that Black people are able to free themselves from racism if they reflect together in solidarity with one another as Black people, and if White people do the same.[11] I am frequently challenged on this point by Black colleagues, 'Who are you to tell me that the past has damaged me, that I have been dehumanised by racism? What about your own dehumanising? Don't speak for me. Speak for yourself.' Such an activity allows both to happen.

Consequently, in this chapter, and the next, I present stories of Black people's pain,[12] anger and outrage as they were related to me in response to two questions: 'How does South Africa's past still affect people today?' and 'How were/are you affected by South Africa's past?' I have made every effort to let the stories speak for themselves. In Chapter 5, I present White people's responses

---

7   Steve Biko and Aelred Stubbs (1978) *I write what I like*. London, UK: Bowerdean Press, p. 91.

8   See Sharlene Swartz, Emma Arogundade, and Danya Davis (2014) Unpacking (White) privilege in a South African university classroom: A neglected element in multicultural educational contexts. *Journal of Moral Education* 43(3): 345–361.

9   Biko and Stubbs (1978), p. 90; Swartz et al. (2014).

10 Biko and Stubbs (1978), p. 21.

11 The #RhodesMustFall movement that emerged in 2015 took these principles seriously as they began their campaign to free themselves from the shackles of racism and colonialism. The movement was Black-led with White students being encouraged to form allied but separate movements.

12 Terrie Williams (2009) *Black pain: It just looks like we're not hurting*. New York, NY: Simon and Schuster.

to the same two questions, but limit accounts to racism's effect on White people despite the fact that many White people commented on how they believed racism affected Black people. I also interpret and comment on their accounts, as I am one of them. While not strictly following Biko's principles, I am at least, as Xolela Mangcu describes it, exercising a 'consciousness of Blackness'[13] and am offering a perspective as an ally in Black people's struggle to end White domination.

Demeaned and dehumanised, whether executive or unemployed

In the study, a number of Black South Africans told stories about how they had felt demeaned in the past, or had witnessed a parent being dehumanised, and how this continues to be part of their current everyday experience. I recount the stories of Mayaya and Luxolo – one a business executive, the other unemployed – of racism in their lives, and as experienced by those around them.

Mayaya – demeaned and patronised

Mayaya is a 34-year-old Black woman, who was born and grew up in a rural village in the former Transkei Bantustan. She, and her three siblings, attended a small private school formed by local parents that she describes as being 'a fairly good school … very small – I think there were 13 or 14 of us in the class'. Her father worked for the post office, and then an insurance company in an administrative capacity; her mother worked as an administrator in a local business. When asked how her parents afforded to send her to a private school, she replied:

> **Mayaya:** I don't think they could afford it actually … [They] did not have much money, but my father has always been very enterprising. I remember growing up, we had a general dealership where we would have to take turns working, making money to

---

13 Xolela Mangcu (2014b). The contemporary relevance of Black Consciousness in South Africa: From Black Consciousness to consciousness of Blackness. In Devan Pillay, Glibert Khadiagala, Prishani Naidoo, et al. (eds) *New South African Review*. Johannesburg, South Africa: Wits University Press.

support the family … So we were never hungry, but we were the
children that could never make it to camp, because there were
many of us to go and he could not really pick which one to send.

Mayaya and all her siblings now have university degrees and good jobs. Mayaya
has an undergraduate degree in computer science and physics, and an MBA.
Her first job was for the company that had given her a bursary followed by a
senior position with a national retailer; she now works for a financial services
provider as a business strategist. Her husband is a financial executive at a large
retail bank. They have two children, one of whom attends an exclusive private
school in Cape Town, the other will follow shortly. Mayaya and her husband
own property in Gauteng and currently rent a property in Cape Town.

I asked Mayaya to reflect on how the past had affected her life, and whether
it still affects her life. Her story was one of anger, humiliation, grit and
determination in the face of past and current racism. It addressed the topics of
affirmative action, how Black executives experience corporate South Africa,
and family life. Mayaya's immediate response to how the past has affected her
was to say, 'I don't know.' Then as she continued to talk, she spoke of how
important education has been in her life and that to value it was something
her father had instilled in her. Her father had gotten 'his very first pair of
shoes when he started working at the post office', and 'understands the value
of education, you know, in his life'. She continued:

> **Mayaya:** It's almost as if for those that never had the exposure,
> things have just gotten worse … And for those that had even
> a crack of light, that sort of knew even a little bit about what it
> would take to liberate their families and their children, things
> have gotten better.

When we talked about her level of political consciousness and awareness
while growing up, she told me that she 'grew up singing the liberation songs
without really understanding or knowing what they were all about'. At family
gatherings, her uncles would educate her about what was going on in the
country in response to her questions. By 1994, when she was 15, she says
she had a good understanding 'that the majority of Black people were under
oppression'. She related an account of her earliest awakening, when they were
stopped and searched at a roadblock in the Bantustan while travelling in a car
with her father.

Mayaya: If you were a Black guy, of course you always were stopped and searched … This traffic officer stopped my dad and my father's demeanour … he almost took a position of 'I'm so subservient to you', you know … And that's an image that has always stayed with me. It made me angry … It disturbed me initially because I did not understand why. But when I realised what was going on, it made me angry and sad at the same time.

Mayaya then used the above story to relate how the past (South Africa's history of Black subjugation) – which she experienced first-hand in this incident with her father, affected her then and still does. She spoke of how this incident made her come to see herself:

Mayaya: I'm as good as anybody else out there. I am more than good enough. I do not owe anybody anything and no-one else owes me anything, and that I have made it this far on a combination of luck, hard work and people supporting me. It has nothing to do with the fact that I'm Black … It's just made me determined to prove [myself] to anyone that looks at me and undermines me based purely on how I look and how I sound. And that's how I think it's affected me … it's also made me very defensive.

She related a number of incidents that have provoked this anger and defensiveness. One concerned a public event when a respected White newspaper editor explained why Black people continue to vote for what he described as 'this very corrupt government'. According to him, it was because Black people had grown up in families and a system 'where everything was illegal, from *shebeens*[14] to illegal bootlegging'. As a result 'Black people see corruption as normal'. Mayaya was seething as she ended her account and said, 'It offended me greatly'.

She told me she has had to deal with White people's interpretation about Black people's lives many times. In her former job at a retailer, her White colleagues, during a strategy meeting, spoke about how 'Black people don't know anything about vitamins and supplements, and that sort of thing because they think taking laxatives is it'. She interjected sharply saying, 'It's not a Black or White thing, it's an education thing'.

---

[14] A tavern or pub.

Her experience of getting her child into a private school also evoked anger. She related how she has frequently asked the school principal why there was only one other Black child in her son's class of twenty, only to be told 'there aren't enough Black children in Cape Town who want to, or can afford to, go to private schools'. She replied cuttingly to the principal:

> **Mayaya:** I know that when we wanted to move from Jo'burg to here, trying to get a place [at this school] you did not welcome us with open arms. No, we had to jump through hoops to get in. So don't tell me there aren't enough Black people … You like keeping things the way they are!

Another incident concerned how she is frequently assumed to be a junior assistant at business meetings, rather than the senior executive she is:

> **Mayaya:** I've gone to business meetings where I've had someone who works with me, but junior to me and they're a White person, and the people I'm meeting with will address this White person and proceed to give me the files to hold and carry. And I'll just smile and I'll take them, and then I'll hand them over to my White assistant.

When I asked Mayaya how she survives the continuous racism in her life as a successful executive, one who has worked hard to earn her success, she told me she speaks out and always confronts it. It is important that she does so, she explained, since working-class Black people seldom resist racist treatment.

To Mayaya, racism remains rife in South Africa. Her message to those who continue to make ignorant comments about Black people is that 'until you've been Black, and a woman, and lived my life, I do not think you have earned the stripes to speak of Black women, or Black people in general'. She acknowledged the difficulty in being outspoken, the psychological effects of always 'being in a state of stress', of always having to be the one to speak out, especially since people 'believe what they believe – that there is White superiority and Black inferiority – they believe it … It's difficult to change someone's belief.' What's the lasting psychological effect of this, I ask? She said,' It's made me not trust White people inherently … any White person that I do not know, I look at them and I watch them with a very careful eye of distrust. So that's what it's done for me.'

Just as I begin to think we've exhausted Mayaya's take on the effects of the past on the present, she offered an analysis of the difference between racism in Cape Town and Johannesburg.[15]

> **Mayaya:** I've found White people from Cape Town to be very patronising. Extremely. I've found Black people in Cape Town to be very timid and very subservient, like they know their place. It's like someone has said to them: "This is where you belong. This is as far as you ever go. Don't you dare step out of these lines.".

Her analysis went further when she told me she can't believe how young Black professionals with whom she works in Cape Town still struggle to assert themselves in the working environment:

> **Mayaya:** They've gone to one of the greatest universities in SA. It's UCT! And they have the same qualifications as their peers, and yet they seem to not believe that they have ... They're not comfortable to state their case. They're not comfortable to disagree or even agree. They're not comfortable to speak up and have a voice.

She says that 'something weird is going on in Cape Town'. In Johannesburg, her experience was quite different. Even those who went to less prestigious universities do not lack confidence in social settings as do Black people in Cape Town. In fact, she continued:

> **Mayaya:** Even the service people in Cape Town – Black, White, Coloured – are very patronising towards Black people ... I understand why they are the way they are ... they believe that I am not as good as a White woman ... They believe that.

Mayaya's stories about racial denigration, being demeaned, rejected and dehumanised were repeated by many of the Black participants in this study. Private school educated, 34-year-old Black man, Vukani, related a similar story to that of Mayaya's childhood experience with her dad. In 1988, when he was travelling with a male family friend, a doctor and a member of the Lesotho royal family they were pulled over by a young White traffic officer:

---

[15] The Western Cape province, of which Cape Town forms a part, is currently led by the Democratic Alliance, a White-majority party, and the official opposition in Parliament. The ANC controls Gauteng, which includes Johannesburg.

Vukani: To see this man … levelled down to, I don't know – It was a very difficult thing to see – like a child. And he had to respond in a way, very apologetic for who you were, sort of thing … You can sense the anger in the man that "I've had to behave this way in front of all of you." … I was very aware, even at that age of maybe seven, eight years old, that this is a very differentiated society that we live in.

Vukani also told of driving through a West Rand Johannesburg suburb in 2008, 14 years into democracy, and stopping at a pub with friends:

Vukani: The establishment ignored our presence completely. No service, just total – [pause]. You go to the barman; he doesn't look at you at all, and just carries on doing whatever he's doing. And there's nobody else being served … It's actually quite a segregated environment where Black people will still be treated as if it's still the pre-1994 era.

He related a similar incident one Saturday afternoon in 2013; this time he was out for lunch with his family and some friends at a popular restaurant in Cape Town. He arrived early and asked for a table for eight, only to be told there were no tables available. A few minutes later his White friend arrived, asked for a table of eight, and was immediately seated. When he and his family joined this White family, Vukani recalls, 'It was quite an awkward situation for the Black maître-d who had indicated there was no table, and suddenly there's a table.'

Vukani: It's a story that's common across Cape Town … I make bookings on the phone and … people don't know on the phone that I'm a Black person. Then suddenly I arrive and they're like "Damn it, we should have picked this up" … And it's sad because the Black populace accepts it … In the Western Cape, they generally choose not to make a fuss about the fact that they're not integrated into this province at all. They remain in their townships.

Zethu, a 40-year-old Black female executive, who had previously said that living through Apartheid had made her stronger, spoke of her outrage at having to cope with racism against her son. Shortly after they moved to the suburbs of Cape Town, he began getting stopped by the police and armed response security patrols when he went out for a jog. At his local suburban school he experienced ongoing racial slurs. After this had gone on for some time, and she had been 'in and out of the school' trying to sort it out, and had written letters to the school with no change, she sat her son down and told him, 'I give you permission to smack them.' She explained:

> **Zethu:** My son is big, he's huge … he plays rugby. I said: 'Punch them and I'm happy to go to the office to have a chat about that.' That's when it stopped. I reflected on that and I thought: 'Gee, until today the only language racism can understand is violence. Really?' … [but] I've never been called in … Anyone who calls him a baboon or whatever, anything racist, you know, he smacks them.

She concluded that she can cope with racism directed towards her, but not her son:

> **Zethu:** From being undressed by security at a Waterfront [shopping mall] shop, and asked for an ID when I'm about to pay, or told something is expensive as if I didn't see the tag … I can deal with that. But when you kick my kid, it just rips me apart.

In contrast to the stories of Mayaya, Vukani and Zethu, that speak of their outrage at the ongoing racism they experience, despite their positions in society as relatively wealthy professionals, Luxolo's story highlighted another effect of racism – a person's sense of confidence, or self-worth. Luxolo's story differed from those of Mayaya, Vukani and Zethu because, unlike them, not having the resources afforded by social class, she has not found ways to resist racism, nor cope with its effects.

Luxolo and the effects of racism on her sense of confidence

Not all incidents of racism are blatant, but their effects are as bad as, if not worse than, those that are openly so. Luxolo, a 28-year-old woman, unemployed and living in a backyard shack on the premises of a family-owned house in a Cape Town township, explained in an extended conversation how she sees the effects of racism on her confidence. She began by saying that she 'wasn't affected as much [by Apartheid] as my parents and grandparents because I just grew up now when everything was already okay'. She paused before continuing to talk about the issue of confidence:

> **Luxolo:** So there's no confidence. It's just something that's not there. It's something that we lack, all of us as Black people. Some of us are

confident enough, but some of us still have that negative feeling
... Especially when you don't have a job, it's hard for you to feel
confident about anything.

I asked her if she felt this had changed in the past years. She responded
obliquely by speaking of the value placed on material gains as a symbol of
self-worth by people living in the township:

> **Luxolo:** People in the townships, they like expensive stuff and they
> like expensive clothes, but I've changed from that. I used to do
> that as well, but now I just don't care. If I have shoes, I just happen
> to have shoes, that's all. Even if I could work right now, I am in
> a different place than I was because I saw that it doesn't make a
> difference wearing R800 shoes and wearing R200 shoes.

We went on to discuss her unemployment. I began by asking her where she
placed the blame for her joblessness. She said it was 'my fault for dropping out
of school in Grade 9'. Because I know Luxolo's story from my doctoral study, I
asked how her mother's death from AIDS-related illnesses, her absent father,
her unemployment and Apartheid were related. She reluctantly responded
saying, 'Ya, it's not what it might have been. If it weren't for Apartheid it wasn't
going to be like this, of course.'

Our discussion moved on to the subject of the xenophobic attacks in both
2008 and 2014. I asked her what she thought had led the perpetrators to carry
out the attacks.

> **Luxolo:** I think because Black South Africans were treated badly,
> some of them, they have that anger. And that anger they put
> towards ... other Black people ... Maybe they want to feel superior
> themselves, so they play big on other Black people – foreigners.

I probed her further on why White people had not been victims of xenophobia,
to which she replied: 'It's easier to pick on a person that's defenceless and you
know that they don't have anything. Black people, I think they're scared of White
people.' She continued to say that many Black people held concurrent feelings of
fear and admiration of White people: 'Even now, some of them [Black people],
if they see a White person it's like they see a prince or king or something ...
They're more obedient, more shy, everything "yes madam, no madam".' Our
conversation moved back to the issue of confidence when I asked Luxolo how
she felt when she saw Black people acting in a subservient way:

> **Luxolo:** I don't like it. I just like people to feel free to be anywhere. Like if we're walking on a pavement and I'm going to move off the pavement to make way for you. Why can't a White person make way for me to pass? … It's because of Apartheid making Black people feel smaller than other people.

Luxolo's explanation of the erosion of confidence, being made to 'feel smaller' and taking it out on those who are 'defenceless' are among the many effects of racism.

Coming to see and to survive a brutal inheritance

Welile and Sizwe, two young university-educated Black men spoke of how they have come to cope with the brutal inheritance of South Africa's Apartheid past. They spoke of their anger as they have come to see how the odds have been stacked against them. They highlighted the erosion of trust within Black communities as competition for scarce resources grows and frequently turns ugly. Both men's stories bring into stark relief the relationship between education, class and confidence when faced with racism.

Welile's brave face and determination in the face of inferior education

Twenty-four-year-old Welile was born and raised in an informal settlement along the N2 freeway in Cape Town. Until recently, he lived with his mom, who works on a contract basis at a printing company, and three sisters. They have now moved into an RDP house for which they've waited almost 20 years; he has remained in the informal settlement. He has no real relationship with his biological father, but has a relationship with his mother's partner. Welile completed both primary and high school education in township schools. He then took an enforced gap year after school while he scraped together registration fees for university. In 2012, he graduated from Cape Peninsula University of Technology (CPUT) with a national diploma in food technology. During his studies, he held various casual jobs, including a job at one of South Africa's premier food and clothing retailers. Immediately after his studies, he did an internship (for a nominal monthly stipend that barely covered his travelling costs), and a few months later he got a job as a sales representative for a company that sells corporate entertainment packages.

Welile had much to say about how the past had affected and still affects him. His first story is one of racial aggression encountered while working at the retail store. A customer had come in asking for goat's milk but since the shop layout had changed recently, Welile was unable to point him to the product:

> **Welile:** He found it by himself and came to me and asked me if I'm blind … 'This is the goat's milk I was looking for *jou bleddie kaffir* [you bloody nigger].' He was a White older guy. He was Afrikaans. Hey, I got angry. I was angry at the fact that he called me a 'kaffir' … I wanted to let it go, but this other lady that was also shopping there – she was Black – she bombed him out. They got into this big argument … [She] asked him to apologise. He did apologise just to get away … At times you still know if you're Black you're Black, if you're White you're White.

Reflecting on the impact of the past on members of the community in which he lives, Welile said that it has resulted in people becoming 'greedy, eager only to help themselves'. The consequence of this is the erosion of trust amongst Black people themselves and the dissipation of community solidarity:

> **Welile:** Our history divided us. Not only by colour, even Blacks divided themselves because of Apartheid. Because there were people that were fortunate during Apartheid times – a few … When we were given this freedom … people did what they thought was best for themselves first, before they thought of other people.
>
> ***
>
> Now people don't trust each other. People are not happy to see other people succeeding in life. They feel like it should have been them. Hence there's a lot of robbery going on [in my community] … People feel like they're owed, so that's why they do certain things. It's sad.

Welile turned to talking about his education, articulating his experiences of the obstacles he faced, from language barriers to resources:

> **Welile:** I went to [township schools] … then after to CPUT. It's not the best education. You start to see that when you get to varsity – that the education that you had is not the same education that other people had. When I got to varsity, I had to work twice as hard

> as another person that went to a suburban school. I didn't have
> any computer knowledge when I got to varsity … The language
> barrier was another obstacle … The level of the education that we
> had – things that other people told me that they learnt in Grade 10,
> I didn't know … When I got to varsity, I realised that the education
> that I had for all of this time was not as good as it's supposed to be.

Despite this realisation, Welile continued to work and made sacrifices:

> **Welile:** I didn't want people to look at me through what I didn't
> have … I don't like people feeling pity for me … I told myself, I was
> already in varsity, it's either do or die. So when other people were
> out partying I had to study. I had to put in that extra effort … I
> needed to study extra.

He made the point that in order to succeed as a young Black South African
who has suffered Apartheid's racism, you have to be exceptional, in terms of
determination, mental health, focus and hard work. This is not the case for
White South Africans.

Welile is a young man whom I have mentored since high school. Despite his
circumstances, he has always put on a brave face. During our interview, he
told me how much 'stress' he was under during his varsity studies, and that he
intentionally kept this from me: 'I was putting on a bold kind of thing. It took
me a lot of guts actually to ask you for money for transport when I was doing
my in-service training, but I didn't have a choice.' He also told me that during
his enforced gap year when he stayed at home, neither studying nor able to get
a job, he would tell me he was working. 'I was trying to make myself feel better
… I don't want people to see me for my failures, you know?'

Welile also gave an insight into the inter-generational effects of South Africa's
Apartheid past. His grandmother was a teacher in the Eastern Cape, but when
she came to live in Cape Town, she was not allowed to teach due to the 'influx
control' legislation. As a result, his grandmother was unable to pay for his mom's
schooling. 'So I feel like maybe if my mom would have had an education, maybe
she would have actually got a better job. That means a better life for us.' He
concluded by saying, 'All of that actually affected the life that I had: growing up
in a shack, [with a] single parent and … [my mother losing] her permanent job
because the company only kept people that had certain qualifications.' He talked
about his sense of self, experienced most acutely in the work place:

Welile: There are times when your colour will make you feel inferior. I mean, even now, there are guys that I speak to who are managers or chief executives that we pitch products to … [and who] will say 'I'm not interested' and will put the phone down … The very same guy will be pitched by another person on the other side of the room that is White. He will listen, and get a sale out of him.

My conversation with Welile was heart-rending. His honesty and self-disclosure took me by surprise, partly because of the front he had put up for the past ten years. We spoke about why he had decided to say so much this time:

Welile: Many people are still angry out there. There are no platforms for people to raise their voices … There are a lot of people in *ikasi* [township] that still feel that White people owe them … [But] people are afraid of raising their voices, people are afraid of talking about their feelings.

Interviewer: Why?

Welile: If you say something now, chances are you're going to hurt someone … [Or] it's going to turn into this political thing or you're going to end up in court … or you're going to get fired from a job because now you've got too much opinion.

I then asked Welile to conduct further interviews on my behalf for the study. I asked him to interview people in his community, especially those who may be reluctant to speak to me. Some opened up and spoke of their anger and their understanding of how the past has affected the future; others did not do so, even to him. Was it a lack of confidence, a lack of understanding, or perhaps just a sense of hopelessness? Sizwe's story sheds further light on racism's effects.

Sizwe describes his journey from fear, to anger, to self-blame and beyond

Sizwe is a 23-year-old Black gay man completing an honours degree at UCT and living in a rented flat with housemates. He comes from a township outside Pretoria where his mother still lives in a shack. He has no relationship with his father. He did extremely well at school – a township school – and received numerous UCT bursaries over the course of his studies. He was admitted on merit rather than on the UCT affirmative action admissions programme. He is active on campus in social justice issues, leading an anti-racism campaign and after I interviewed him, he became active in the #RhodesMustFall collective. He began by talking about poverty's effects on his life:

> **Sizwe:** I used to go to church on Sundays but [now] have issues with religion because they would preach things like it's okay to be poor ... For me, poverty on its own – beside racism and Apartheid and whatever – messes you up. It takes something from you that you can't get back, I think. Secondly, I'm gay and I used to go to a church where it's wrong.

His interview indicated how clearly he sees the need for restitution in South Africa, drawing on his own experiences at UCT in which he has had to work on White people's terms in order to succeed. He also shared indelible impressions when he saw his mother on her knees before her White employees, and of being called 'a kaffir' by his mother's boss for whom he did some gardening work when still at school. In describing the incident and its impact on him, he told me of his realisation as a 16-year-old that he needed to rise above his circumstances, for his own sake and that of his mom.

His direct response to the question about how the past had affected him was to acknowledge the material and economic conditions he faced that were informed by his mother being a domestic worker and the schooling he received. He continued:

> **Sizwe:** For me it was more than poverty. It was the emotional, mental, psychological, internal issues that I've had as a Black child, as a Black man. To come into the world and have to constantly think that you're Black and have to constantly work on your mental emancipation.

Echoing Welile and Luxolo's description of the fear felt towards White people, Sizwe spoke of 'a phase' when he was 'scared of White people ... not want[ing] to upset them or something', which was soon replaced by anger:

> **Sizwe:** [As a child] I would see White people and run away 'cos I was like: 'Oh my gosh, God is coming' ... Then I started being angry at White people. I'm not scared of them anymore ... That was in my teenage years from like 13 until I was 19. Then when I came to UCT, I still had that anger. I won't lie. Then all of a

sudden, you land up in a situation where you are equal to White people somehow. Obviously socio-economically, they come from Constantia, they have wealth, you have nothing. In this institution, you're supposed to be equal and I remember how I would go to class and think: 'Well, he's White, I'm Black. He's more intelligent obviously' … For me Apartheid messed me up because I remember how my mom reveres White people. It trickled down to me.

While for Welile and Luxolo fear translated into pain, Sizwe's mutated into rage. He expanded on his experiences at UCT beginning with Black students being called 'kaffirs' by White students at the residence to which he was assigned. He related an outrageous practice where 'White students paid *the Black receptionist* [said emphatically] money to make sure that … she makes it a Whites-only block.' In class, his outrage continued: 'You can tell the way they [lecturers] speak to you in class. That they think you are stupid because firstly, you don't speak the way bourgeois people speak. You don't look the way bourgeois people look.'

I met Sizwe when I was teaching the sociology class on race described earlier. He sat in the front row and was extremely vocal. He told me that just prior to taking my class he had read Steve Biko's book on Black Consciousness and how it changed his life:

> **Sizwe:** I realised I'm not an appendage, I'm an equal. It's a constant project, though, because for me Apartheid messed my family up, messed me up as a person … to think, for most of my life, that I'm sub-human. Now, having read that book and now being a Black Consciousness scholar … I try and free other people as well.

The realisation that came from reading Biko was one that allowed Sizwe to regain his sense of worth. He resolved to excel at UCT – which he has done, frequently receiving the class medal for achieving the highest marks in class, and winning a prestigious scholarship to study at Oxford University in 2015. The project is ongoing he tells me, 'It's not like: "Oh, I'm mentally free now." It's a constant thing, even today.' This constant project to escape the shackles of Apartheid's dehumanising messages 'is exhausting. Yo! It's tiring'. He reflected candidly:

> **Sizwe:** The past is not really past. Yes, it's the past in terms of the Constitution. That's the political rhetoric that we hear … As for my

socio-economic conditions [long pause] … The past has tangible, present, current, real effects. And sometimes I'm like: 'Oh, we should move on', but it does affect me. I used to sometimes try and deny it and shut down, but I can't because it's the truth. The past for me has shaped and still shapes my life. In the decisions I make, in the way I am, my future … What I'm going to do in life is to try to redress the past.

Sizwe's reflection carries with it a burden that no one should have to bear – the constant struggle to be equally valued, to be equally human. This struggle has been obvious in all the stories related so far: from Luxolo's lack of confidence, Welile's understanding of his inferior education, the daily struggle to escape race in the workplace and its effects on his family, as well as the stories of Zethu, Mayaya and Vukani – to ensure that their children get past gatekeepers into elite schools, that they are safe and not bullied or harassed, and that they themselves are not demeaned by security guards in retail outlets, in boardrooms, or in restaurants.

Inferiority and superiority

A key theme that runs through the stories of many Black participants about how the past affected their lives is concerned with the issue of attributed value, of inferiority and superiority. Thirty-four-year-old Nobuntu, an executive at a well-known South African food retailer says that the past affected her 'psychologically' from a young age. She related how as a child, she grappled with the issue of 'why I couldn't be a member of the library in town because it was The Republic of South Africa … where White people stayed, where the best library was … [whereas] I lived in a Homeland'. Nollie (32, a helpdesk assistant) says that the past has resulted in people being 'stuck in that whole mentality that we Blacks are not good enough'. Palesa (22, a business graduate) speaks of the 'mentality, the way we were raised up – the things instilled in us that White is better … We still think the Western way is the better way than our cultural ways'. Twenty-four-year-old Lwethu, who works as a shop merchandiser made the wry and insightful comment:

> **Lwethu:** When a Black child is asked what they want to be when they grow up and their answer is he or she wants to be a White person, we know we are still in trouble, and that equality has not

fully arrived … We are trying to move away from that mind-set
that the White race is the better and more superior race.

Sibu and Haley provided further insight into how this inferiority and
superiority are experienced.

Sibu's account of subservience and being judged for being Black

Sibu is a 27-year-old Black woman who lives in a shack 40 km outside of Cape
Town while waiting for her RDP house to be built. She has been trained as an
auxiliary social worker but was unemployed when I met her. While looking
for work she volunteered at her church in an administrative capacity and
did some cleaning. I met her when she filled in for her cousin who was off
on maternity leave and she came to clean my house every Saturday for four
months. When I asked her how the past had affected her life, she started by
explaining that the past had had a positive effect on her:

> **Sibu:** I'm Black and I don't feel ashamed just because I'm Black,
> because I'm strong and I'm beautiful and I can push the walls. If
> those women back in those days pushed the walls [and] they were
> heard, that still means that I can do the same. There's power behind
> Black. There's strength behind Black. So I love being Black even
> though sometimes I feel like people just have to … take me as I am
> rather than looking at my skin, you know?

She then spoke of the negative effects of the past and what it means for her now:

> **Sibu:** If I sit in a room where there's Coloureds and White people,
> and then there's R200 missing, I don't want to feel guilty because
> I'm Black … The R200, they're going to say it's stolen by me just
> because I'm Black. I don't want that. I wish we could reach a
> point where we don't judge each other according to the colour of
> our skins.

Sibu attends a racially integrated church (one of very few in Cape Town) but
says that even there people still equate 'being Black with being poor … and a
charity case' or being criminal:

> **Sibu:** When I come to you or ask for something and then you hold
> your purse tighter because I'm Black. I wish our relationship could

go beyond that ... I'm not going to steal from you. I'm not going to break into your house. I'm not going to hijack your car.

We returned to the topic later, when we spoke about what Apartheid had taken away from Black people, to which she unhesitatingly responded 'power, dignity, self-esteem' and she related two examples:

> **Sibu:** My grandmother ... she wouldn't call you 'Sharlene'. She would call you 'Madam', you know? And she would ask me also to call you madam because you're White. For me now, it absolutely doesn't make sense ... [but] she's seeing herself as less of a human than you just because you're White. Even though she's not saying it out loud. By saying madam to you, it shows how she feels about herself.

The second concerned Black people's 'obsession' with material things as a symbol of self-worth, as Luxolo had also mentioned. Sibu told me she had heard from family that it was, and remains, one of the very few options available to poor Black South Africans to 'feel human':

> **Sibu:** If you go to Gugulethu you would see people on weekends, they dress up nice. They get expensive clothes even if they don't have food in their cupboards ... [They buy] expensive cars and pay R600 for premium DSTV, whereas they are sleeping in a small bed and sharing a half loaf of bread. They're trying to show their status. 'We are people. We deserve these things.' Because of something that was communicated to them in the past, 'That you are less of a human, you don't deserve this' ... Unfortunately now it's affecting them economically because they can't save ... and get into debt.

Sibu's analysis of the subservience of her grandmother, the automatic suspicion of wrongdoing her Blackness evokes, the way in which Whiteness is the standard by which all things are judged, and the ways in which some Black people believe they have to prove that they are human through what they own, demonstrates her recognition of the vast injustices of Apartheid's racism. Sibu saw clearly the effects of the past on her life and on that of other Black people in her community.

Haley's explanation of inherited beliefs of racial inferiority and superiority in South Africa

Haley, a 42-year-old Coloured woman and Anglican priest, offered a detailed explanation of how the feelings of inferiority and superiority came to be entrenched in South African society through the Apartheid past:

> **Haley:** Very bluntly, I think there are people who still have an inferiority complex that they live with, no matter how old they are. And 20 years later, they're still … victims of that. And there are still some people who have a superiority complex that they suffer from, and they're not even aware of it … Relationally that whole dynamic is messed up. It makes connection and social cohesion impossible.

Echoing Welile and Sizwe's experiences at university, Haley spoke of the fallacy of linking achievement and intelligence to being White. She tells of a conversation she had with a Coloured academic friend:

> **Haley:** There's a colleague of mine who says [when] he walks into a room and he's the only person of colour – and he's an educated man with a degree, quite senior in his work – [he] loses his voice … feels like he's pinned against the wall and wants to burst into tears because he doesn't feel like he has anything to say … It was just the first time in a while that he found himself a minority in a group [of Whites] and he completely defaulted to the inferiority complex. Like automatically. And I think the same thing happens to White people around superiority issues. I think White people default to superiority, and Black and Coloured people default to inferiority.

Haley emphasised the need for people to acknowledge these unfounded feelings of inferiority and superiority as part of restitution, saying that 'until you take responsibility to believe that you are equal in this country, you're sunk'. Not that this is easy, she continued. We have all been 'brainwashed into believing this rubbish'. She spoke of how the church's teaching aided such attitudes by inviting acceptance and complacency:

> **Haley:** My great-grandmother's response to the forced removals was *God se water oor God se akker* [God's waters over God's lands]. Very Calvinist. That it's God's will and we must continue to pray

for the government and God will eventually bring justice … You mustn't resist Apartheid, not passively, not violently. You must accept it because obeying your government, this is God's will. So anybody resisting Apartheid was like: 'Yes, can you see what happens to those people? They don't want to listen to the word of the Lord' – when they were jailed or killed.

Haley drew attention to the complicity of Christian theology not only in defining policies of separateness, and inferiority, but in entrenching it.[16] This is not dissimilar to Sizwe's strong response to his church preaching about accepting poverty as a Black person.

Black South Africans understand the deep effects of the past on their lives

What has been clear in these stories is that Black South Africans across all levels of education and from all age groups understand the depth and extent to which South Africa's racialised past has affected their lives. The selection of stories I have told are only the tip of the iceberg of the soul-wrenching stories that this study elicited from people. The clarity with which these Black South Africans see comes across superbly in Zethu's summary of Apartheid as a 'superb system of social engineering' and in Lwethu's description of Apartheid's legacy as an exhibition of 'emotional scars … humiliation and degradation'.

Twenty-five-year-old graduate, Sindiswa, concluded her interview by saying: 'I feel – honestly – a bit bitter … there are some big consequences we are facing because of the past.' Thirty-six-year-old Aloz spoke of the 'psychological problems' that Black people experience because of ways in which their hopes for a changed life have been dashed ('promises aren't happening'). The reflections on the pain of the past by both Mayaya and 56-year-old struggle-veteran, Sipho are further evidence of this clarity of insight:

---

[16] The Truth and Reconciliation report goes into detail about how Christian churches were complicit with, and in fact established, the political practice of Apartheid through doctrinal interpretations. See Truth and Reconciliation Commission (1999b) *Truth and Reconciliation Commission of South Africa Report* (Vol. 5). London, UK: Macmillan, p. 251.

Sipho: It's very difficult to talk about the Apartheid era because it brings so much pain and I might even go to bed without eating because I just lost my appetite talking about the past ... [But] I don't mind even though you have opened old wounds that haven't properly healed ... Our past left us with so many emotional scars as well as physical scars ... I just wish that no person who was part of the struggle would live in poverty ... I feel that Apartheid still exists.

Mayaya: On a psychological level, there are lots of scars and wounds that people still carry that will take time to heal. There is still a lot of prejudice against differences. There's a lot of anger. There's a lot of hope for certain people, like me. There's a lot of opportunity as well ... You feel a sense of gratitude because you cannot imagine living in the South Africa that [older] people describe ... There's a sense of helplessness as well. So the past has made me grateful, but also given me a sense of helplessness.

Their stories illustrate Mamphele Ramphele's concept of the 'persistent wound of racism': that we as South Africans are a wounded people in denial about our wounds; that there has been a 'scarring of the Black psyche', the effects of which are 'a socially induced inferiority complex, self-hatred, low self-esteem, jealousy of those seen to be progressing (both Black and White), suppressed aggression, [and] anxiety'.[17] These accounts also serve as a counterpoint to the amnesia about the past White people seem to exhibit. This was graphically illustrated by Jonathan Shapiro,[18] the political satirist known as Zapiro, who penned a masterful cartoon shortly after the TRC depicting how accounts of human rights violations, state terror, subjugation and murder went into one ear and out of the other for White South Africans.

There are three reasons why remembering our turbulent history of racial subjugation is important. I have already referred to how popular the 'forget the past and move on' refrain has become with two-thirds of South Africans

---

[17] Mamphela Ramphele (2009) *Laying ghosts to rest: Dilemmas of the transformation in South Africa.* Cape Town, South Africa: Tafelberg, p. 16.

[18] See 'White South Africa hears the truth about Apartheid' by Zapiro. It appeared in the *Sowetan*, 30 June 1997.

across all historical race groups agreeing with the statement as reported in the *Reconciliation Barometer.*[19] The second is a growing call to frame redress in South Africa based on levels of poverty and inequality, rather than on what caused it in the first place, as reported but not espoused by academics Steven Friedman and Zimitri Erasmus:

> Framing redress in racial terms only is not the strategically most effective way of securing White people's compliance … [since] redress is least likely to face resistance where measures that serve to redress racial inequities can be phrased as anti-poverty measures rather than as means of reversing racial power and privilege. [20]

The problem with such a stance is that it contributes still further to the entrenched amnesia of White South Africans about how the present came to be. Remember too, the *Reconciliation Barometer's* report that White South Africans are less likely than any other group of South Africans to admit that current levels of impoverishment amongst Black South Africans are a direct consequence of Apartheid's legacy.[21]

The third reason for remembering history is one that Biko puts forward, that 'as long as Blacks are suffering from [an] inferiority complex – a result of 300 years of deliberate oppression, denigration and derision – they will be useless as co-architects of a normal society'.[22]

We dare not forget the enduring effects of racism. We dare not focus on poverty without focusing on racism as its root cause. We dare not attempt to build a 'normal society' without addressing the outrage and pain of entrenched racial inequality.

---

[19] Kim Wale (2013) *Confronting Exclusion: Time for radical reconciliation South Africa Reconciliation Barometer Survey: 2013.* Cape Town, South Africa: Institute for Justice and Reconciliation.

[20] Steven Friedman and Zimitri Erasmus (2004) Counting on 'race': What the surveys say (and do not say). In Adam Habib and Kristina Bentley (eds) *Racial redress and citizenship.* Cape Town, South Africa: HSRC Press, p. 346.

[21] Wale (2013).

[22] Biko and Stubbs (1978). p. 21.

4 Apartheid's costs: Education, opportunities, assets and wellbeing

South Africa's demeaning and dehumanising history of racism affects the current inequality[1] we experience between Black and White, and all our challenges – those of poor education, high crime and extraordinary unemployment – disproportionately affect Black South Africans. As with the previous chapter, the missing element in the South African discussion about the past seems to be a national consciousness about how these effects of the past remain in our present, and why restitution is an essential response.

This chapter therefore deals with how the past has influenced people's sense of self as it relates to opportunities for education and meaningful work, and how Black South Africans, across all age groups, interpret and understand South Africa's huge inequalities in relation to the past. It offers accounts of real people's encounters with opportunity ceilings, belonging, the physical (often deadly) effects of poverty and inequality, and the hurts and limitations of being the recipient of an intentionally inferior education.[2] What is clear is that Black South Africans, young and old, are fully aware of these consequences. This chapter, like the preceding one, intentionally focuses on the stories of Black South Africans. The effect of the past on White South Africans will be considered in the next chapter.

---

[1] The South African Gini co-efficient which measures income inequality is currently 65 (expressed as a percentage, or 0.65), the highest in the world along with Seychelles. See United Nations Development Programme (2015) 'Human Development Report' (United Nations Development Programme).

[2] 'Bantu education', the policy of the Apartheid government, was formally abolished in 1994, but its effects remain, with poorly educated teachers, too little teaching contact time, poor infrastructure and insufficient family support noted as contributing factors. See Nicholas Spaull (2013) *South Africa's education crisis: The quality of education in South Africa 1994–2011*. Johannesburg, South Africa: Centre for Development and Enterprise.

The results of an intentionally unequal and inferior education

Mbali, Nontembiso and Lwethu come from varying circumstances and find themselves in different places today in South Africa – as a business woman with a finance degree, a domestic worker with nine years of schooling, and a precariously employed woman in the retail sector with a Matric certificate. All three women both illustrate and clearly recognise the effects of poor quality education on their lives. They also understand why the quality was poor,[3] and how it contributes to ongoing inequality between Black and White South Africans.

Mbali is a 28-year-old Black woman from Soweto who, after graduating from university, works for a financial services institution. When asked how the past has affected her and still affects her, she began with the familiar litany, 'our education system … the education barrier' and offered a penetrating explanation about the quality of township education:

> **Mbali:** The level of thinking and how people get taught things. If you are in the township, there are a lot of things that you will never know about and that you will never be exposed to just because your parents are not informed about these things.

Nontembiso is a 48-year-old Black woman from the Eastern Cape who lives in a shack on the outskirts of Cape Town with her husband and six children. She exited school in Grade 9 and has worked as a domestic worker in private homes since then. She spoke of the 'huge gap in the living standard between Blacks and Whites' that she attributes to Apartheid-era minister of 'Bantu Affairs', Hendrik Verwoerd's policies, and how in the present 'township schools might be free but they offer poor education':

> **Nontembiso:** Verwoerd said Black people will not only have Black skin but a Black-stupid mind also … [So now] there is a huge

---

3   South Africa's education achievement remains amongst the lowest in the world: last for numeracy and second last for literacy according to international surveys. See I Mullis, M Martin, P Foy et al. (2012a). *TIMMS 2011 International Results in Mathematics.* Chestnut Hill, MA: TIMSS & PIRLS International Study Center, Boston College; I Mullis, M Martin, P Foy et al. (2012b). *TIMMS 2011 International Results in Reading.* Chestnut Hill, MA: TIMSS & PIRLS International Study Center, Boston College.

difference between a child who went to a suburban school and a child who attended a township school. Township schools are at a disadvantage ... I can say that we as Blacks, we are still oppressed in terms of education especially if you can't afford to send your child to a suburban school.

Lwethu, who grew up in a shack, speaks of the gap between Black and White South Africans:

Lwethu: We as Black people still have a mountain to climb. Take me for instance as a 24-year-old Black person – I am not educated so I can't better my life whereas a 24-year-old White person has a degree at this age and is establishing a career. A White person has an upper hand, so we will never be on equal ground.

The stories of Welile, Sizwe, Mayaya, Zethu and Sibu in the previous chapter need to be recalled. While the parts of their stories that dealt with the blatant racism they encountered were highlighted, they all spoke of the ways in which being recipients of inferior education had affected their lives. Sibu, the 27-year-old woman now trained as an auxiliary social worker, after a long period of being under- and unemployed picked up the theme of the 'education gap' as she explained:

Sibu: It also goes back to the gap that I'm talking about ... because if you look at Cape Town now it's so divided ... You won't see any White person, you know, running to catch a taxi or running to catch a train. [White] people don't understand why Black people *toyi-toyi* [protest] because they ... always had water, they always had electricity, they always had a proper toilet, they always went to school ... If you go to our schools then you would see. If you would have a conversation with a Grade 10 from Khayelitsha that's going to a local school and then go to Rondebosch Boys' [a suburban school] to a Grade 10 and then have a conversation, you would see that there's a huge difference.

Sibu articulated very clearly that the effect of her education had been to make her feel 'chained by the past' especially 'when I go search for a job and then it says you must have ... and I don't. I still feel very Black'.

Both Andiswa (25, call centre worker) and Palesa (22, financial services administrator) are young Black women with good jobs. Palesa, the first in her family to go to university, spoke about the generational effect of receiving what she recognises as an intentionally inferior education: 'If my mother's generation were the generation that went to varsity … I feel like I would have had a better life today.' Andiswa spoke specifically of the poverty in which many households live because grandmothers receive 'only grant money' and do not have 'the opportunities to succeed in life, because of their skin colour'.

This younger generation of respondents clearly captured the legacy of a poor quality education, a generation after Apartheid's formal end – and a full year before the advent of the #RhodesMustFall and #FeesMustFall movements. Besides the obvious effects of poor skills and hence low paying work, if work is to be had at all, there are other forms of capital that suffer – what sociologists call cultural, social and symbolic capital.[4] These include the ability to know the rules of the game, to draw on connections when it comes to opportunities for advancing in the world, and the importance of being held in high esteem by peers and society.

Opportunity repeatedly denied

The theme of opportunities is another area in which the past and the present are inextricably intertwined for Black South Africans. Many speak of their own experiences, others that of parents. Thirty-four-year-old finance executive, Vukani, spoke of his mother who was a medical doctor, but who was restricted by Apartheid's laws. 'The rules of the time indicated that Blacks could not open practices outside of townships' he explained. He added that he can't imagine what it must have been like to know that no matter how hard you worked and how good you were, there was still 'a ceiling on your opportunities'. Ricky and Fundiswa, despite being two generations apart, told stories (repeated by many others) about their own work experiences that were littered with thwarted dreams and the frustration of denied opportunity, because they are Black.

Fundiswa – I'm a cleaner, this is not my dream

Fundiswa is a 26-year-old Black woman from Cape Town's largest township. As with Welile, I first met her during my doctoral studies and have kept in

---

4   Pierre Bourdieu (1997) The forms of capital. In A Halsey, H Lauder, P Brown et al. (eds) *Education : Culture, economy, and society.* Oxford, UK: Oxford University Press.

touch with her since then. She is the mother of a seven-year-old child and lives in an RDP house with her parents and two younger sisters, one of whom is still at school, the other is unemployed. Fundiswa goes through periods of employment and unemployment. At the time of her interview, she was employed as a contract cleaner with a large company. She explained that she is often moved around, was placed under new supervisors and had been paid late on many occasions, while also battling to get paid for the overtime to which she is entitled. She described her meandering employment trajectory as follows:

> **Fundiswa:** In 2009 I was struggling to get a job and I went for some interviews. I never found any luck. So I got a job as a cleaner at the Waterfront in 2010 … a cleaning company … I'm working there but I'm having a problem there. Every month I have to cry for my pay … The salary is R15.67 per hour … If we're sick, we don't get paid, even if you bring a sick certificate.

Fundiswa described in some detail how hopeful she felt after she completed Matric and was accepted into a technical college to study mechanical engineering. Her hopefulness soon turned to despair as money to pay fees evaporated, and the cost of textbooks and transport became prohibitive. Consequently, she dropped out and took whatever work was on offer, eventually ending up as a contract cleaner working for a low wage:

> **Fundiswa:** I sacrificed for my family to become a cleaner. I never wanted to be a cleaner. I wanted to be at school, finishing my studies. I was so looking forward to being that mechanical engineer … I had to quit college and go to work for my family.

Although Fundiswa was only six years old in 1994, she understands very clearly how South Africa's Apartheid past has affected her and her family:

> **Fundiswa:** To compare us with White people: firstly for education our parents didn't go to school at that time because of Apartheid. … [So] they worked as gardeners, maids. They have poor jobs. And the Whites, they have everything because they are educated.

Fundiswa continued bitterly, 'So the Black people – what can I say about us? Because we are not educated – we don't think, we only make babies … and then we are suffering too much.' She spoke of the past affecting the money, jobs and housing Black people currently have:

> **Fundiswa:** The past is still affecting Black people, because they don't have the *money* that the Whites have. They don't have proper *jobs* like the Whites have. At least some Black people can afford to take their children to high class schools … our family doesn't have *land* like White people. If you go to the suburbs you will see this big house. If you go to a township that one house can maybe be divided into four people's homes.

Fundiswa's analysis is rudimentary but completely accurate. An average suburban house of around 120m2 to 300m2 is between three and eight times the size of a 36m2 RDP house. These inequalities, like those in education that participants reported, conform to racial lines. For example, Black youth are twice as impoverished as Coloured youth, four times as impoverished as Indian youth and eight times as impoverished as White youth.[5] Black youth complete school on average two years later than White youth, and only 35% of Black youth have 12 years of schooling compared to 80% of White youth.[6] The university enrolment rate of White and Indian youth in South Africa is four times that of Black and Coloured youth.[7] It is therefore no surprise that the unemployment rate amongst Black youth (aged between 15 and 24) is four times that of White and Indian youth, and amongst Black youth aged 25 to 34 this doubles to eight times that of White youth.[8]

However, Fundiswa's analysis about inequality in connection with unemployment and the type of work Black South Africans are forced to take, is not the complete story. When finally you do find employment, there are other Apartheid-legacy challenges to overcome, such as discrimination in the work place and little job security: 'White managers, Coloured managers, who are still having that thing of Apartheid … threaten[ing] you that you're going to lose this contract if you don't follow their instructions.' Fundiswa's father

---

[5] Statistics South Africa (2012). Census 2011 Statistical release – P0301.4. Pretoria, South Africa: StatsSA.

[6] Southern Africa Labour Development Unit (2011) National Income Dynamics Study, ed. by Development Research Unit. Cape Town, South Africa: University of Cape Town.

[7] Statistics South Africa (2012).

[8] Statistics South Africa (2013). Quarterly Labour Force Survey – Quarter 1. Pretoria, South Africa: StatsSA.

had an accident in 2008 and broke both his legs. As a result he had to give up work and survives on a disability grant. Shortly after his accident, he stopped going for rehabilitation treatment at the hospital due to the lack of money needed for transport. She shared the despair and shame she feels because of her father's present condition:

> **Fundiswa:** My own father is collecting cans to have cash every day ... He's supposed to be at home, sitting nicely and treating his legs and stuff, but he's busy pushing a trolley on the roads and collecting. You see your father having a big bag collecting dirty stuff? ... Can you imagine how I feel when I see that?

Fundiswa concluded pessimistically by linking the poor living conditions of Black South Africans to the absence of decent work: 'I only see people living in good conditions when I'm in the suburbs ... there are no opportunities for us as Black people.'

Ricky – job reservation and the opportunity ceiling

Ricky, a 66-year-old Coloured man from Cape Town grew up in two different Coloured communities. He worked for a time in what was South West Africa (now Namibia) and now lives in a rented apartment in a formerly White suburb. He has a Grade 10 education, has held many jobs over his lifetime and attends church regularly. He began the interview by saying that as a teenager growing up in Cape Town during Apartheid, he had been taught, and had believed that 'the way things were, were the way they were meant to be'. He explains that you grew up 'not knowing' and you were taught to 'respect the law ... you respected the policeman'. He tells me he only became politically conscious in the late sixties when he repeatedly came face to face with discrimination while working and being denied opportunities for advancement.

Ricky's first recollection of work was helping his father buy and sell fresh produce. Each morning they travelled to the Epping market, collected the day's goods and then took the train to Salt River to sell it. One morning he tells me they were 'chucked out of the train, out of first class, and told to go sit in second class' which was for Coloureds.[9] His second encounter concerned a restricted career path choice:

---

9   Third class was reserved for Black Africans.

Ricky: I did bookbinding as a subject at school ... I could do it! And I thought wow, I could go into the bookbinding business and the printing trade. But no – closed shop. White man's job! ... [As a Coloured] you get the driver's job or sweeper's job, or a cleaning job only.

Nearly 45 years later, Ricky is still clearly upset and angry. His animated, 'I could do it!' spoke of denied opportunities. For the remainder of the interview, Ricky gave me a detailed account of his career trajectory, each job punctuated by the visible presence of Apartheid's job reservation laws and discriminatory treatment.

After selling fresh produce for his father, he got his next job, 'at sea as a greaser, an engine room apprentice, and then I qualified as second engineer, chief engineer by the time I married ... there were no Africans'. He eventually left 'because there weren't any opportunities there ... you were just a cleaner', and because of the discrimination he experienced. He described it jokingly: 'I gave it up because the Whites were having *lekker* [nice] food upstairs ... but we had to just eat what we were given downstairs.'

From one company to another, Ricky kept moving looking for better opportunities. Each time he hit a barrier in the form of a colour bar ceiling in the way he was treated, the position he was allowed to occupy, the salary he was paid, or the benefits he was denied. There was 'No medical aid, there was no pension, there were no benefits'. After taking a job as a fisherman on a boat, Ricky described how he was injured when a seal, slipping out of the day's catch, fell on him and sent him to hospital. Once he had recovered, he returned to the boat still limping badly. His employer, a White Afrikaner, shouted at him telling him to '*Loop rêg!* [walk straight]' and peppered his insults with expletives about Ricky's mother, and threw objects at him. Recounting this, Ricky says dismissively, 'He was evil. But anyway, I survived that.'

From fishing, Ricky turned his hand to mining. He told me: 'On the mine ... there I met Apartheid again head-on ... *Staff* were all White and they were monthly paid. *Day rate* was weekly paid ... and they were only Coloured and Black ... Never mind what qualifications you had'. He related an incident about the day the toilets became segregated. Someone had put up a yellow cardboard sign, saying 'Staff only'. His response was to 'get out my little spray can with Black paint ... and I sprayed over the little yellow board because it wasn't an official company board'. He then used the toilet. Upon emerging, he was confronted by a White staff member who, as he recounts, said to him: "'Did you spray that?" I said: "Yes". He said: "That's for staff only". I said: "What makes you think I'm not staff?" "No, you're Coloured" he said'. Eventually a supervisor confronted him and made him face disciplinary charges for 'misuse of company property'. Ricky's indignation about the episode was still evident.

Next Ricky told me about another job, this time a government job at the Department of Fisheries. After an interview, and being told the job was his, and travelling 2 000 km to begin the job, he received a letter saying: "'Dear Sir, sorry we do not as yet employ non-Whites as officers on our vessels". *Nog 'n klap in die gesig.* [Another slap in the face].' Ricky recounted tragedy upon tragedy in his career, before turning to a story about finding a decent school for his children while working in South West Africa. He described how he visited a local White English medium school to enrol his children for the following year. The Coloured school in the area was Afrikaans speaking and his kids and family spoke English at home. He visited the school principal and made arrangements for them to begin in the new term. The principal said it was 'no problem' and to return a few days before school began with his children's report cards, which he duly did.

> **Ricky:** Get to the school a day before school opens. Greet the principal. 'Oh oh, new principal!' ... School reports in those days had different colours for different races. Even the school reports! It was green. And as I pulled it out ... the principal said to me: 'There's a problem. I cannot take your children in because of their race'. And I said: 'But the [former]principal told me to bring the kids'. 'Sorry, he's gone'.

Ricky took up the matter with the education minister, writing letters and visiting until finally someone got back to him, only for him to be told, 'This matter is for the White administration ... Education is in their hands' and there's nothing they could do about it. Defeated, Ricky sent his kids to school 2 000 km away in Cape Town, where his mother-in-law looked after them. I asked him how this had made him feel:

> **Ricky:** It's a terrible feeling. To think that this man, who has all this power to scratch stuff off the statute books, he couldn't help you ... We stayed another little while in Namibia and then came back home again.

When Ricky arrived back in Cape Town he continued to move through jobs, without benefits, for low wages because of his skin colour, and with the ongoing humiliation of being denied jobs for which he had qualifications. Yet another job was offered to him, then retracted, because he was initially mistaken for White. His address in a Coloured residential area gave him away. Ricky concluded by summarising how the Group Areas Act affected his life, how Coloured people were exploited in the work place, and were not given the same opportunities for training as White men were. Almost half-heartedly he said 'But you cannot blame everything on Apartheid.' He told me that it was his choice to drop out of school early and that this action no doubt also affected his career trajectory. 'Now you see, that is a choice. An uninformed choice, not a proper choice … there were no role models to learn from.'

Ricky is clearly intelligent and his career 'flatline' has been the source of much frustration and humiliation in his life. After a working career of 45 years, he still does not own property and his son-in-law contributes to the small business he now runs. He ended his narrative by telling me how job reservation for White people has now become affirmative action for Black people, of which again he is not a part: 'Getting jobs is now absolutely difficult for Coloured people. First we weren't White enough, now we're not Black enough.'

The issue of belonging

An important feature of this study, and the previous two chapters is that several of the Black people whose stories were being told are professionals. They are people over whom the past ought not to exert such an influence. But it is apparent in the stories of Mayaya, Zethu, Sizwe and Haley, who are either people in professional careers, or on their way, as in Sizwe's case, is that the past does catch up with them in multiple ways. The stories of Thamsanqa and Olivia further deepen our understanding of the way in which the past remains present in the lives of Black and Coloured South Africans, even though, to all external appearances, they have 'made it'.

Olivia – rising above expectations, feeling like an alien

Olivia is a 41-year-old Coloured woman who has a doctorate and is one of four children. She lived and worked internationally before marrying a White man and settling in a wealthy, formerly White suburb. She and her husband own two properties, and her two children attend a local ('very White') private school. She switched careers from that of an academic at a prestigious university and chose to work for, and then run, her own non-governmental organisation. When I asked her how Apartheid had affected her life, her first response was to refer to her father:

> **Olivia:** My father is highly intelligent but was never allowed to work above his status and so he was always frustrated ... So we actually grew up with quite a frustrated man because he was never allowed to dream and live out who he was supposed to be. And so that affected our family because we lived under a man who was belittled.
>
> ***
>
> The ripple effect of [this] ... in our family continues now ... Because my father was dishonoured and was a victim of injustice, my siblings and I are still having to carry him financially. And my siblings have not gotten out of the cycle. So one or two of us have, but some haven't because he was not able to provide for us.

Olivia went on to explain how she is reminded of the influence of the past on her parents' opportunities when her White friends talk about their 'family holiday homes' and 'inheritances' which she does not have: 'You're just reminded that actually your parents didn't have the opportunities that others have had ... We're not equal. Even though it looks equal, we're not.'

In explaining how she feels about the private school her daughters attend and her interactions with other parents there, Olivia begins the narrative of 'alienation' that characterises much of our interview. She explained how she feels like she does not fit in – not with her family in the Coloured area, in which she grew up, nor in her current suburban social circle:

> **Olivia:** Even though I managed to get an education and move out, and improve my circumstances, the people around me who I grew up with never did. And so I, through my education, separated myself from people I grew up with and used to live with, and have immersed myself in a different social sphere where I'm not one of them because they're not my friends from high school ... So it's just like a totally different world and so I always feel like an alien either in the friends that I had or the friends that I now have. I'm

just always different. So that's for me the biggest challenge in my current life – being the outsider in both worlds.

Olivia tells me she copes by limiting her time in both contexts. When she goes to family gatherings or parties she often leaves early because, 'I have to deny that I have a PhD … dumb myself down … not talk about stuff that's important to me now … stuff that might intimidate others in the room'. When in the suburbs with friends 'and they're all chatting and they all have familiar things in common and you're just – I know you guys now but I can't contribute to that conversation because I didn't go to [the same suburban school]'. Olivia tells me she is constantly aware that White people 'don't understand … don't want to understand' what it means to have grown up Coloured in Apartheid South Africa. She also tells me she has to stop herself reflecting the racism of many of her suburban neighbours. After a recent burglary at her home, she says she had to be 'very deliberate about not assuming, like so many suburbanites do, that the burglar was Black'. 'Why am I so racist' she asked 'after all I've experienced?'

Olivia's sense of alienation extends to her church involvement. When she first settled in the suburbs, she attended a predominately White church where few people made an effort to befriend her. She then moved to a church filled with 'historic Coloured families who've been coming there for years … [and] White justice fighters'. Still, she told me, she does not feel like she fits in, because she is not 'a White justice fighter' but a Coloured one; nor is she from the same community as the Coloured families in the church. 'So I never quite feel like I belong in that community either.'

Besides her 'leaving early' and self-censoring responses to her experiences of alienation, she employs two other strategies to cope with her feelings of not belonging. The first is to 'debrief with people who have the same experience as me … the Black intelligentsia in this world, because they've come from the same background, they've gone to university and it has separated them from their families'. The second is to be a 'pioneer' and remind people growing up in suburbia that not everyone shares the same privileges, especially parents at her children's school. She concluded by telling me how 'lonely' and 'tiring' it all is: 'I don't want to be viewed as the angry Coloured woman because I don't fit in and things aren't just right … I always feel like I don't belong. And until I feel I belong I'm not restored in my context'. Olivia's comment about belonging is an important theme in considering how the past remains present, one to which I return in Chapter 8 in the discussion of personhood.

Thamsanqa – forced to live in a world not my own

Thamsanqa is a 32-year-old Black man currently completing a Master's degree at the University of Cape Town. He is also a colleague of mine at the HSRC. He currently lives with friends in a rented apartment in the Cape Town City Bowl, but grew up in what he describes as 'the deep rural Eastern Cape'. He is one of five children. He does not have a relationship with his father, and was raised by his mother who was a domestic worker. Thamsanqa's story of not fitting in focuses on the cultural and social aspects of his university and workplace experiences, and to some extent his social life.

He said a key feature of receiving an education under Apartheid in a rural area was the limited access to 'sport or other extramural activities … because the resources were not there' which resulted in 'never getting being able to explore and develop these other talents' He said he realised at an early age that 'your only option was to do well academically for you to be able to uplift yourself'. Which is what he did.

Doing well academically meant moving to Cape Town in 1994 to continue his schooling since his mom had heard schools 'were better in Cape Town'. In South Africa's new democracy, moving was now possible. When he arrived he found it difficult to fit in since the 'city kids were more in tune with the world'. Nevertheless he did well at a local Cape Town township school and was accepted to UCT. This transition, however, was a lot more traumatic:

> **Thamsanqa:** When I went to UCT there was another huge gap from township education … As much as I was able to get the marks to get a university entrance, in terms of being able to deal with university education, I feel actually I was cheated.

The first colossal barrier was language. As an isiXhosa speaker he was not accommodated. Instead he had to learn English, and like Welile, Sizwe, Vukani and Mayaya, told me he had to 'work twice as hard to gain half as much':

> **Thamsanqa:** There was a whole group of us from different provinces and they had an extra class … which helped a lot. But it always felt so unfair that we came from an education system that did not equip us with skills to deal with this work. And we're competing with kids that went to schools that equipped them.

The second barrier, Thamsanqa explained, concerned the social and cultural world he encountered, and had no choice but to embrace if he was to be successful at university:

> **Thamsanqa:** It was frustrating because what I realised was not only did I have to learn the material I was given in class, but I had to learn the socio-cultural background upon which it was based. When I expressed my socio-cultural background, I felt it wasn't understood because the people I was interacting with, or the people that were marking my work did not understand that world where I come from.

Thamsanqa explained at some length how he experienced huge dissonance between university and township life. This, he said, was further complicated by the fact that he is a gay. He described how on the train between university and the township he would notice himself physically changing: the language he spoke, how he spoke it, his hand gestures, the topics of conversation. At UCT, he could be openly gay but struggled to communicate in class. In the township he could communicate but not be openly gay for fear of violence. At UCT, he worried 'about how I sound when I speak ... about whether my ideas are smart enough'. He spoke of his 'struggle ... travelling between these two worlds'.

> **Thamsanqa:** It was a consequence of the type of education I got – the divide that was created by the Apartheid government. You get a particular kind of education, you live in a particular type of house, you live in a particular type of environment which is different from some others in the country. And then here we were. Now we're in the same space. We're expected to engage the world at the same level. And it was frustrating and painful ... and unfair, because there were other people who just occupy this world without having to qualify themselves. They have this sense of belonging and sense of ownership that you just never feel.

Thamsanqa provided perhaps the most graphic metaphor when he talked about what it means to be a Black person living and working in a space in which people, including some of his friends 'aspire to Whiteness'.

> **Thamsanqa:** Last week [a friend] ... posted a picture on Facebook of a Black bear taking off a White onesie type costume. The caption

was something like: "Nine to five is done now so I have to take off my Whiteness". That's what I'm talking about, and I was so surprised that other people feel like that as well.

He describes his experiences of UCT and the HSRC as places where you 'speak English and express yourself in certain ways that are dictated by Whiteness ... if you don't then you don't get acknowledged'. On the streets of Cape Town, he told me he feels frequently 'misread ... seen as a potential criminal, a dangerous Black man'. One way to overcome this is to wear your 'White polar bear suit', he said. To go out of your way to 'act non-threatening, not seem so tall, smile a lot'. Moreover, it's not just White people who expect him to forgo his culture and history in order 'to be heard' but it's also the younger 'born-frees who look down on what it means to be African in terms of culture, tradition ... and believing in ancestors'. He concluded:

> **Thamsanqa:** It's like there's no effort to understand me ... The past Apartheid structures are still in place ... Sometimes not even physically – in people's minds ... it's very clear that we actually still look at each other through the lens of Apartheid, which is sad.

The economic costs of Apartheid

In the previous chapter I related some of Haley's observations – a 42-year-old Coloured woman and Anglican priest – about how the past and the present remain intertwined. Haley spoke of the automatic default Black people have to feelings of inferiority and White people to feelings of superiority, and how flawed theological understandings of fatalism and obedience to authority, then and now, keep Apartheid's legacy in place. I now recount her story in greater detail to show how the physical, financial and health effects of Apartheid's policies of job reservation, the Group Areas Act, and an intentionally inferior education all converged in one person's life, and how their effects remain to this day.

Haley – the compounded tragedy of expropriated property, wealth and inheritance

In her initial response to my question Haley summed up the effects of the past on her life by reciting a list of differences: 'If I was born White ... the kind of education I could have got, the kind of pension my dad would have had, the kind of life we could have had, the property we would have owned.' She then began again, by telling me that whenever she drives past the beach, her mother never fails to speak about how 'White people got to swim in the nice beaches and we had to swim in the rough seas … [My] dad just refused to go to the beach.' She continued:

> **Haley:** My aunt and her daughter were both domestic workers in [the suburbs]. So we used to go and fetch them once a month. They got one weekend off … they came and stayed with us and we were eleven people in a three-bedroomed house for that weekend … We would drive into these beautiful green leafy suburbs and my mother always used to comment about 'these Whites who have stolen everything from us'.

Haley talked about the effects of the past on her parents' lives, explaining how her mother's career had been limited by the Apartheid education she received and the jobs which were open to her as a Coloured. Similarly, for her father; he ended up in a job, doing the work of a professional but having to be content with the title and salary of a clerk. When Haley was 12, her father passed away, and the company hired two people to do the job he had done. 'If he had been born White he would have been a senior engineer … I was affected by that because when he died, he didn't get the pension of an engineer, he got the pension of an "expediter", whatever that is.'

Haley told me three stories about land and property that are worth repeating since they help to quantify the financial cost of Apartheid's policies for an average South African Black family. The first concerned her family home and the effect of the Group Areas Act on her mom's current wealth, and consequently, her own inheritance; the second was about land restitution claims in the Eastern Cape made by her family for land forcibly removed from her grandfather; and the third was about the reward her grandfather received for serving in World War Two. All three speak volumes about the tangible effect of the past in the present.

Haley grew up in a house that her mother had inherited in Wynberg, a modest Cape Town suburb, and that was fully paid off. In 1976, 'parts of Wynberg were declared White … and we had to move':

> **Haley:** [My parents received] R5 000 for a four-bedroomed house in Wynberg and we ended up buying a three-bedroomed house in

Mitchells Plain that was about half the size for R12 000 at a fixed interest rate for 25 years. So we had to take out a bond. We owned a big house and we had to take out a bond to buy a *pondokkie* [a shack] in Mitchells Plain. And my dad had to add on an extra 50 km round trip every day to work.

In 1997, three years into South Africa's new democracy, her mom eventually sold the house in Mitchells Plain for 'R90 000 and a couple of months later [our original] Wynberg house was on sale for R400 000'. Her mom then took out another bond of R60 000 to buy a 'two-bedroomed flat in Kenilworth for R150 000 – when she's in her fifties ... after selling a three-bedroomed house in Mitchell's Plain for next to nothing'.

Haley provided enough information for me, with the help of an economist colleague at the HSRC, to do a calculation to quantify the financial cost of Apartheid in property terms on Haley's family's wealth. In making this calculation we assumed that the money used to pay off the additional bond through the involuntary move from a fully paid off house in Wynberg to Mitchells Plain was invested at prime interest rate at the time.

By 1997, without the move they were forced to make, the potential value of this investment would have been R260 000. With the value of the Wynberg house at R400 000, Haley's mom's net worth would have been R660 000. Instead she received only R90 000 for her Mitchells Plain house when it was sold. This is a seven-fold loss due to Apartheid in terms of wealth accumulation measured solely on the basis of property.

In 2015, this investment and the money saved on paying the new Kenilworth bond would have grown to R2.8 million. The value of the house in Wynberg is currently R1.3 million. Their net wealth would therefore have been R4.1 million.

Instead, Haley's mom's net worth in terms of property is R1 150 000 – the current value of the now paid off Kenilworth flat. This represents a 3½ fold loss compared to what her wealth might have been – R4.1 million. So if we want to know how much Apartheid has cost Haley's mom the figure is R2 950 000 million. As one of three siblings, assuming Haley stands to inherit an equal share of her mom's wealth, one-third of R1 150 000 is R383 000. Without Apartheid this would have been R1 366 666. Apartheid has cost Haley R983 666. If we need restitution to have a figure placed on it for one individual – in property terms alone – this is that figure.

This is only one cost of the past in the present for Haley – yet a very tangible cost measured in property and lost investment. I do not have the skill to quantify the loss to Haley and her family based on her father's low earnings because of his colour rather than his skills, the inferior pension paid to her mom on his death, the cost of the increased commute due to the Group Areas Act, the loss of earnings her mom incurred due to her restricted education and limitation on her own employment, nor of the effect on Haley's own education and health. However, what becomes very clear in Haley's second account of a *successful* land restitution claim is that current structural restitution, when it is claimed, comes nowhere near to addressing the real costs of Apartheid's effects. Instead, it adds insult to injury and so the story is worth recounting in some detail.

Haley described a land restitution claim made by her family in respect of two farms in the Eastern Cape from which her grandfather was forcibly removed when the area was declared White. If it weren't for its extreme injustice, it would read like a comical farce. Haley and her two siblings put in a claim under the Restitution of Land Rights Act:

> **Haley:** We were now all allowed to claim for land that we were dispossessed of. So we put in a claim and it took about six or seven years with the paperwork, and writing, and waiting and waiting. And then out of the blue we got a letter to say we had to come to Port Elizabeth to sign so that our claim could be settled.

The officials insisted that she and her sisters travel 800 km to sign the document and receive the money. Despite the expense and time off work they needed, they did so and received the following settlement:

> **Haley:** We each got paid out R5 874 ... R17 622. Two weeks later we got a phone call to say that we had to return more than half [the money]. They said there was a miscalculation ... For *two farms* in the Eastern Cape! ... so R8 573. You can't even build a garage or a toilet for that!

I was in such disbelief that I asked Haley to show me the letters she received from the Commission on Restitution of Land Rights. She did; one was dated January 2010 and the other a month later, asking for a refund of R3 016 from her and each of her two siblings. Still in disbelief, I asked how big the farm was:

Haley: [My grandfather] had maize that he grew. He had cows. He had a tractor. There was a big farm house and a few other out buildings … My dad looked after cattle. They used to plough the fields, they used to sow seeds, they grew potatoes. There were orange orchards. [So quite big!]

This was beyond belief. I can't begin to imagine what other White South Africans think about how the land restitution process is going. Many know there is a land restitution process, but very few know just how dismal the actual compensation is.

Haley tells me she tried to fight the case but to no avail. She never paid the money back but told me 'I have a sneaky suspicion my siblings paid back my bit'. Haley's land claim eventually ended up costing her more than the amount she received once a flight to Port Elizabeth, accommodation and car hire were factored in. Looking up the value of property in the Eastern Cape is an easy thing to do. Currently, farms are being sold for between R2 and R3.8 million. Since there were two farms that Haley and her sisters were claiming compensation for, the loss to Haley, at the most conservative valuation, is R1 330 475, a one-third share of two farms valued conservatively at R2 million each, less what she received from the Commission on Restitution of Land Rights (R2 858).

Haley's story about these two properties – the house in Wynberg and the two farms in the Eastern Cape – highlights the intergenerational cost of Apartheid. By an accident of birth in Apartheid South Africa, she will inherit less than one-third of what she is due had Apartheid not been in place. This amounts to around R2 314 141. Haley, at the age of 42, still does not own any property. For many other Black South Africans this loss is even higher, or more commonly unquantifiable when property ownership occurred without title deeds in rural areas, Bantustans and townships.

Haley's final property story concerns her maternal grandfather who fought in World War Two. Upon returning home from the war, Coloured veterans were given bicycles, African veterans bibles, in gratitude for their service. Their White compatriots were given pensions or property, frequently in coastal areas, that have since seen vast increases in value, and are the original source of many holiday homes for White South Africans. These unequal 'rewards' have contributed to the intergenerational transfer of impoverishment through property. Haley knows this and it angers her deeply. In particular, she is angered by the lack of acknowledgment these elements of South Africa's past receive, and how far from the consciousness of White people these facts are.

The intertwined effects of race on health, education and volunteering

Haley completed her account of how the past has affected her by walking me through some of her education, health and community volunteering experiences. Because I've known Haley for over 25 years, I know she's dyslexic and suffers from chronic asthma. I asked her about how her health might have been different without Apartheid. The issue of her asthma is simple: much less waiting to see doctors and better medication if she and her family were able to afford private medical care instead of having to rely on the public health system. Her dyslexia is far more complicated and has effects more difficult to pin down.[10] These effects are also completely enmeshed in the education she received. As a Coloured child, Haley was educated under the House of Representatives education policy, not as bad as that designed for African children, but nowhere near the elite education White children received. Haley described the instability of her learning environments:

> **Haley:** We were like forty-something children in my Grade 1 class, so how can a teacher pick up something like that [dyslexia]? They can't. … The teachers were in survival mode plus there was unrest going on. I mean, I went to school just after the '76 riots had started … High school in the early '80s … [In] my first year of high school, schools closed for three months … There was no way they were going to pick it up.

When I asked Haley how her untreated dyslexia had affected her life she responded:

> **Haley:** I've never developed a love for reading. Even the discipline of sitting down with a book. It was always just hard work, so it was never a thing I wanted to do or thought about doing … But I

---

10 Like Haley's undiagnosed dyslexia, many more childhood conditions such as attention deficit hyperactivity disorder, foetal alcohol spectrum disorder amongst Black children went, and still remain, undiagnosed and untreated. This results in long-term consequences, including violence that arises out of frustration from being bullied, left out or left behind.

love learning, so when there are things I really want to learn then I make a plan to find out what's going on.

Despite Haley's dyslexia she completed high school, did a diploma in theology and later returned to theological college in order to be ordained as an Anglican priest. Initially, her mom had said there was money for one year of post-school study for her and each of her siblings. That meant no money for transport, food, or books. Haley and her siblings took part-time jobs to fund their studies and frequently hitch-hiked from Mitchells Plain to their respective campuses. Part of her 'making a plan' to cope with her dyslexia included forming study groups, getting friends to read to her, and finding audio books and podcasts. She has developed an almost photographic memory since her chosen career relies heavily on the written word. Her current success as a global public speaker and thinker has been hard won.

A further impact of the past on her life concerned her involvement in a local youth organisation with many volunteers coming from Coloured communities and townships. She told me that planning meetings for events were held at the organisation's offices in the suburbs, 20 to 40 km away from where most volunteers lived, resulting in many needing to take public transport to get there and hitch-hiking home if the meetings ended after dark. For Haley, it wasn't the long walks in the dark, or the pressure to find money for camp fees, it was the fact that White staff members (with cars and who lived nearby) seemed oblivious of the additional effort required to attend training meetings or to raise money for camp, when 'you were already hitch-hiking to college and paying for so much already'.

Haley's personal experience of the legacy of the past illustrates how deeply the effects of inequality and intentional impoverishment are interwoven. She counts herself 'lucky' because she at least was able to finish school, follow the career path of her choice and overcome her disability through grim determination and some ingenuity. Many others she knew from school were not as able or as exceptional:

> **Haley:** In Grade 9 we were 42 who wrote exams ... and 16 passed. ... And the reasons why people didn't get past Grade 9 is not because they're stupid ... Some of them had to go work because there was no money in the family ... Some were in the wrong place at the wrong time: one falls pregnant; the other one is involved in a robbery ... If it's a White kid it doesn't matter how smart they are,

they're going to finish high school ... It's a given. So you project that reality onto their future and you just know what kind of jobs they're going to get, where they're going to be able to live.

Haley concluded: 'These consequences of repeated injustice [long pause] you can't fix.'

Wellbeing, stories and agency

The effects of the past on education, careers, belonging, and health have been clearly told through the stories related in this chapter. Thwarted dreams, continued feelings of frustration, alienation, widening economic inequality, these are all legacies of unjust gains from job reservation, preferential access to land, and education for servitude, still evident in South Africa today. What was less taken into account, and of which my respondents only spoke briefly and in passing, concerns the physical and mental health effects of poverty. Health disparities between Black and White South Africans are a critical part of the long arm of the past on the present. We probably know this intuitively – when we hear about children who die under the age of five, and of teenagers who fall pregnant, women who are assaulted and raped, twenty-somethings who die of tuberculosis, and fifty-somethings who die of diabetes or hypertension. This burden of ill-heath is disproportionately borne by Black South Africans.

Globally, there are a number of studies and papers written about the knock-on effects of social and economic inequality on health.[11] Michael Marmot[12]

---

[11] Lee Jong-wook (2005) Public health is a social issue. *The Lancet* 365 (9464): 1005–1006; Ichiro Kawachi and Bruce Kennedy (1997) Socioeconomic determinants of health: Health and social cohesion: why care about income inequality? *BMJ*, 314(7086): 1037–1040; Vijaya Murali and Femi Oyebode (2004) Poverty, social inequality and mental health. *Advances in Psychiatric Treatment* 10(3): 216–224.

[12] Michael Marmot (2005) Social determinants of health inequalities. *The Lancet* 365 (9464): 1099–1104; Michael Marmot (2007) Achieving health equity: From root causes to fair outcomes. *The Lancet* 370 (9593): 1153–1163; Michael Marmot, Sharon Friel, Ruth Bell et al. (2008) Closing the gap in a generation: Health equity through action on the social determinants of health. *The Lancet* 372 (9650): 1661–1669; Michael Marmot, Carol Ryff, Larry Bumpass et al. (1997) Social inequalities in health: Next questions and converging evidence. *Social Science & Medicine* 44(6): 901–910.

has documented this extensively: 'Gender, education, occupation, income, ethnicity, and place of residence are all closely linked to access to, experiences of, and benefits from health care.'[13] Furthermore, the literature reports that the lower the social position that a person occupies in society the higher the probability of ill-health,[14] the worse the treatment for major diseases,[15] and the lower the access to health facilities.[16] Goran Therborn eloquently documents how poverty and inequality are literally 'a killing field', with millions of people dying premature deaths. [17]

The calamitous impact of race on people's wellbeing is also specifically and separately documented in the academic literature, but is seldom discussed in everyday conversations (nor by participants in this study). David Williams states categorically that, 'Racial segregation probably has its largest impact on health status'[18] and that this effect is not just about access to resources but through the 'stress induced by personal experiences of racial bias in the larger society.'[19] This experience of stress from racism is in addition to the stress experienced from poverty. So apart from the physical outcomes of poor health and access to medical care, racism results in psychological outcomes of 'anxiety, depression, suicide and also severe mental health diagnoses, including psychosis ... [and] schizophrenia.'[20] Furthermore, the World Health Organisation[21] has shown that experiences of racism and anger[22] entrench and worsen existing mental health problems.

---

13 Marmot et al. (2008), p. 1664.

14 Marmot et al. (1997).

15 Marmot (2005).

16 Kawachi and Kennedy (1997).

17 Göran Therborn (2013) *The killing fields of inequality.* Cambridge, UK: Polity.

18 Parliament of the Republic of South Africa (1996). The Constitution of the Republic of South Africa. Pretoria, South Africa: Parliament, p. 4.

19 David Williams, Harold Neighbors and James Jackson (2003) Racial/ethnic discrimination and health: Findings from community studies. *American Journal of Public Health* 93(2): 200.

20 Sophie Wickham, Peter Taylor, Mark Shevlin et al. (2014) The impact of social deprivation on paranoia, hallucinations, mania and depression: The role of discrimination, social support, stress and trust. *PLoS ONE* 9(8): 1–2.

21 World Health Organization (2001) *Mental Health: New understanding, new hope.* Geneva, Switzerland: World Health Organization.

22 Anger and resentment underlie a number of mental health disorders including depression, suicide and violence.

The encounters and experiences documented in this chapter and the previous one have offered real and everyday stories from Black South Africans who are able to see the injustices of Apartheid and their present day effects clearly. It has demonstrated that 'race is always … present in every social configuring of our lives'[23] and extends beyond particular incidents of racism described in Chapter 3. These stories, ranging from Sibu's experience of suspicion, Fundiswa's subtle victimisation at work, Mayaya's disrespect from White colleagues, Welile's anger, Ricky's frustration, Olivia's alienation and Haley's loss all indicate how entrenched and interwoven struggles against racism are despite the changes that have occurred.

I relate these stories in order to raise the consciousness of White South Africans. And while it may be true that single stories about loss and adversity are seldom the whole story, they remain stories that must be heard. In the words of Nigerian author Chimamanda Ngozi Adichie:[24]

> Stories matter. Many stories matter. Stories have been used to dispossess and to malign, but stories can also be used to empower and to humanize. Stories can break the dignity of a people, but stories can also repair that broken dignity.

There are many, many more stories that go untold. Furthermore, while Black people's stories are never only stories of pain, damage and outrage, these stories must be told. There are other stories: stories of grace towards those who have wielded unjust power, patience in exercising anger, the resilience to overcome, and the commitment to rebuild from the ashes. These will be told on another day, when we are closer to another country. For now we need to sit with, and reflect upon, the stories of the long tendrils of the past that encroach on South Africa's present.

---

[23] Gloria Ladson-Billings (1998) Just what is critical race theory and what's it doing in a nice field like education? *International Journal of Qualitative Studies in Education* 11(1): 7–24.

[24] Chimamanda Ngozi Adichie (2009) *The danger of a single story*. TED Talks. Accessed 10 July 2015 from https://www.ted.com/talks/chimamanda_adichie_the_danger_of_a_single_story/transcript?language=en.

5 White privilege and responses to South Africa's past

One of my earliest memories comes from 1972, when I was four or five years old.[1] It is a memory about race. My dad owned a big 1958 model cream Vauxhall. I used to love driving with him to the garage in Lansdowne Road to fill the car with petrol for two reasons. There were always stickers or plastic decals to buy and add to my collection, and because the men who worked the petrol pumps were always so friendly to me, frequently giving me 'doubles', stickers that others had left behind. I called them *mdala*[2] and always left happy. My dad frequently told me not to call these men 'uncle'. 'They are Black' he said, as if that explained everything. I ignored him. I called these men 'uncle' because they were older than me. My parents had taught me to respect my elders, and to be polite. I was a child, they were my elders, and besides, they were nice to me.

A few years later, in 1976 – the year of the Soweto student uprising[3] – my dad, a storeman in a government job was promoted, and we moved to Johannesburg. On the 21st June, we packed up and left Cape Town. After what seemed to an eight-year-old an interminable drive filled with squabbles and games up the N1, we suddenly pulled over to the side of the road. We were near Uncle Charlies, a large intersection outside Johannesburg, and my mom had been

---

[1] By then the National Party had been in power for 24 years and South Africa's Apartheid policies were fully entrenched. Armed resistance to Apartheid had started and South Africa was increasingly isolated from the world.

[2] IsiXhosa for 'Uncle' – a word I learned from my grandfather.

[3] The June 16 uprising of 1976, now commemorated as the symbolic turning point in the struggle for freedom, was a peaceful youth protest. Fifteen thousand unarmed township school pupils, some as young as 11, protested against Afrikaans as the medium of instruction in their schools and the White domination this exemplified. It is estimated that 575 young people lost their lives that day – shot by security police, many of whom were also young White army conscripts. See Swartz (2009) for further details.

taking a turn to drive. 'Look, it says "Warning Bantu Township Ahead"', she whispered, panic evident in her voice, as she pointed into the middle distance. My dad slid over into the driver's seat, and we drove in silence the last 40 km to our new home in Edenvale. My parents frequently spoke in whispers about that day, about 'riots', 'Communists',[4] passbooks, stayaways, and about Black people and danger in the same breath. My parents were afraid, and somehow their fear began to seep under my skin, along with belligerence towards Black people. That year was also the first time we had a Black woman domestic worker in our house.

By 1979, at the age of twelve, I was a converted racist: hateful, fearful, privileged and entitled. How did this happen, and so quickly? Fear was certainly one way. My parents were genuinely fearful for our safety in our first years in Johannesburg. My mom, working in the retail sector, experienced first-hand the stayaways and violence against members of her staff who did not participate in the mass action. Our domestic worker, who worked tirelessly, cooking, cleaning and babysitting while my parents were at work, soon became the object of derision and scorn from my brother and I. We dropped our dirty clothes on the floor when we took them off, left our plates unwashed and beds unmade, and generally taunted her. When we found her sleeping during working hours, we bribed, teased and threatened her. When she was arrested for being without a passbook, and was jailed for the weekend, we mocked her and stole money from her; and when she had been drinking, we ridiculed her, made her stand still and threw darts at her feet. We were never told off by our parents who, admittedly, were seldom around to see our base behaviour.

---

4   After the Soweto students' uprising in 1976, there was increased militarisation on both sides of the struggle. Many Black South Africans went into exile to avoid arrest, and to prepare for an intensified armed struggle; the South African Defence Force increased the period of compulsory military service for all White men over 18, and these conscripts were deployed to South Africa's townships and borders in what become known as the Border Wars against a 'Communist Insurgency'. In 1977 Steve Biko was killed by security police while in detention.

Going to *Veldskool*[5] later that year reinforced my right to treat Black people badly. The messages were clear: guard duty was necessary at night to protect our camp from 'Black terrorists'; reverence was shown for God who gave White South Africans this land 'under covenant'; and it was a duty to fight for our country against the 'ungodly Communists' who were seeking to take it over. Later that same year, I had my first letter to a newspaper published. It concerned, what I termed 'the unfairness' of the public transport system. It was school holidays, and I had just finished watching *Star Trek* (I think) and was waiting for a bus to go ice-skating at the Carlton ice-rink with friends. Twelve Putco buses designated for Blacks-only passed where I was waiting before a Whites-only bus arrived. Completely indignant, I wrote and complained. How dare there be more buses for Black people than for me! Of course, I was oblivious to the facts: that White people had the privilege of owning motor cars, and that White people comprised a much smaller proportion of the population. Nor did I give a thought to the many opportunities I had for entertainment that were unavailable to Black South Africans. What was I thinking of by writing such a letter? What was *The Star* thinking of by publishing it? My sense of entitlement and privilege was by now so ingrained that it took over three years before I eventually cringed in horror at the arrogance of my letter, and my behaviour towards our domestic worker.

The year I turned 15 was a momentous year for me as a White South African. It marked a number of awakenings. My brother joined the South African Police Force as a permanent member hoping to avoid the two year call up as an army conscript. It nearly destroyed him. By the end of his basic training, he was so filled with hatred for Black people that my dad had to twice physically restrain him from driving his Opel Kadett into a group of Black men walking on the side of the road. My parents eventually 'bought' him out of the police and he was promptly sent to Phalaborwa to train as a South African Defence Force sapper responsible for laying and clearing mines.

---

5 *Veldskool* [bush school] was an invention of the South African National Education Department, and can only be described as a week of brainwashing and militarisation for White school pupils in Standard 5 (now Grade 7) and again in Standard 8 (Grade 10). The role of the *veldskool* as a quasi-military and religious conditioning tool as part of Christian National Education for White youth under Apartheid has not been sufficiently interrogated.

Later that year, as a result of a spiritual awakening, I became involved with Scripture Union, a Christian youth NGO. One evening I attended a meeting in a Johannesburg suburb, where for the first time in my life Black and White people sat together, as equals, in the same lounge. The group was planning a conference to bring together people from the townships and suburbs to talk about the state of our country, and also to run holiday camps for young people across the colour bar. Towards the end of the meeting, people were suggesting topics for prayer. A middle-aged White woman said, 'Let's pray for the boys on the border,' and the woman sitting opposite her, also middle-aged, also White, asked, without skipping a beat, 'Which side of the border?' That sunk in.

I spent a lot of time that year meeting people not like me, in houses in the suburbs and on camps. I learnt about a South Africa, of which I was until then quite oblivious. My history teacher at Sandringham High School, a member of the banned South African Communist Party, introduced me to Phambili Books in Plein Street, Johannesburg. The bookshop was near to the NGO where I volunteered in Harrison Street, and so frequently after school I would visit both. They had a discreet basement where I read a copy of the *Freedom Charter*, and later bought a copy of the *Communist Manifesto* keeping it hidden, together with a newly acquired Bible, under my mattress. I read about justice and compassion in the Bible, and about racism, struggle and inequality from the books I acquired from Phambili. I used both approaches in the youth groups and camps I ran over the next few years. I stopped singing the national anthem at school.

By the time I arrived at Wits University in 1985 at the age of 17, I was involved in contact camps with Scripture Union, anti-racism workshops with the Human Awareness Programme, community development programmes with the South African Council of Churches, and discussions about liberation theology in Soweto. These all helped develop my critical consciousness. At university, I watched the wave of student activism and attended some protests and rallies, but always felt a little young to aspire to a leadership role in student politics. There were also epic moments of failure in those years; times when I just did not get it and where I behaved like the many other privileged White 20-year-olds of my generation. Frequently on campus, I would attend a protest rally, and then once clashes with riot police became uncomfortable, I would beat a hasty retreat to a shopping mall in my brand new Toyota Avante with a few White friends. When it came to voting in 1987,

I asked some of my Black friends who I had met through church activities who they would vote for if they had the vote. I was trying to do something about their disenfranchisement. To my surprise, they said none of the candidates. Looking back now, I am horribly ashamed that I could have thought that such an act was useful. In the next election, in 1989, a little wiser, I spoiled my vote as an act of protest.

When Sibu, the 27-year-old Black woman and social worker, commented during her interview: 'I would say somebody who is racist has lost their humanity' and looked at me questioningly, I knew that she needed to hear my story of growing up White in South Africa; a story of slipping in and out of consciousness of injustice and racism, of being born with a strong sense of humanity, of losing it, regaining it, repeatedly failing to apply it. Afterwards, when she asked me, 'what do other White people have to say about the effects of the past?' I knew that this chapter was important, a chapter about White Consciousness, or inverting Mangcu's phrase, about White people having a consciousness of Whiteness, of their white privilege.[6] So the question this chapter asks is, do White South Africans realise the magnitude of their privilege under Apartheid, and still today? Do they ever consider themselves as leading lives of careless ease, an ease conferred by an accident of birth, being born into a country set up to give them every opportunity to succeed just because of the colour of their skin? Do they connect the dots between their privilege and the racism, inferior education, opportunity ceilings, lost wealth and growing inequality Black South Africans experience? Do they slip in and out of consciousness, or are they completely conscious or completely unconscious? Do they see, experience, feel and know the cost of their privilege? This seeing is important since many scholars argue that for redress to happen, first there needs to be 'recognition'[7] of the other as a human being and of the factors that lessen their humanity. Only then is solidarity possible – standing together to ensure just action, including restitution.

---

[6] Xolela Mangcu (2014b) The contemporary relevance of Black Consciousness in South Africa: From Black Consciousness to consciousness of Blackness. In Devan Pillay, Glibert Khadiagala, Prishani Naidoo et al. (eds) *New South African Review*. Johannesburg, South Africa: Wits University Press.

[7] Iris Marion Young (2003) From guilt to solidarity. *Dissent* 50(2): 39–44; Iris Marion Young (2006) Responsibility and global justice: A social connection model. *Social Philosophy and Policy* 23(1): 102–130.

'Seeing' the past as the starting point for restitution

I begin with Graham and Rose's analysis of the effects of the past since both displayed multiple ways of seeing. While Graham at times sees clearly, for the most part his vision is distorted or he refuses to see. Rose mostly sees but at times in our conversation she also experienced new insights. Later, I offer a wide range of White perspectives that further illustrate how White South Africans fall in multiple places along the spectrum of 'seeing' (distorted seeing, refusing to see, coming to see and seeing clearly) that I described in Chapter 2.

Graham's ambivalence – beneficiary and government critic

Graham is a White 29-year-old marketing graduate currently living in a large industrial town 80 km from Johannesburg, and running a family-owned business. Straight after graduating, he got a job working for a well-known retail sports brand. Graham comes from an upper middle-class family, grew up in Cape Town, went to a prestigious government school and studied at Stellenbosch University. In 1994, Graham would have been nine years old. He tells me he 'proudly ... voted for the DA' in the 2014 election because:

> **Graham:** I looked for a party that actually cared about the future of our country with equality for all ... that had integrity and was not involved in constant corruption ... that would win a large enough majority to make a difference and challenge the ANC.

His interview was characterised by strong criticism of the current ANC-led government, a theme to which he constantly returned. 'We are in a slump or depression and unless our government changes to uphold integrity we will stop progressing as we should,' he pronounced. When asked how the past affected and still does affect him he answered:

> **Graham:** I don't feel negatively affected. What the past has given me is a greater sense of compassion for the previously disadvantaged. I want to help in small ways and understand what they are going through.

Graham's interview was filled with hesitation and ambivalence. So despite 'wanting to help in small ways' he also said, 'I don't honestly feel I have a responsibility to become a national activist of restitution.' Later on he described himself as 'an inheritor of benefit' with regards to his education and standard of living but also said he dislikes being accused 'of creating the injustice and unfairly benefiting from the situation as ... I had no involvement or input or control over Apartheid'.

So while Graham acknowledges that various problems the country currently faces are as a result of past injustices, he lays the blame on the present government and its levels of corruption, and firmly believes it is the role of the government to fix the past:

> **Graham:** The repercussions of the past are still very much affecting people in South Africa ... The past inequality has led to previously disadvantaged people thinking that the well-earning White people owe them something and that the corruption is therefore okay. These people don't even think that the amounts of money being spent on Zuma's personal homestead are wrong. They think it is his right as the president.
>
> ***
>
> The government needs to stop thinking of themselves and use the resources of the country to invest much more into creating equality through still better infrastructure in schools, hospitals and housing and job creation. Most of this has to sit with government but maybe we can privatise some of these items to speed up restitution.

Here Graham displayed both distorted seeing and narrow vision. Do Black South Africans believe corruption is okay? Are they looking to White people for redress? The evidence presented in Chapter 2, and later in Chapter 9 does not support these views. His vision is narrow in placing responsibility solely at the feet of government that has an enormous backlog to address. And it must be remembered, the present government inherited these problems; they were not of their making. But his ambivalence was also apparent when I asked him what are the hindrances to redress:

> **Graham:** [It is] the inability of the previously advantaged to realise how much they benefited from the past and to be a part of the restitution process – big or small.

Here Graham gets it. A little later, close on the heels of saying the past has not negatively affected him, he told me he has 'suffered when it comes to finding work since so many appealing jobs are only for affirmative action applicants although you may have all the education and experience'. From what I know of Graham, he has always had work and often had multiple job offers at any one time. He has chosen to go into his wife's family business. Why is this not apparent to him? I wonder too, how many serious conversations about South Africa Graham has engaged in since his move to a conservative South African town, and whether anyone has challenged his perceptions.

Why does Graham not take more responsibility or show more remorse for the past? Agreed, this was partly because he was a child under Apartheid. But he certainly benefited from Apartheid's laws. This he admits. But why the ambivalence, the reluctance to take responsibility, to act? I suspect this is because Graham has very little contact with Black South Africans – apart from those he employs in low-skilled jobs or helps 'in small ways'. He is unlikely to be familiar with many of the stories shared in the previous two chapters. Instead, he shifts the blame from any form of personal culpability to blaming the government's inefficiencies and corruption. I also suspect that Graham is not unlike many other White South Africans. He is not without compassion, and is not overtly racist (although his comments about honesty and corruption are borderline), but he has large blind spots when it comes to acting to make things right.

Rose's account of deference, complicity and shame

Rose is a 36-year-old White woman, part-time lecturer and mother of two children under five. Her partner is a medical doctor and they live in a Cape Town suburb and own their house. Rose is about to embark on a doctorate in education. Her response to how the past has affected her life, and how it affects the present – both corporately and individually – was comprehensive and encompassed many facets of other people's responses. She undoubtedly sees clearly the effect of the past on the present and articulates it extremely well referring to issues of power and deference. She began by talking about how she is perceived by Black South Africans because she is White. She says that Black South Africans see her as 'different … and have certain negative ideas about me'. The opposite is also true as she explained:

> **Rose:** White people believe they know what kind of view I hold about a topic … If they're telling a racist story … they'll say, "You

know what I mean" ... They'll draw me in as if I'm completely complicit in that thinking without questioning. That, because I'm White, I would automatically agree with them and have a racist position.

Rose told me how, in her view, relationships in South Africa have become irreversibly tainted by assumptions about what the colour of a person's skin means. For her it means automatically receiving 'deference' from Black people and she offered three examples: from older black people despite her belief that 'there should be a sense of deference towards seniority, towards age'; from a young Black couple with whom there is no 'usual banter and disagreement, argument and debate that might happen in a friendship between equals'; and from Black and Coloured construction workers involved in her house renovation who 'gave me deferential, short answers ... rejecting my advances of friendship'.

I asked her how White people's assumptions about race and being on the receiving end of deference from Black people affect her:

> **Rose:** I feel guilty and very ashamed as well, because I feel I'm made complicit in the injustices of the past because of that deference ... Deference is about power. The giving and not owning of power. So if someone is being deferential towards you then they give you all the power and then they become powerless ... There can't be equality in the relationship if there's deference.
>
> ***
>
> I remember having a conversation when I was younger than ten [with my mom], about wanting to be Black ... I can remember feeling ... that then I'd be free of the guilt of being White.

After this explanation Rose slumped in her seat, the emotion of talking about the effect of the past on the present physically enacted. After a while she continued, and talked about two further features of the past in the present for her as a White South African:

> **Rose:** Poverty tends to have a generational effect. And poverty is inherited and it's prolonged ... Society under Apartheid was designed to cater to a rich ten per cent and a large labour force of essentially poor Black people.

***

> Our geographical separation militates against transformation and restitution. As long as we are separated geographically, our health systems, and educational systems created under the past regime remain in place and are very difficult to change … even if the people have changed or the laws have changed.

Rose's analysis concerning the inherited and generational transmission of poverty and wealth, and the effects of geographical segregation and social distance was repeated by many other White people I interviewed. Rose sees the past clearly in the present. The ways in which she came to see during the interview concerned being able to articulate insights about power and deference that emerged in our dialogue.

Experiencing the past – rupture and racism

Both Rose and Graham offered insight into how they see the past. Graham's view of the past is rife with ambivalence regarding responsibility and blame. Rose's considers the effects of the past on her – as producing regret, guilt and shame. Both their responses were visceral and emotional. In trying to summarise how the White participants in my study experience the past, the best summary I can offer is to distinguish between their accounts of racism, and the genuine rupture they feel both geographically and socially.

Geographical separation and ruptured relationships

Across generations, roughly a quarter of White respondents spoke about the ongoing geographical separation experienced in South Africa, from 21-year-old student Hillary, to 38-year-old development worker Heather, and 78-year-old retired architect Michael:

> **Hillary:** Geographically, the way South Africa is constructed, it is still very segregated.

> **Heather:** In Cape Town, where I live, it is almost as if the Group Areas Act is still in existence … I was unaware while growing up … how long it would be before I would experience socialising, living and working with people of other race groups as normal.

Michael: The big ongoing problem in South Africa is that the Group Areas policy was so good that after the collapse of Apartheid, the country is left with segregated cities and towns that will last indefinitely.

Leo (46, non-profit organisation director) said we like to see ourselves as 'the rainbow nation' as depicted in 'beer commercials [but] … relationally, we remain a divided society, largely unable to build relationships beyond the superficial sense'. Sarah (37, primary school teacher) echoed this when she said the past hasn't affected her, then stopped mid-sentence and added, 'But I haven't got any Black friends'.

Implicit and overt racism

Most people spoke of being racialised and racism as being a strong legacy of the past with at least half of the White participants drawing attention to it. Thirty-six-year-old businessman Luke summed it up succinctly when he said: 'We remain a very racialised society. Race is still important all the time … I'm still gobsmacked that we measure race all the time.' Most participants admitted racism still existed, some in their own behaviour and attitudes, while others spoke of it in their parents. Twenty-three-year-old Thomas, a recent graduate, who comes from a wealthy propertied family and who attended a private school was perhaps the most honest:

Thomas: You see a White beggar and think: 'Shit! Hey what's happened there?' You think about the person in a more compassionate way as opposed to: 'It's just another Black person' kind of attitude. As terrible as that attitude is, it pervades your thinking. You do lose your humanity … the fact that there's four homeless people, but they're Blacks – it's standard, it's to be expected. It's a terrible thought but it does creep in.

He was not alone in confessing his racism. Thirty-seven-year-old doctoral student Angela spoke honestly of still being racist in terms of the assumptions and stereotypes that are internalised, and how she has to catch and correct herself. Thirty-year-old Rebecca who works for a car dealership was perhaps not intending to be quite so forthright when she bemoaned the fact that she had to work with 'men in the Black community who are – I hate to say this – are stupid'. In the conversation that followed, she conceded that much of her opinion of Black men was due to the frustration she experienced because they were both not able to speak each other's language, their low levels of education and because of sexism – rather than race itself. Rebecca is engaged to a Coloured man but seemed oblivious of how her racist comments might affect him. Later in this chapter and in Chapter 7, I show how Rebecca came to see some of her racism during the course of the interview. For now, her honesty was helpful as representative of many White South Africans who see through distorted lenses.

Twenty-one-year-old student, Hillary from East London, spoke of her parents' racism:

> **Hillary:** There's still an 'us and them' mindset. I know personally my parents' mindsets haven't changed. They're from that certain cohort of South Africans that believe the country ran better pre '94 … I see it in my parents when helping our nanny. It's like an 'Ag shame' mentality.

Twenty one-year-old Jane, active in DA student politics on campus, spoke of how racism, although constitutionally illegal 'is still very prevalent … and is understated to a large extent, especially by White people'. Leo concurs when he talks about how the past has resulted in both 'White arrogance and racism', with White people believing themselves to be 'richer, more dominant because we are better, sharper, more intelligent' rather than as a result of unjust laws and systems of oppression and privilege.

Only Luke spoke of 'coming across less and less racism', and when he does, 'It has become properly offensive.' He explained: 'I think … as enough people are as offended as I am by real racist talk, that either people are socially electing to not voice their racism or actually, we're dealing with the racism issue'. Luke's comment was a real revelation to me. I've known him since he was nine years old, and his outward persona is one of a politically incorrect joker. He tells homophobic and racist jokes regularly – or certainly that was my impression of the younger version of him I have known. So now, his comment about finding racist talk offensive, alerted me to something that needs further exploration: how social behaviour and actual convictions can be dissonant; and that serious conversations about race and other injustices have been rare in South Africa.

Inheriting the past – privilege, parents and affirmative action

Affirmative action and the effect of their parents' non-involvement in South Africa's anti-Apartheid struggle came up frequently as a legacy of the past. However, by far the most frequently referred to effect of the past on the present by almost all of the 26 White participants across age and educational divides was the notion of unearned privilege – of being a beneficiary of past injustice in multiple ways.

Acknowledging the benefits of White privilege

The acknowledgment of privilege happened unprompted, before I asked participants to choose labels for themselves that included 'beneficiary' (see Chapter 7). Jane was particularly eloquent and straightforward in her response, as were 21-year-old student Noah, 23-year-old recent graduate Thomas, and 38-year-old year old businessman Luke:

> **Jane:** I'm privileged by the experiences of my parents under Apartheid … My parents were elevated in terms of their opportunities … I can't help but feel guilty about this inherited White privilege that was the result of my being a beneficiary of injustice … this advantage overwhelms any kind of reverse disadvantage … against me as a White person because of policies like Affirmative Action.

> **Noah:** I've benefited … I've had better schooling and opportunities than most South African kids … Having grown up in a free South Africa, I have to say that not too much has changed for me in socio-economic terms. I still live in a mostly White society and experience White privilege on a daily basis.

> **Thomas:** Theoretically, there are equal opportunities, but not really … I'm able to fulfil my potential in a way that other people can't … Let's be honest, the White base has maintained its economic strength.

Those at the older end of the age spectrum also had clear insight into the levels of privilege experienced under Apartheid, as evidenced by 74-year-old

Ann and 63-year-old Harry (who had initially stated that the past had no effect on him):

> **Harry:** To say I was affected by South Africa's past you must understand the privilege that we lived in in the 60s, 70s and even 80s. We had the best jobs. We got easy loans. We got houses. We got nice cars. And we weren't even clever ... So the privilege of that time for that White generation was fantastic.

> **Ann:** I suppose I was extremely privileged while other people were denied everything. In every way – education, jobs, whatever ... So I'm still privileged ... Living in [the suburbs] ... you didn't come into contact with the world, really.

Those in the middle generations, while also speaking of education, jobs, wealth, security and health care, made profound points about the meaning of privilege:

> **Luke:** So I'd go as far as to say that I think my middle-class stimulation from school, sport, extramural activities, parental support and opportunities has made me a more intelligent person than I would have been if I'd grown up in poverty, despite the fact that I would have the same number of grey cells. I think that if you were born into poverty you'd probably just stunt the whole process.[8]

> **Heather:** I enjoy the security of an inheritance that should keep me comfortable throughout my life ... I will never know what it was like to grow up without the subtle message always given; that I was top of the pile ... one of the masters.

> **Angela:** A gap year after school ... University fees were paid for ... a flat to live in. And I still reap the benefit of that past in terms of my access to knowledge, ways of being in the world ... Never

---

[8] Luke's observations reflect a whole literature on the effects of poverty and adversity on children's health and wellbeing, including their cognitive development. See Jack Shonkoff, Andrew Garner, Benjamin Siegel et al. (2012) The lifelong effects of early childhood adversity and toxic stress. *Pediatrics* 129(1): 232–246.

feeling a question about whether it's appropriate for me to occupy any public space … There are very few places where I know my voice does not matter, where I am not valued. And that's a legacy of our past.

For 43-year-old doctor David, his privilege has been to 'travel in the lucky part of the river':

David: We have always been the owners of social, ethical, intellectual capital of varying inclinations. I have almost never been discriminated against. *In fact I have been so privileged that I mostly understand myself as being without colour.*

These are honest and profound observations, and the fact that most White respondents could articulate and acknowledge their privilege is encouraging. But how far does this understanding extend to the general White population in South Africa, and to what extent does this consciousness of benefit translate into action for making things right? These remain the larger questions.

Thirty-four-year-old Dylan, in the final stages of his doctorate, offered a counterpoint to the issue of acknowledging privilege when he said, 'there isn't a group consciousness that we've all benefited immensely from a system of privilege'. Instead White people have come to 'feel that in some way they've earned the right to that privilege' and 'that either their parents have worked hard towards the privilege they have or that the bad people, who did the exploitation, weren't us'. Furthermore, Dylan continued,

Dylan: White people have come to see their high standard of living as 'normal'. A school where teachers teach for eight hours a day … each family has two cars … no potholes … expecting that others be brought up to this level, rather than being content to earn R5 000 a month … and living in something between a shack and a dilapidated house – which is normal for most South Africans.

He concluded that if White people truly had a collective consciousness about the extent and origin of their privilege they would not 'whinge, whinge, whinge' about the corruption, poor governance, and lack of jobs for White men. Dylan's view is probably only partly accurate. Graham, whose responses I related at the outset of this chapter probably comes closer to current White group consciousness[9] in the portrayal of ambivalence – at times embracing privilege, at others arguing for government to establish his version of normal – rather than outright denial of it.

Peter, a 39-year-old small business owner, clearly grasped the depth of the privilege he experiences. He trained as a medical doctor and wanted to specialise in ophthalmology but did not get a place because he was White. He is quite matter of fact when he tells me that was one of the factors that contributed to his leaving medicine and pursuing his other great love – music, and turning it into a business in which he employs 'over thirty people … some from previously disadvantaged backgrounds'. Peter understands that it was his privileged background, the fact that he had a family able to absorb both paying for his medical studies and then able to offer him the support he needed to finance a new venture, which made it possible. But it is in the following statement that Peter's deep understanding of the nature of privilege is shown:

> **Peter:** In many respects, the inequalities of the past ironically still create the opportunities for the future because our society is still unorganised … So out of chaos it's easier to create your own future. In a very rigid, organised society, when you're in a pool of people who have all been very well-educated … who've had the same opportunities as you, I think it's much harder for an individual to rise above the average.

Later on in the interview when Peter talked about his experience of Black people, especially in his business as 'entitled and lacking drive to succeed' I wanted to point him back to why the opposite was true for him – an enormous privilege of financial and social resources that Black South Africans have not automatically inherited from families and their environment.

A further irony in Peter's story is that his grandfather, as a White returning serviceman after World War Two, received a pension as reward for his contribution. Peter and his two siblings were ultimately the beneficiaries of this payout. This pension contributed to financing, among other things,

---

[9] Benjamin Roberts (2013) Your place or mine? Beliefs about inequality and redress preferences in South Africa. *Social Indicators Research* 118(3): 1167–1190. doi: 10.1007/s11205-013-0458-9

Peter's ability to choose and change careers. This is in stark contrast to Haley's grandfather, who received a bicycle as a reward for his service in the war, and who lost two farms to Apartheid. The intergenerational transfer of privilege and injustice is clearly illustrated here.

Mixed inheritances from parents

So far, I have reported on White participants' references to their parents' overt or subtle racism, education, networks and finances that have been inherited. In the next section, I describe some of the more nuanced inheritances from parents that White respondents spoke of. For some this brought relief (Chris and Thomas) and gratitude (Dylan), for others a sense of disappointment (Luke).

Thomas spoke both of his own inheritance from the past and how his father had 'dodged military service under the Apartheid government' and that this had left him with 'a slightly easier conscience'. He also told of a friend whose grandfather was the former head of the Conservative Party under Apartheid but argued 'what your parents did is not necessarily who you are'.

Luke spoke of the fact that although he grew up in a family where his father had given up legal practice to work in a non-profit organisation, he still felt 'isolated and unconscious' about what was going on in South Africa until the 1992 referendum[10] (when he was 15 years old). He says that 'prior to Nelson Mandela's release and the '92 referendum I must admit I would describe myself as just having my head in the ground'. He described his parents as not politically vocal and found himself 'perplexed' because of my parents' silence:

> **Luke:** I would like to ask my parents why they weren't anti-Apartheid activists ... And although they were involved in non-profit work and things like that, they were non-political ... And I think they are representative of the White church mind-set that was apathetic towards the ills of Apartheid and non-active against Apartheid.

By contrast, 34-year-old Dylan's recollection of his parent's activism was hugely appreciative. While he says he did not fully understand what was

---

10 In 1992, the then President, FW De Klerk, called a Whites-only referendum to ascertain support for his plan to end Apartheid.

happening when he was a child, he was aware that the situation was complex. He tells of the time his father was arrested and jailed for a night when he was seven, and another incident where his father took part in a march and wanted to take him and his sister along but his mother objected. In speaking of metaphorical inheritances from their parents as part of how the past had affected their lives, no-one mentioned the largest inheritance of all – that of the material wealth and property they are likely to receive upon their parents' deaths. The silence on this topic was puzzling and one to which I will return in Chapter 9.

A complicated response to affirmative action

Perhaps the most complicated responses I recorded were White people's reaction to affirmative action as a legacy of past injustice. Thomas told of how despite affirmative action, White people have retained their economic superiority although 'governmental work is almost impossible to find'. Graham said that it had prevented him from getting the job he 'really wanted'; and Peter said that he decided to change careers when faced with an affirmative action dead end – and he could easily do so because of his family's resources. Noah (21), Luke (36) and Harry (63) spoke of affirmative action, not with fear but as a matter of fact, quite accepting that their futures lay in the private sector, or in running their own businesses because of it. None had any doubt about their ability to succeed given their high levels of educational privilege, family support and social networks:

> **Luke:** I feel, as a self-employed person, I've managed to kind of dodge the bullet.

> **Noah:** I probably have limited opportunities in certain areas‾ like politics and would have to work harder in order to climb a corporate ladder, for example.

> **Harry:** I'm retired, but I would be unable to get a job now. But I think that's fair because we had our chance.

It was only Jack and Chris who showed a fear of affirmative action, yet both their stories are complex. Jack is a 71-year-old retired man from a lower middle class Cape Town suburb. He spent most of his working life as an administrative officer in the civil service, rising through the ranks until he held a 'chief admin officer' position. He has a Grade 8 high school education, making him a prime example of a beneficiary of White affirmative action under the Nationalist government. He described how he landed the position:

> **Jack:** It was 1968. I had two children to support and I was without work … So, I went to the labour department, which was all White then, and that man there sent me to the abattoirs or to a hospital … So I went to the hospital first and I didn't go to the abattoirs, and I got the job straight away.

When I asked Jack about this job and whether he was aware at the time that jobs were reserved for him as a White male he said: 'I didn't even actually think of that,' instead, he just saw it as 'a lifesaver'. When asked how South Africa's past history had affected his life overall, he answered by talking about South Africa's transition during which he was still a government employee. He said he was initially afraid: 'First I thought we were going to be thrown to one side, but the respect was there after '94, between the Whites and the Blacks, especially who I worked with'.

Jack retired from the civil service in 2002, eight years into democracy. Since then he says, 'I see the changes, definitely. They actually employ more Blacks than Whites nowadays.' Jack contradicts his initial statement and says, but now 'things have changed for the worst, a little bit'. He then contradicts himself again, and tells of two recent experiences with the Departments of Home Affairs and Social Development. He had to get a new identity document at the first and register for an old age pension at the other. Both impressed him he tells me. First, they treated him 'with respect', second 'there were not just all Blacks' but a mixture of Black, White and Coloured staff at both departments, and 'the service was very good, very professional'. So maybe things have not 'changed for the worst' as Jack feared. In the end he tells me that actually, 'its crime that's gotten worse', rather than employment or services.

What I learnt about Jack in the course of this interview was similar to what I learnt about Luke. In the course of everyday interactions, White South Africans seem to make a sport of putting down the government, making racist jokes and in Dylan's description, of 'whinging'. But sitting down and having a serious conversation, albeit in a formal research interview, provided deeper and more nuanced responses. Jack seemed to be working things out as we spoke. Is Jack still *racist* in his attitudes and actions? Without a doubt. But is he *only* racist, or *always* racist? I think not. Many of my respondents portrayed this multi-faceted attitude towards the past, towards 'the other' that is worth noting. We are seldom one thing. Of course, there are some who are hardened, committed racists, who are closed to other perspectives; but these were not the people I met in my study – perhaps those people refused to be interviewed. To what extent are incorrigible racists representative of the general White populace? Probably more than I'd like to admit, but likely less than we see reported in the media, or represented by those who troll online news sites.

Only 78-year-old Michael and 34-year-old Chris, a chef with a high school education, were openly critical of affirmative action, Michael bemoaning the wholesale replacement of qualified people with 'zombies' instead of allowing new incumbents to be 'mentored by the people who were leaving', and Chris calling it 'reverse racism'.

Dylan added a further nuance to White views on affirmative action. He had just submitted his doctoral thesis when I interviewed him, and he was about to embark on a post-doctoral fellowship in the US. With him was his partner, a 34-year-old Black woman who had resigned from a senior position in government to begin a prestigious leadership programme for young Africans sponsored by US President, Barack Obama. They had both applied to the same programme, but Dylan had not been accepted. He offered a complex view of the way in which he is affected by affirmative action, and draws together the intersections of privilege, opportunity and aspiration:

> **Dylan:** I'm of a particular age so these issues have direct implications for me, my partner, our lives and the way that we have opportunities or don't have opportunities … This Young African Leadership Initiative … There's no doubt that she deserves this but … It's a complex question about the opportunities that are available to her than what are available to me.

While acknowledging the assistance he has received from having contacts and the opportunities that came along with them, Dylan goes on to speak of his conflict when people speak only of privilege without acknowledging his own hard work:

> **Dylan:** It makes me feel a little bit frustrated sometimes when people say: "Oh, of course, but everything you've done in your life is the result of privilege" … In terms of feeling like I've achieved stuff in the world, it sort of takes away from it a bit.

It is also clear that Dylan experiences an inner conflict and frustration when he compares his opportunities to those of his Black partner:

Dylan: [She] doesn't have a PhD. She doesn't have that much experience. I'm not saying she's not hugely talented and deserving and good at her job, but just to get into that position ... I want to be a Young African Leader! I don't think that I'm demographically seen as someone who Barack Obama would see as desirable to be a Young African Leader right now.

Affirmative action is a complex feature of the past in the present for White South Africans. Those who want to contribute to another kind of country might just have to wait it out for now, and do so in good grace. Of course, the evidence is that White South Africans are virtually no more or less employed than prior to 1994; in fact, there are many more in skilled positions than in semi-skilled positions when compared to 1994.[11] Affirmative action has simply pushed White South Africans up the skills ladder rather than out the door.

'Feeling' the past – fear, guilt, shame and anger

A number of responses in answer to the question how has the past affected your life could be categorised as strongly emotional. I've already mentioned Rose's shame, Graham's indignation, Dylan's frustration, Michael's suspicion and Chris's resentment. Yet others spoke about fear and anger, and quite a few more about shame and guilt, in relation to how the past has affected them.

Fear about violence, revenge and losing wealth

Not many respondents spoke about fear as an effect of the past on the present, apart from 38-year-old part-time teacher Sandy's fear of 'Black revenge' (Chapter 1). Rose related a dream she had had when she was a child, and which

---

[11] White unemployment (narrow definition) has increased from 7% to 8%. For other groups this is much more, for example from 40% in 1994 to 43% in 2014 for Black Africans, with an overall rate of 22% in 1994 and 25% in 2014. See Statistics South Africa (2015) *Employment, unemployment, skills and economic growth between 1994 and 2014*. Accessed 28 March 2015, http://www.statssa.gov.za/presentation/Stats%20 SA%20presentation%20on%20skills%20and%20unemployment_16%20September.pdf.

had stuck with her over the years: 'A dream about the military occupying the road outside my church because there was going to be a civil war.' She tells me that even though she 'didn't fully understand what it was about at the time', in retrospect she thinks she was 'taking on the fear and anxiety of the 80s' – the height of the Apartheid struggle. Luke spoke of the impact of crime on his everyday life and the levels of stress experienced by South Africans due to it. He said that crime has resulted in, for example, 'not being able to go for a run or a walk in your own neighbourhood without fear'. He also says laughing, 'If my alarm goes off in the middle of the night, I'm quite certain that the fortress is being compromised, you know?'

Heather spoke rather frankly of the fear instilled in White people towards Black men; the 'fear of the other that our history' has spawned. She continued, 'I am usually unaware [of this fear] until I am right in a situation that exposes fear.' This fear of violence and crime at the hands of Black people, especially Black men is pervasive in South Africa, as it is in many other parts of the world. Of course, South Africa does have high levels of crime and violence, but as Leo explains, the situation is more complex since:

> **Leo:** [We are] a traumatised society across all the economic and racial spectrums … The violence, both personal and structural, leaves its mark in deep ways which show themselves most obviously in some of the darker parts of our society, for example child rape, but also in some of the more mundane areas, for example our aggression levels on a rugby field.

Leo's analysis of fear spawning aggression is insightful and borne out in the literature.[12] Dylan drew attention to a frequently overlooked issue regarding White people's fear of crime[13] and violence when he said:

> **Dylan:** It's only that White South Africans have been exposed to crime more recently. Black South Africans have always lived with

---

12 Derek Gregory and Allan Richard Pred (2007) *Violent geographies: Fear, terror, and political violence.* London, UK: Taylor and Francis.

13 Benjamin Roberts (2010) Fear factor: Perceptions of safety in South Africa. In Benjamin Roberts, Mbithi wa Kivilu, and Derek Davids (eds) *South African social attitudes second report: Reflections on the age of hope.* Cape Town, South Africa: HSRC Press, pp. 250–275.

large numbers of criminal acts ... a part of daily life ... And that's a result, in my opinion, largely of our history of the majority of people struggling and needing to survive.

Guilt and shame

About a third of the White participants spoke of feelings of guilt and shame about how the past has affected the present. Without differentiating between these two emotions, a task for another occasion,[14] they also gave very different examples of how this shame or guilt operates. What was clear was the link to 'being White'. Many in fact referred to these emotions as 'White guilt' and 'White shame'.

Twenty-one-year-old Noah put it succinctly when he spoke of feeling 'guilty for being White ... [for being] the oppressor ... a perpetrator of atrocities ... having atrocities done in my name'. He said, 'I worry that people resent me because of the colour of my skin and my wealth, even though I wasn't directly involved in past injustices.' Thomas, the 23-year-old recent graduate from a wealthy Cape Town family, echoed Rose's sentiments about shame. He spoke of being ashamed of being unmoved when seeing Black people sleeping on the street in the middle of winter; of never having been attracted to Black women (until recently when he started dating a Black woman) because the only 'Black women I have been exposed to were domestics'; 'the fact that I can't communicate with the rest of my countrymen'; and having 'an older Black male ... calling me a sir'.

The interesting fact to note in respondents' talk of guilt and shame was their ages. No older respondents spoke of a sense of guilt or shame, while many of the younger ones did so, along with a few in the middle generations. These responses of guilt and shame included thoughtful insights about how productive such emotions can be, especially in the questions they raise for these young White South Africans:

> Hillary (age 21): If you want to label it, constantly grappling with White guilt. I'm constantly faced with trying to reconcile the heritage that I am born from, which was the oppressors within the country, versus me trying to be an active member of society.

---

[14] June Tangney and Ronda Dearing (2003) *Shame and guilt*. New York, NY: Guilford Press.

> **Cara (age 21):** I don't think that White people know how to handle that guilt. … Who should speak up against injustice? … Because I'm White, can I fight against this or can I speak up against that?

Sandy linked being 'ashamed of White people for what they allowed' with having 'empathy … to want to help to achieve equality'. Twenty-one-year-old Jane concluded that 'White guilt' had the possibility to be either productive 'let me give back and uplift the masses', or could simply result in 'anger and denial'.

Thirty-year-old Rebecca, who grew up in one of Cape Town's grey areas, speaks of a different kind of shame, for being mistaken for a Coloured person: 'I was always afraid to tell people I lived in Lansdowne [laughs]. I was ashamed … and friends at school would say, "Oh, you live in a Coloured area." And I was like, "But I'm White. I'm White, I'm not supposed to live in a Coloured area."' Hers is the only account of shame that demonstrated deeply entrenched racist attitudes instead of a healthy and productive emotion. Rebecca, like Graham and many others who participated in this study, probably had also not had an opportunity to examine many of her beliefs about race, the past and its impact on her life. During the course of the interview, and in subsequent conversations she demonstrated a growing realisation of some of these racist attitudes:

> **Rebecca:** The changes in South Africa have been a good thing; otherwise, I wouldn't have been able to marry Donovan. [We met] after '94, but my parents' mind-set at that time was, "You don't know inter-racial relationships". So I was too scared to tell them about us … And then ten years down the line – we're getting married soon.

Later she began speaking about affirmative action. Rebecca slipped in and out of consciousness: 'The whole job thing – BEE … I think is unfair to a certain extent', but then she pauses, stops and adds a caveat, 'But, then again, I don't know how it was to live in the times when White people got everything and Coloured and Black people had nothing'.

Anger towards other White people

While there were people with some conservative views in the sample, none of them expressed anger about South Africa's transition or current circumstances. Instead, about a quarter of White participants spoke of the anger (and disappointment) they felt towards other White people, mainly over their racism and reluctance to make things right for the past.

For Leo, White people's refusal to take collective responsibility for the past made him 'sad and angry':

> **Leo:** People are happy, even sacrificially keen, to act charitably in addressing poverty in South Africa. But turn the conversation into one about relationship and about taking collective responsibility … and people's defences go up and their hackles are raised … This isn't from crazy right-wing racists; this is from largely progressive people.

Leo's point is well made. White people seem to be happy to be charitable; they are less eager to take the same actions as a moral obligation, as acts of restitution.

Johan is a White 48-year-old man who has spent his life working for social justice in South Africa: initially as a church minister in a Black community in rural KwaZulu-Natal, and more recently as the head of a non-profit organisation focused on restitution. For him, one of the overarching effects of the past on his life was of always being the odd one out. From choosing to go and work in a Black congregation as an Afrikaner and 'not ever really being one of them' to being regarded as 'less ambitious' by his White peers for doing so, and never being acknowledged by the Afrikaner community for the work he does on restitution. Johan, like Olivia, felt 'alienation on both sides'. He describes his anger towards White people:

> **Johan:** I realised I have been hugely angry towards White people … I am affected by the past in seeing signs every day that we are not a normalised society yet, in many ways. We are carrying the wounds of the past very clearly. I hate it that we go to the gym and all the people that are doing the cleaning jobs are Black people … I despise it when I'm in a conversation with Black people and they focus all their attention on me just because I'm White.

Johan describes how this anger started 'early on in my life' as a student member of the National Party which frequently led to conflict with the right-wing AWB and the Conservative Party on the university campuses he attended in Potchefstroom and Pretoria:

Johan: When I was in the residence, I was very small. The majority of people were quite far right wing. They once put me in the tumble dryer because they wanted to shake my head so that I can get rid of my liberal thinking.

How clear seeing comes about

In reading White people's responses to how the past affects the present, and how it has affected them personally, I marked some as 'seeing clearly' while others I marked as 'not caring to see'. Sometimes I realised that people were seeing through a 'distorted lens' (blaming the current government when in fact it was a legacy from the previous government, for example). Frequently, I noted within an interview how people 'came to see' as they spoke – that it was the act of thinking about, and responding to questions that helped them 'come to see'. Rebecca provided a clear example as she came to see her own racist attitudes about Black men as 'stupid', as being ashamed of being thought of as Coloured when she was White, of biting her tongue when she realised that affirmative action and racism still affects her Coloured fiancé. Hillary provided another example of 'coming to see'. She began by saying, 'being a White female from a middle-class family I'm not affected by the past', then she said, 'Well, not directly affected', then 'I have inherently benefited from South Africa's past'.

As I applied these labels, I was hoping to find some trends. Was it the older generation who saw through distorted lenses or who did not care to see? Was it the younger generation who saw clearly, perhaps because they were at greater distance from our awful history, and less emotionally complicit? What made someone open to coming to see as we spoke? My conclusion is complicated. Yes, certainly the younger participants often saw more clearly, but almost everyone was open to coming to see. Those who saw clearly were frequently those who had done some prior reflection, and whose knowledge about the details and history of South Africa's past went beyond the superficial.

White South Africans who refused to see, or who saw through distorted lenses, had mostly not had these sorts of conversations before. Their knowledge of the past was based on limited perspectives, self-fulfilling complaints and media-shaped opinions of 'corruption and entitlement'. Very few in this group had a deep understanding of the past's pernicious effects. I suspect that many who read Black South Africans' accounts of the effects of the past on their lives will do so for the first time.

To be sure, White South Africans know that the past affected their superior education, employment status and wealth, and the reverse, the poor quality education, unemployment and poverty of Black South Africans. Some have inklings of Black South African's frustrations and anger, but few articulated knowledge of the dehumanising effects of racism, job reservation, opportunity ceilings and alienation; the demeaning frustration of being refused service at a restaurant and being made to act like a child when faced with a young White official; or the indignity of not being able to provide for family; nor the life-shortening effects of despair, poor services and violence on the mental and physical health of Black South Africans.

It is my hope that these three chapters will help White South Africans reject the superficial call to 'let's just move on, and forget the past' as a privilege not afforded to Black South Africans. Cara summarised the problem well:

> **Cara:** You can't ignore White privilege. I think it's everywhere. And I think that it's even more evident to Black people. I think they see it more clearly … I think there's a lot of White guilt and a lot of Black resentment. I think there's a denialist mentality in many White people who think that: 'I wasn't a part of it or I didn't benefit – we must all kind of move on'. I think that mentality of moving on is doing us all a disservice, because I don't think we're ready to just move on. I think there's a lot of work to be done.

White South Africans need to deepen their understanding of the way that South Africa's segregated past continues to affect their lives – in multiple areas of unearned privilege, fear and shame. They need to know our history, see its effects and feel the shame that galvanises action. Seeing, feeling and knowing the past has the potential for 'undoing' the past and 'doing' restitution.

To return to Sibu's question, and to paraphrase it, 'What do White people have to say about the effects of the past, and how is the past still present?' The stark answer is that the past is not really present. For most, their wealth and privilege has protected them from the effects, unless they make a conscious choice to choose to see. Many are wary of talking about the past, perhaps because, like Sandy, they fear Black people's anger and desire for revenge.

Perhaps they are not sure what to do about the past, apart from the anxiety of having to give up their material wealth, so the less said the better.

There are some cracks of light, however. The candour with which people I interviewed spoke, corrected themselves when realising how thoughtless their views were, and sweated through challenges to come up with new ways forward, all point to this. Despite all my categorising and labelling, it was also apparent that these White South Africans did not ever hold only one intractable view on all issues. They are not only conservative or only progressive, only right or left wing, racist or egalitarian. This offers hope for our future, for building another country, and why it is time for a new conversation about restitution. Opening up such a dialogue is what the remainder of this book endeavours to do, by discussing in detail how the word restitution might be able to help us let the light in, so we can better see past and present injustice, and opportunities for healing. I will argue that it offers an opportunity for us all to locate ourselves in the conversation in ways we have possibly not done before, and to embark on actions to repair South Africa's tragic past.

PART 3

TURNING TOWARDS TOMORROW

6   Restitution: A new conversation

When we got to the question about restitution, Rebecca and Donovan, a couple who were about to get married and who were interviewed together, laughed nervously. 'When you asked if you could interview us about restitution, we didn't know what it meant. We've heard about *restitution restitution restitution* before but we don't really know,' began Rebecca, a White, 30-year-old car sales administrator. To which Donovan, a Coloured 30-year-old retail sales manager responded, 'So we Googled it the other day'. Rebecca interjected, 'But to be honest with you, I don't remember what we came up with' [laughs].

Rebecca and Donovan were not alone in not knowing what restitution means. Forty-eight-year-old contract cleaner Lyanda candidly responded: 'I don't know. Am I supposed to know? Is there a word like that in isiXhosa?'[1] 'I don't know' was the answer given by half of all participants. Nor is it unusual to forget once you've Googled the word, since Googling results in loads of technical and legal definitions, including at the very top of the list, from Wikipedia, 'the law of gains-based recovery' and then refers to land being restored to rightful owners after conflict or injustice in some form. Another quarter replied saying, 'something about land', and a further quarter of the participants offered explanations that included legal definitions, land claims and sometimes more broader understandings. For most people though, the topic of restitution for South Africa's past is not a common part of our conversation.

So far, I've been using the word restitution rather broadly, saying it means 'making things right' and noting from time to time what a difficult word it is – both in its technical meaning and in the emotional responses it elicits. I've also offered people's stories that illustrate the very many effects of the past in the present as well as the common vision we have for South Africa.

---

[1] The practice of paying damages is common in African traditions, for example, when a young woman falls pregnant outside of marriage (*ukuhlawula*). This is a form of restitution and may be a helpful way to begin a discussion of restitution on a broader scale.

In this chapter, I focus attention on the complex meanings of the word restitution: how it has been used historically by lawyers and other thinkers more recently, how the people I interviewed understand and respond to it, and how – with a little tweaking – it can be a really useful everyday word for us in South Africa as we embark on a second journey to deal with our past. The chapter ends by considering why, as helpful as the term might be, a conversation about restitution is uncomfortable, and for some unnecessary and unwanted. The reasons for this include believing that the TRC was enough, an obsession with moving on, leaving redress to government, confusing charity with restitution, fearing it will never end once we begin, dreading the loss of personal wealth and privilege, not knowing how it can be done, and not fully understanding our roles in, and therefore our responsibility for, the past. I begin with what the people who were interviewed in this study understood by 'restitution', as well as the varying perspectives about it from law, history and other thinkers.

The meaning of restitution

About one-quarter of the people interviewed had some innate understanding of restitution before being prompted (as I will later explain); this group comprised both young and old, as well as Black, White and Coloured people. Most had been involved in some form of activism with NGOs, on university campuses or had dealt with restitution as part of their employment (in government and business). These respondents generally agreed that restitution involves making amends for past wrongdoing. So for Portia (Black woman, 26, financial services administrator) it was about 'making things right and restoring what is broken'; for Heather (White woman, 38, non-profit) restitution is about 'Giving back what was stolen. Making right'; and for Ricky (Coloured man, 66, small business owner) it's about right-making action, right-making, 'The Afrikaans words are much nicer: *regstellendeaksie*, *regstellend*' he said.

A few personalised their responses and alluded to themselves and their families either as having been wronged or having committed the wrongdoing. Mayaya (Black woman, 34, business executive) reflects, 'It means the things I lost I will regain them one way or the other, in terms of lost finance or lost property.' For Johan (White man, 48, non-profit), 'Restitution is about saying: "We did wrong and we need to make right for what we did wrong."' Some spoke of the multiple dimensions of restitution that went beyond material giving back. So for Nontembiso (Black woman, 48, domestic worker) restitution was about receiving 'compensation for the emotional pain that we suffered at the time'. In a similar vein, Peter (White man, 38, business owner) said, 'For me restitution's got to do with restoring a person's sense of self-worth and value as a human being primarily.'

Some also elaborated on the goals and processes of restitution. So for example, Haley (Coloured woman, 42, priest) spoke about how 'restitution is about justice for me ... [and] kindness' and explained what she meant:

> **Haley:** If there was a pizza with eight slices and four of us, we don't give two slices to each person. We ask: "When last did you eat and when are you going to eat again". And we divide the pizza that way, because equality is not justice.

Leo (White man, 46, non-profit organisation director), on the other hand, spoke of equating restitution with the Hebrew word 'shalom' or 'peace'. He explains that shalom is 'not simply an absence of violence but a rightness and togetherness in all directions for people ... with other people, their society and the world at large'.

Zethu (Black woman, 40, business executive) cautions against hasty definitions of restitution when she said, 'I'm so scared to give it one line.' Instead, she described it as follows:

> **Zethu:** Restitution is a process ... an open-ended concept that goes beyond our own imagination of what needs to happen to achieve it ... [It] starts with *engagement* ... really *listening*. Some meeting of minds, but also so much of heart ... Then there's *re-engineering* the future if I can call it that – looking forward and imaging how you do it together.

Zethu then spoke about the 'different languages of restitution', drawing on a popular contemporary book *The Five Love Languages*[2] that describe how people respond to different ways of giving and receiving love in intimate relationships. Some respond to what is said (language one – words of affirmation) or what

---

2   Gary Chapman (1992) *The five love languages.* Chicago, IL: Northfield Publishers.

is done (language two – acts of service; language three – physical touch) or through what is given (language four – physical gifts; language five – quality time). Her comparison is helpful; those giving and receiving restitution might have a need for different forms of restitution – what is said, done or given – if it is to be meaningful and contribute towards making things right. For Zethu, even if the process of engaging, listening and re-engineering the future is followed, there may still be different outcomes. She explained:

> **Zethu:** You must just acknowledge that if you want to show ... sorry-ness to a group of people – the one might just want that you give them something and will be genuinely okay with that. The other one might just be happy with you saying stuff, but the others would want you to be part of them in an ongoing way ... People will have their own barometer of what is needed.

For Zethu, for restitution to succeed, the expectations and needs of both the giver and receiver must be considered in the process; clearly something that cannot happen without a process of engagement with each other. She further warns that such a view of restitution requires unhurried and non-predetermined amounts of time:

> **Zethu:** If I'm born to circumstances that were created by somebody else, then the next person can never be the judge of how quick I heal from that ... You actively engage me to understand me ... before you quickly think we can move on.

Jane (White woman, 21, student) echoed this when she emphasised the importance of restitution 'achieving a level of satisfaction and fairness to all parties, mostly the victims'.

Each of these people had an instinctive sense of restitution; one that went beyond a legal view of returning land or even making compensation, but that included addressing the loss of dignity and emotional pain as part of its hoped for outcomes. Key to making things right was a process of listening, mutual engagement concerning what actions are appropriate, along with a shared vision of the future. For those who had no idea of the concept or thought of it only in terms of land redistribution the next activity I asked them to engage in – a consideration of two stories that served as simple analogies for what had happened in South Africa and its results – elicited much more conversation and discussion regarding its meaning and implications.

Understanding restitution using two analogies

In the introduction to this book, I described the following two analogies that might be helpful in thinking about South Africa – *The Stolen Bicycle* and *The Unlevel Soccer Field*. During the course of each interview, participants were either given a copy of both stories, and asked to read them, or the interviewer read the stories aloud.

'The Stolen Bicycle'

Jabu and Johnny are two boys who live next door to each other. Both have bicycles. One day Johnny steals Jabu's bicycle. Jabu tries hard to get it back but can't. Of course, they stop being friends. A year passes and they do not talk or even look at each other. But Johnny misses his friend, goes over to Jabu's house one day, and says, 'Jabu lets be friends again'. Jabu agrees and so they shake hands and make up. A few days later Jabu says to Johnny, 'Johnny, what about my bicycle?' to which Johnny replies 'Look Jabu, this is about becoming friends again, not about bicycles'.

'The Unlevel Soccer Field'

Imagine two teams are playing a soccer match, but the pitch is tilted at a 30-degree angle. The side playing downhill is unfairly advantaged and is able to run up a score of 19–2. At a certain point during the match, the advantaged team is helped to realise that the match is not fair and that the playing field must be levelled before the game can continue. Some want the score to remain in place and think it's fair merely to carry on playing on a level field. Others want to level the scores as well as the pitch and start again. Yet others do not want to continue the game but want new rules and time to let the team who have been playing uphill recover from their exhaustion, injuries and sense of hopelessness, before replaying the match.

The participants were then asked to say what they thought about the stories 'both of which try to describe what has happened in South Africa's past' as the interview question put it. Once their initial responses were exhausted, they were asked how stories like these were helpful in talking about the past. I'll describe their responses shortly. Of course, for me, the key objective was to get respondents to talk, to discover the meaning of restitution if they didn't already know what it meant, and to deepen their understanding as a motivation to do something about it. Their responses were abundant; they could have filled an entire book. People reacted emotionally – with jubilation and anger – raising concerns and problems, developing clarity and insights as they spoke.

The Stolen Bicycle

This story generated enormous discussion, with people liking or disliking it, and spending lots of time debating what the bicycle represented in contemporary South Africa, as well as the flaws in the story. Some participants, both Black and White, simply retold the story when asked what they thought and offered no analysis. Others gave short, visceral responses but went no further. Ann (White woman, 74, retired salaries clerk) immediately responded by saying, 'If Johnny's now got two bicycles why won't he give one back? I mean, that's crazy.' But when asked if this related to South Africa and how White people have benefited from Apartheid, she said, 'No, I don't know what to say about that.'

A few people shook their heads and said the story was about 'forgiving and forgetting', about 'friendship not bicycles'. Chris (White man, 34, chef) said: 'I'm on Johnny's side because it's about forgetting about the past and if Jabu had already dealt with a year of not having his bicycle then surely he could carry on.' So whereas Chris's empathy with Johnny is not surprising given his other views about affirmative action, for example, others like Naledi (Black woman, 21, unemployed) and Robyn (Coloured woman, 33, administrator) were more surprising. Both interpreted the story as a call to move on despite their own experiences of racism in current day South Africa:

> **Naledi:** I think going back to the past is holding us back from moving forward because if we don't move on we will be holding on to unnecessary grudges. We should forgive and forget.

> **Robyn:** People are still having grudges of other people doing certain stuff to them or in the past their forefathers doing stuff to them. So that grudge needs to be gone.

Across all race groups and generations, the story evoked strong emotional responses, and many agreed that something further needed to be done to address the past:

> **Rebecca:** I would want my bicycle back.

Sibu (Black woman, 27, social worker): I think it's not fair and it's unjust. Because you can't carry on with the friendship knowing you've been robbed.

Ricky: Let's just forget the past and move on ahead? That's what that story's saying … But that is bull. We can't write off history by forgetting the past.

Thomas (White man, 23, recent graduate): Johnny is not even prepared to discuss the bicycle issue and in no way wants to make amends for something he's clearly done wrong – it's going to make it difficult to be friends.

Many respondents articulated clear ideas about what needed to be done to resolve the issue of the stolen bike. For Manny (Coloured man, 48, university administrator), 'Johnny needs to give Jabu's bicycle back, otherwise it's not a real friendship.' For Mbali (Black woman, 28, financial administrator), material restitution is the only sign of serious intent: 'I feel since Johnny came to Jabu and asked for peace, he is supposed to come with the bike as a token to show that he is really serious.'

About making the jump from a bicycle to what it represented in South Africa, participants were quick to explain that the bicycle is land, wealth and education but also the intangibles of dignity, confidence and social connections:

Welile (Black man, 24, sales rep): [It's] everything that we owned, from the land to our dignity. I mean, it's everything that we had … We're not getting anything back except now we're friends.

Cara (White woman, 21, student): It's opportunities [like] education, employment, standard of living. It's both capital and social capital because it's everything that has been gained in this period of time, from when they weren't friends to now.

Olivia (Coloured woman, 41, non-profit): Confidence, education … twenty years into our democracy the young Black kid still feels that he can't speak to a White person … Yes, give bicycles back but also just teach a kid to do maths and English.

Luxolo (Black woman, 29, unemployed): You can't give back self-confidence and pride, and stuff like that … There are some people who lost parents to Apartheid and you can't give that back.

Fundiswa (Black woman, 26, contract cleaner): The White people have two bicycles because they stole our land and Black people have nothing ... The stolen bicycle is how you can't represent yourself as a Black person ... You cannot stand in front of people and explain yourself as a Black person.

Leo aptly summarises the point of the analogy when he says that the story 'forces economics to be a conversation piece' and that 'without that on the table very few other things will shift'.

The Stolen Bicycle story also provides an opportunity for people to discuss the complexities in South Africa's history and the problems in trying to address these now. For Heather it was that 'in South Africa we were never old friends, and so there are no places of remembered trust to return to'. For Thomas it was not simply about returning a bicycle since 'it may have been upgraded ... What about the time lost riding the bicycle and potential wear and tear?' 'What if Jabu used the bicycle to deliver newspapers and earn an income?' asked Johan. He referred me to the *Restitution Toolkit*, a document produced by the Restitution Foundation, that uses *The Stolen Bicycle* story to provoke discussion about restitution:

> A man's bicycle is stolen. This now means he has no transport, and cannot get to work; thus, he loses his job. Without a job, he cannot educate his children or support his family. Perhaps he used that bicycle to run errands for the homebound elderly woman next door; now she is affected by the loss as well. Jobless and frustrated, he becomes a drain on his community rather than a resource. What would restitution look like in this situation? Certainly, it is not just returning the bicycle. He is not the only person who has been affected by the crime; his family, his neighbours and his community have also suffered. Now imagine that theft not only of resources such as land, education and money has occurred on a broad scale, but also of intangibles: dignity, a sense of safety, self-worth, an understanding of one's rights, and a sense of belonging in one's own country.[3]

---

[3]   Restitution Foundation (2010) *Restitution toolkit*. Cape Town: South Africa.

Mayaya (Black woman, 34, businesses executive) addressed the inter-generational effects of South Africa's past by saying that it was now not in fact Johnny who owned two bikes but Johnny's grandchildren: 'How do you now make Johnny's grandchild understand that actually the bike was never hers in the first place? She may have inherited it, but it was stolen to begin with, which is the case in South Africa.'

Other participants raised problems regarding the relationship between Jabu and Johnny. For Vukani, it was a matter of power: 'The story seems to suggest that it's Johnny who decides it's time for them to reconcile as opposed to Jabu who's been trying to get his bike back all along. So it almost seems like Johnny's the hero.'

Ted (White man, 67, leadership non-profit) says the story fails to address 'the history behind … why Johnny stole Jabu's bicycle and why he thinks he's entitled to keep it'. Ted here was not excusing Johnny but wanted the story to show how the supremacist ideology of Apartheid had led Johnny to believe he is entitled to keep the bicycle – and challenge him to denounce it.

The Unlevel Soccer Field

The Unlevel Soccer Field story provoked less debate about whether the story was a good interpretation of South Africa's situation as was the case with *The Stolen Bicycle*. Instead, people leapt straight into what should be done about this unlevel and unequal state of affairs. Unlike *The Bicycle Story* that merely described a scenario, *The Unlevel Soccer Field* story made claims about the fairness of the match, prescribed that 'the playing field must be levelled' and offered options for how this should be done, such as:

Level the field, keep the score as it is, and continue.

Level the field, level the scores, and then start again.

Level the field, make new rules, allow exhausted players (who have been playing uphill) to recover, then replay the match.

Unsurprisingly, all respondents, across race group, age and level of education and current work circumstances, quickly agreed that the game had been unfair and that the field should now be levelled. They also easily chose from amongst the options given, or offered their own.

Lyanda: There is still inequality between the Black and White populations. There should be redress so that all South Africans can be on the same level.

Luxolo: Level the playing field and then start over.

Connie (White woman, 71, retired): I would say that I agree with the person who wants to stop the game and start again because one always has an unfair advantage.

Donovan, a little more creatively, added: 'I would only start counting the score maybe fifty games in, when things are really fair'. The idea that the disadvantaged team needed to rest was noted by a few, such as Manny, who said, 'It's essential to give the disadvantaged team time to recover before continuing the match so that they are on equal footing because the injustice is quite patent'.

What was clear was the fact that these multiple options – more than just 'level the field' – stimulated great reflection and discussion. Rose (White woman, 36, part-time lecturer) commented on how apt the analogy is: 'I like that it shows the … diversity of views and the struggle that we're all having. How do we deal with the past?' So, whereas *The Stolen Bicycle* story was criticised for being too simple, yet still made a point about the need for restitution and of what sort (material or intangible), *The Unlevel Soccer Field* story opened up the discussion even further regarding what kinds of action might be taken to address past injustice. What does 'recovery' – in terms of skills development, education and general health and wellbeing – look like? What does levelling the scores mean in term of affirmative action? How do we 'start over'?

Of course, participants also raised other complexities, criticisms and dilemmas inherent to this story. A number of Black and Coloured participants' reflected on how it would be nearly impossible to level the playing field in reality. Sizwe (Black man, 21, graduate student) remarked, 'There's no way of levelling it'; Welile argued, '[White people] don't want us to start at 0–0 now … They don't want us to start again'; and Haley lamented:

Haley: It leaves me feeling quite hopeless because we know that the score is never going to be levelled again … If you take a White South African, a Black South African and a Coloured South African and give each one of us R200 and say: 'Go grow this money', what a Black kid will be able to do with that compared to what a White kid will be able to do with that – you can't compare. Black kid goes home with R200 – they might not even get home. They might be robbed. And the kinds of things they could think of. How do you grow R200? 'Oh, I'll buy some sweets to sell, maybe' compared to the things that White kids can think about like buying shares in Google. Because of the resources and life experience that they have at their fingertips … So what restitution means to me is, I think, first of all acknowledgement that we can't begin to appreciate the complexity.

Both Leo and Noah had a further reflection:

Noah: I take issue with the idea of two 'teams' … where the opportunities for the 'teams' are changing, and those who inherit or benefit are changing.

Leo: The second story conveys this complexity better. Though I think it's unhelpful in that it locates the story as two teams *in opposition* to each other even though the fields need to be levelled. This is true but it might be truer that we're actually on the same team and hindering our own success by our continued refusal to even out the resources available to all of us. That way the restitution I make is about our shared future success, not simply about sacrificing until such time as we can go at it again.

For Noah, it was about allowing individuals to access opportunities off an equal base, although he did explain he wasn't against 'a time of redress' for groups. Leo's point about being on the same team *now* is an important one to make. Restitution allows for us to be on the same team – the well-being of each one of us depends on all our well-being.

Stories as a means of 'coming to see' restitution

The variety of responses came from people of all backgrounds. That was a key strength in using stories to provoke discussion. These responses reflect how analogies can remove defence mechanisms and overcome reluctance to talk about a sensitive topic, while also being engaging and allowing people to formulate complex points of view in response to short vignettes (both were under 140 words). Noah, Haley, Donovan and Leo all pointed out how complex reality is compared to stories or analogies. However, what was clear from these stories was that they allowed a space for the conversation to open up, become richer, deeper and more meaningful than when participants were only asked to say what restitution means, and responses were largely limited to, 'I don't know', 'No idea' or 'Something about reclaiming land'.

As the interviews progressed, and after we had discussed these stories, the comments from participants become more focused, stronger, more confident and more practical. Lyanda provides a clear example of a developing consciousness about restitution, a growing ability to articulate it, and ideas to apply it:

> **Lyanda:** I have never heard the word [restitution] anywhere.
>
> ***
>
> There is still inequality between the Black and White populations. There should be redress so that all South Africans can be on the same level.
>
> ***
>
> White people and government should pay back and provide houses and better services, then this restitution would be achieved.

And for Donovan who began with Googling the word 'restitution' and immediately forgetting what it meant, to subsequently offering an insightful analysis based on *The Unlevel Soccer Field* story of 'I would only start counting the score maybe fifty games in, when things are really fair' showed he was also able to develop a growing consciousness, to 'come to see', as I called it.

An important contribution that this book hopes to make is in fact to help people come to see, and see more clearly, how to address our past history of injustice and its ongoing consequences. These stories help. They may also help us tell our children about the past since they are easily understood, and children will be able to apply these stories in increasingly complex ways, as they grow older. In addition, stories are also useful with adults – across all backgrounds – as these rich responses attest. For Leo, these are 'good and helpful stories in that they evoke emotions and get questions going well'. Welile, reflecting many other views, concluded: 'These stories reflected exactly what is going on.' Fundiswa put it more poignantly, 'These stories ... they are trying to tell me that the White people still have more advantage and we are lacking things because we never got them from the past.' Rose, referring to the story of returning the bicycle, said she found it to be a very good metaphor:

> **Rose:** A very good story to tell people who I meet often who say –
> and I hear this refrain often – 'We must forget the past and move
> on' ... mostly from beneficiaries of Apartheid ... It's much easier to
> see that Johnny is unfair and mean spirited in his response ... than
> it is to say to a White person that says 'Let's move on from the past',
> 'You are wrong'.

Only a very few thought of them as too simplistic, like David (White man, 43, doctor) who felt 'mild irritation at the simplification and lack of nuance'. Dylan (White man, 34, graduate student) observed that it is precisely their simplicity that offers space for reflection: 'They are thought-provoking stories, not mainly for the stories themselves but as a comparison between the story and the South African context'. These stories, though they may fail to capture the full complexity of South African society, served in our conversations as important mechanisms to help people see the past more clearly, and the many possible ways it can be addressed. They offer an entry point into a new conversation about restitution.

The legal and historical practice of restitution

The scholarly literature has much to say about restitution. In this next section, I offer an overview of ideas about restitution, starting with the legal and historical view before expanding it to the more social and every day ideas.

Restoring

Restitution has historically and legally been defined by the International Law commission (ILC) as restoring 'the situation which existed before the wrongful act was committed'.[4] Such an aim is not easily achieved: where people have been killed, land has been stolen and developed, people have been enslaved and geographically relocated over generations, racial superiority has become institutionalised and engrained into the psyches of whole groups, or children have been sexually abused, what was lost is almost always irretrievable.

---

[4] International Law Commission (2001). Articles on Responsibility of States for
Internationally Wrongful Acts.

Compensating

The ILC continues to say that where such *restoration*, the most fundamental meaning of the word 'restitution', is impossible, reparations and compensation should occur until the injured party is content (the legal term says until there is 'satisfaction'). Reparations and compensation, and hence also restitution, may therefore include 'an expression of regret, a formal apology or another appropriate modality'[5] – in other words, symbolic actions. Other vehicles for creating satisfaction may include memorials or even truth commissions, but the key feature of legal restitution is that the injured party must be content with the action. It cannot be decided by a court without asking whether those injured are satisfied.

Gain-stripping

A further and key element in restitution law is that no one should enjoy the benefits of unjustly gotten gains. Not only should victims be compensated,[6] but perpetrators should be stripped of any benefit received through wrongdoing (so called 'gain-stripping' or 'the law of gains-based recovery').[7]

Acting symbolically

What is clear is that even in law, restitution is not to be limited only to material compensation, although this forms an important part of it. Frequently, offering an injured party satisfaction as a response to injustice is not achieved through financial means. So for example, in 2008 the Spanish parliament passed the Law of Historical Memory that aimed to end 'amnesia' about Spain's civil war (1936–1975) and the 36-year long brutal dictatorship that followed under Francisco Franco. It condemned the Francoist regime, made it illegal to hold political events at Franco's burial place or display Francoist symbols. It recognised victims of violence, rejected laws passed in this period,

---

5   International Law Commission (2001).
6   Peter Birks (1985) *An introduction to the law of restitution.* Oxford, UK: Clarendon Press; Daniel Butt (2009) *Rectifying international injustice: Principles of compensation and restitution between nations.* Oxford, UK: Oxford University Press.
7   Sam Doyle and David Wright (2001) Restitutionary damages: The unnecessary remedy? *Melbourne University Law Review* 25. Accessed 14 April 2011 from http://www.austlii.edu.au/au/journals/MelbULawRw/2001/1.html.

and declared findings of military tribunals during this time null and void. It offered state help to trace the remains of those killed, and allowed those forcibly exiled under Franco's rule to return.[8] These acts aimed to end Spain's shameful history under Franco, and to restore an accurate account of events, through a restitutionary law, based not on material compensation but on symbolic actions.

Returning rights – civil, political and property

Restitution of an individual's or a group's civil, political and property rights has also formed an important part of the transition from an oppressive regime to a rights-based and democratic one.[9] For example, *The Pinheiro Principles*[10] is a well-known and key UN document that sets out 23 principles to guide post-conflict property restitution. Frequently, legislated restitution programmes have played a prominent role in returning land, enshrining civil and political rights in a new constitution and instituting various symbolic acts of remembrance– including national days of recognition, return of refugees, and protection of minority groups.[11]

---

[8] Omar Encarnación (2007) Pinochet's revenge: Spain revisits its Civil War. *World Policy Journal,* 24(4): 39–50.

[9] Ruti Teitel (2007) Transitional justice genealogy, *Harvard Human Rights Journal* (16): 69.

[10] Centre on Housing Rights and Evictions (2005) The Pinheiro Principles: United Nations principles on housing and property restitution for refugees and displaced persons.

[11] Derick Fay and Deborah James (2009) *The rights and wrongs of land restitution: Restoring what was ours.* Abingdon, UK: Routledge; Jorgensen Hans and Olof Stjernstrom (2008) Emotional links to forest ownership: Restitution of land and use of a productive resource in Põlva County, Estonia. *Fennia,* 186(2): 95–111; Charles Puttergill, Nolunkcwe Bomela, Janis Grobbelaar et al. (2011) The limits of land restitution: Livelihoods in three rural communities in South Africa. *Development Southern Africa* 28(5): 597–611; Cherryl Walker (2005) The limits to land reform: Rethinking the land question. *Journal of Southern African Studies* 31(4): 805–824; Rhodri Williams (2005) Post-conflict property restitution and refugee return in Bosnia and Herzegovina: Implications for international standard-setting and practice. *New York University Journal of Law and Politics* 37: 446.

Rehabilitating offenders – restorative justice

Restitution can also be seen as having as a key aim the rehabilitation of offenders. This is how the notion of restitution and restorative justice[12] are most easily seen to be linked. In South Africa, the amnesty process that occurred as part of the TRC did not include the rehabilitation of offenders. Perpetrators who gave a full and frank disclosure of the human rights abuses in which they were involved received amnesty and were not subjected to criminal prosecution, as long as they could show that their actions were politically rather than criminally motivated. However, at least 300 applications were refused and handed over for prosecution, although only a few cases were tried.[13] Those who were imprisoned are now up for parole, and some have participated in the Department of Correctional Services' Victim Offender Dialogue programme prior to parole being granted. With young offenders, restorative justice frequently replaces imprisonment. Instead, apologies to victims and community service placements form part of the restorative and restitutionary process.

Albert Eglash, American psychologist, refers to such a practice in which offenders are rehabilitated as 'guided' or 'creative restitution'[14] and describes it as a model of justice that offers perpetrators the possibility of improving their 'self-control and judgement'.[15] He suggests that this kind of restitution need not only occur between individuals, but can be a group practice too. John Braithwaite describes such a group process as 'restoring victims, restoring offenders, and restoring communities as a result of participation of

---

12 Barry Fields (2003) Restitution and restorative justice in juvenile justice and school discipline. *Youth Studies Australia* 22(4): 44–51; Peter Schneider, William Griffith, and Anne Schneider (1982) Juvenile restitution as a sole sanction or condition of probation: An empirical analysis. *Journal of Research in Crime & Delinquency* 19(1): 47–65.

13 Political interference is blamed for why this was the case. See Franny Rabkin, Political interference blocked TRC prosecutions, *Business Day*. 22 May 2015. Accessed 28 March 2016 from http://www.bdlive.co.za/national/2015/05/22/political-interference-blocked-trc-prosecutions.

14 Albert Eglash (1958) Creative restitution – A broader meaning for an old term. *Journal of Criminal Law and Criminology & Police Science* 48(6): 619–622.

15 Eglash (1958), p. 622.

a plurality of stakeholders'.[16] Current research on the outcomes of restorative justice suggests it reduces repeat offending and that the majority of victims who participate are satisfied with the outcomes, more so than in traditional justice procedures.[17]

Contemporary ideas around restitution

These components of restitution: restoring to its original condition, compensating or making reparations, satisfying the injured party symbolically or materially, stripping the perpetrator of unjust benefit, and returning civil, political and property rights is restitution in its legal form. The law makes allowance for each of these facets of restitution, and also allows for programmes that rehabilitate offenders. Legal approaches to restitution are based on strict *liability* for an injustice (that can be proved in court). Approaches that are more contemporary focus on the idea of *responsibility*,[18] broadening our understanding of individual versus corporate accountability, widening our vision for expected outcomes, and offering nuanced views of what it means to restore matters. These views come from scholars across disciplines apart from law, including historians, political scientists, philosophers, psychologists and sociologists. These larger understandings are important since, in South Africa's case, many of the original architects of Apartheid's injustices are no longer alive, although many live with the benefits of unjustly acquired gain and loss.

Restitution as shared moral obligation across generations

Central to the approach focused primarily on *responsibility* for injustices is the view that injustice requires a moral response, one that includes inter-

---

[16] John Braithwaite (1999) Restorative justice: Assessing optimistic and pessimistic accounts. *Crime and Justice* 25, p. 1.

[17] Braithwaite (1999).

[18] While the law does not recognise responsibility across generations, a number of scholars speak of a moral responsibility. See for example Elazar Barkan (2000a) *The guilt of nations: Restitution and negotiating historical injustice.* London, UK: Johns Hopkins University Press; Todd Calder (2010) Shared responsibility, global structural injustice, and restitution. *Social Theory & Practice* 36(2): 263–290; and Iris Marion Young (2006) Responsibility and global justice: A social connection model. *Social Philosophy and Policy* 23(1): 102–130.

generational responsibility, and the notion of indirect benefit. Key here are the levels at which responsibility – individual, communal and institutional – could be taken.

US-based historian, Elazar Barkan describes a growing trend of voluntary (rather than coerced by law) acts of restitution as an emerging response to large-scale global injustices. He ascribes this trend to 'a social moral theory that binds universal values to social realities.'[19] At the core of these values is a sense of moral obligation borne out of 'principles in his nature, which interest him in the fortunes of others, and render their happiness necessary to him, though he derives nothing from it, except the pleasure of seeing it.'[20] More pragmatically, putting forward restitution as a moral obligation allows people to tangibly embrace the idea of a common humanity in which an injury to one is an injury to all; and to deal with public senses of guilt and shame over atrocities committed by other human beings, including the benefit that may be derived from that act. Such voluntary acts of substantive or symbolic restitution, Barkan argues, *are the precursors for reconciliation*.

A number of scholars[21] focus on this continuity of obligation to act across generations and time.

Political scientist James Booth declares that 'we are our past as well as our future.'[22] In doing so, he is arguing, like many others, from a moral perspective that the political identity of communities is consistent across generations and so responsibility does not evaporate.[23] Instead, we need to be 'the bearer

---

[19] Barkan (2000a), p. 309.

[20] Here Barkan quotes from Adam Smith's treatise on Moral sentiments, Barkan (2000a), p. 308.

[21] William Booth (1999) Communities of memory: On identity, memory, and debt. *American Political Science Review* 93(2): 249–263; Daniel Butt (2006) Nations, overlapping generations, and historic injustice. *American Philosophical Quarterly* 43(4): 357–367; Daniel Butt (2012) Repairing historical wrongs and the end of empire. *Social & Legal Studies* 21(2): 227–242; Renée Hill (2002) Compensatory justice: Over time and between groups. *Journal of Political Philosophy* 10(4): 392–415.

[22] Booth (1999), p. 259.

[23] Susanne Buckley-Zistel (2009) Transitional justice in divided societies – Potentials and limits. In *5th European Consortium for Political Research General Conference*. Potsdam Universität, Germany; Alasdair MacIntyre (1981) *After virtue: A study in moral theory*. London, UK: Duckworth.

of responsibility for the past and a custodian for the future.'[24] Alongside the attention paid to the continuity of political identities, political science and philosophy literature also emphasise how individuals who *indirectly* perpetuate socioeconomic inequalities and the ill-treatment of others become responsible for paying restitution to victims of injustice. The most prominent arguments for restitution based on collective responsibility for benefiting at the expense of others emphasise the individual's role in supporting processes of structural injustice.[25] Both feminist political scientist Iris Marion Young's 'social connection model' and Canadian philosopher Todd Calder's notion of 'shared responsibility' for global injustices show how structural injustice becomes embedded in society because *we assent to it through accepting its benefits*. Even those who cannot avoid the benefits of structural injustice still have a moral responsibility to repay unjust gains. Calder[26] uses the example of a Western, middle-class woman, Janis, who through lack of interest or ignorance in global affairs, persistently perpetrates acts of injustice through using goods made in sweatshops that exploit children: 'In sum, Janis tacitly supports structural injustices suffered by sweatshop workers living in developing countries through her actions, omissions, and attitudes. For this reason she shares responsibility for these injustices.'[27] As Calder notes, Janis would be liable for moral, not legal, restitution; she has, after all, not done anything *unlawful*.

Young argues that, since people frequently become overwhelmed by the sheer amount of injustice with which they are confronted and then do nothing, we need to share responsibility as a social group. So instead of isolating individual liability, she focuses on the responsibility of the individual to act *as part of a group* to rectify injustice. In the context of grand-scale, institutionalised injustice, Young contends that isolating individuals is impractical, if not impossible. She states, 'Under a social connection model, agents share responsibility with others who are differently situated, with whom they usually must cooperate in

---

[24] Booth (1999), p. 249.
[25] Calder (2010); Iris Marion Young (2004) Responsibility and global labor justice. *Journal of Political Philosophy* 12(4): 365–388; Young (2006).
[26] Calder (2010).
[27] Calder (2010), p. 268.

order to effect change.'[28] In sum, Calder and Young focus on individuals' often unwitting involvement in global injustice to highlight how *individual* actions are inextricably linked to *structural* factors that underpin domestic and global injustice and that responsibility is best shared if people are to be motivated to act.

Restitution as backward- or forward-looking

Given these understandings of moral obligation, social solidarity and connection, it is also important to state the ultimate purpose of restitution. A number of scholars[29] address the issue of whether restitution should punish the perpetrator, compensate the victim, or restore one or both parties. The liability and culpability approach resulting in punishment is primarily described as backward looking since it focuses on responding to a specific harm. Compensation, too, is strictly just and does not address larger issues of what it means to be restored after an injustice has occurred. In contrast, forward-looking restitution resonates with Booth's notion that we are bearers of the past as well as custodians of the future. Forward-looking restitution is Janus-faced in that it looks to the past in order to remedy injustice but primarily considers the future in formulating a response.[30] This perspective tends to come to the fore in studies considering the nature of structural injustice, namely, 'an ongoing set of processes that ... is likely to continue producing harms unless there are interventions in it.'[31] In short, forward-looking restitution emphasises restoration, for both victim and perpetrator, frequently through satisfaction for the victim (rather than only compensation) and rehabilitation for the perpetrator (rather than only punishment).

Restitution as 'making good' versus 'making right'

Contemporary scholars also contribute to the problematic aim of legal restitution as returning a situation to the way it was before the injustice

---

[28] Young (2006), p. 130.
[29] Calder (2010); Leif Wenar (2006) Reparations for the future. *Journal of Social Philosophy* 37(3): 396–405; Young (2006).
[30] Thom Brooks (2008) A two-tiered reparations theory: A reply to Wenar. *Journal of Social Philosophy* 39(4): 666–669.
[31] Young (2006), p. 122.

occurred, as well as to how the intergenerational transfer of benefit as a result of injustice could occur. It does so by distinguishing between restoring to the way things were (or 'making right' as I have described restitution thus far), to something more akin to repairing – what I will call 'making good'. It is almost always impossible to make things right after injustice. Time has passed, and Johnny no longer owns the bicycle; rather, it is owned by his grandchildren. Jabu has not just lost a bicycle but a livelihood, along with his dignity. Levelling the playing field does not take into account fatigue, injury or a broken spirit.

Two German words translated as restitution help us here.[32] In the case of legal restoration or compensation, the term *wiederherstellen* has been favoured – to restore to the original state and to pay back. However, the term, *wiedergutmachung* which directly translated means, 'making-good again' is closer to the notion of restitution I advocate for South Africa. Here the phrase 'good again' must not be confused with 'how it was'. A construction analogy is perhaps useful in explaining the difference. When I renovated my kitchen, I got a group of friends to do the demolition work with me by removing old cupboards and a wall to make the space more open. Unfortunately, after the cupboard fitter had completed his work there were unsightly gaps between walls and ceilings, and the ceiling itself sagged due to the absence of a supporting wall. I then had to employ a builder to 'make good again' – the term that appeared on his invoice. His job was not to return everything to its original state, nor was it to reinstall the cupboards. Rather it was to work with what had already been achieved, and to ensure that the resulting space was made fit for purpose. He did not just paper over the imperfections, rather he inserted a new structural beam, plastered and repainted the wall and ceiling, and installed a new cornice between the wall and ceiling. He then asked whether I was satisfied with the result. Through a concerted effort and consultation, he made the space good again.

Restitution, thought of in this way, comprises voluntary acts and attitudes towards making good what our past history of injustice has damaged. While it includes efforts, predominantly by government, to compensate people for what was lost, to return rights, and to ensure nobody benefits unjustly from the

---

[32] Tony Judt (2005) *Postwar: A history of Europe since 1945.* New York, NY: Penguin; Mark Sanders (2007) *Ambiguities of witnessing: Law and literature in the time of a truth commission.* Stanford, CA: Stanford University Press.

past, it recognises that satisfying those who were affected by these wrongs and rehabilitating those who were responsible is a better aim for individuals and communities to pursue as a moral responsibility rather than as a legal liability. This kind of forward-looking restitution invites all parties to acknowledge the past, and to work together to repair it through symbolic and material, conceptual and emotional actions. The motive is our shared humanity, and the goal is a restored humanity of all involved. This I call social restitution. How it should be done will be addressed later, but for now let's turn to what obstacles need to be overcome in order to embark on such a journey.

Obstacles to making restitution

There were a number of answers that participants gave to why restitution has not been a larger part of South Africa's transition to democracy.

Believing the TRC and 'reconciliation' was enough

The first answer was that the TRC was enough. That hearing victims' accounts of torture and killings, along with (miniscule amounts of) compensation paid to very few victims, and amnesty for perpetrators who came forward, was enough. When Archbishop Emeritus Desmond Tutu called for 'a social dynamic that includes redressing the suffering of victims … [to] meet the ideal of restorative justice',[33] he made it clear that the TRC itself was only a beginning, and that civil society and government needed to become involved in doing the work that the TRC showed was needed. Such a social – as opposed to government-led – dynamic has never emerged in South Africa. To be sure, there is lots of good work being done by individuals and communities in the name of development and charity, but not as intentional restitution.

There is a growing consensus that the 20 years after democracy has been South Africa's reconciliation project, our 'rainbow nation' moment. However, the widespread protests against ongoing inequality and impoverishment are proving Barkan correct when he says that restitution needs to form the

---

[33] Truth and Reconciliation Commission (1999a). *Truth and Reconciliation Commission of South Africa Report* (Vol. 1). London, UK: Macmillan, p. 131.

bedrock for reconciliation.[34] Consequently, every effort at nation-building is thwarted by an absence of socioeconomic restitution. We remain stuck in our current state of inequality, dispossession, pain, outrage and amnesia. The TRC was clearly not enough.

A chronic case of 'moving-on-itis'

As I have shown so far at least two-thirds of South Africans[35] suffer from chronic 'moving-on-itis'. Perhaps this is unsurprising since confronting the past is and will prove to be difficult. The Economic Freedom Front and the many student movements begun in 2015 have done an outstanding job of challenging this condition and reminding the country of the inequalities that persist. The medicine they propose, including nationalisation, land expropriation without compensation, and a change of government is difficult for many to swallow.

Leaving it to government

The people I interviewed for this study, across all races and ages, had a general working knowledge of what the government had done and continues to do in terms of redress and restitution. While people mentioned the three main areas of affirmative action, the TRC and land redistribution, the most frequent response concerned the role of affirmative action and how it was helping to level the playing field in terms of access to wealth through employment, education and business ownership.

Many Black South Africans, like Fundiswa and Sibu spoke of widespread government efforts to bring about equality, although limited by money:

> **Fundiswa:** Government has made everybody equal. Everybody can do whatever they want. They can go to any job that they studied for ... Our children are going to school for free now ... And the houses ... we can now stay in the suburbs with White people if we have money.

---

34 Barkan (2000a).

35 Kim Wale (2013) Confronting exclusion: Time for radical reconciliation. *South Africa Reconciliation Barometer Survey: 2013.* Cape Town, South Africa: Institute for Justice and Reconciliation.

> **Sibu:** Building houses and providing infrastructure. Working towards making the health system better. So I think I'll give credit to government for that and the roads. Especially in the small towns, you know, things are getting better.

When asked what should be done regarding the dehumanising conditions faced by many of South Africa's poor and mostly Black people, Jack (White man, 71, retired government administrator) noted, along with many others, 'The government should do it.' Johan spoke of 'the fact that social grants have been extended' as 'a good example of some redistribution of wealth.' Black South Africans also tended to want government to improve service delivery in these areas. Few spoke of expecting White South Africans to do anything about restitution. However, that conversation has changed somewhat in 2015 and 2016.

Taking charity for restitution

Participants reflected on what the various organisations and institutions they knew – large and small – were contributing to change, to making a difference in people's lives:

> **Manny:** There's a myriad of NGOs working in South Africa ... to enact social upliftment ... that essentially give services to people in the poorer townships.

> **Luxolo:** There are many NGOs and projects that go to the township, and go and help people with skills. And they train people to do stuff for themselves.

A few spoke of the work of Raymond Ackerman, founder and owner of a large South African food retailer, who also runs a training academy for young, mainly Black, entrepreneurs. Many others spoke of young people who they mentored, or whose school fees they paid. Ted tells of how he and his wife 'have been sponsoring a boy from a township into, you know, a much better school' and how he's discovered 'how many other people say, "You know we've also got a youngster that we're helping, that we are sponsoring", and that's fantastic.'

Almost everyone had stories to tell of individuals who were doing all sorts of things to help improve the lives of those impoverished by South Africa's past. When I asked whether they saw these actions as acts of restitution, some did, or did now after our conversation. The majority saw these as acts of charity or development; seeing a need and meeting it because it was in their power to do so – an obligation of those who *have* towards those who *do not have*.[36] The difference between *doing good* rather than *making good* concerns one of power. Doing good is valuable, but is its own reward. It is frequently done on the terms of the one doing the giving, hence the power differential. Restitution, or making good, is a moral obligation. A duty towards those who have been wronged. It comes with no power or kudos; it is a duty.

Fearing the 'camel-in-the-tent' syndrome

A further obstacle to restitution, and the one most commonly spoken about, was fear. According to Thomas, 'there's still a sense of fear … we're scared of what might happen'. Welile agreed on the issue of fear and expanded: 'They don't know what's going to happen … [Those] that are actually willing to give up a piece of their farm are afraid government will go to them and ask more'. I call it the 'camel-in-the-tent' syndrome based on a folk tale about a camel asking if it could place its nose in the tent because it is cold outside, then progressively asks if other parts of its body can also come into the tent; until it wholly occupies the tent and the tent-owner is forced out into the cold. It aptly illustrates this fear of restitution.

Greed and self-enrichment

Somewhat related to a fear of losing everything, was greed. 'Wanting more for me' is how Ricky described it. Nollie (Black woman, 32, financial administrator) calls it 'self-enrichment … everybody is trying to get themselves to be on top', and here she is speaking about White reluctance to make things right, rather than government corruption. 'They forget about the other person,' she continued. 'They don't really want to make things right.'

Not knowing what could be done

Another obstacle to restitution concerned ignorance and was only spoken of by White and Coloured participants: people either not knowing what can be

---

[36] This is commonly known as *noblesse oblige* – the obligation of the nobility for those under their rule, an expression from feudal times.

done to make restitution, or being ignorant of its necessity and importance. Harry, a 63-year-old retired White business executive, said: 'If we don't have restitution we can't go forward. But having said that, there's also no understanding of what restitution is or how it can take place.' Dylan covered other obstacles in his response along with that of 'not knowing what to do ... feeling like how much can they give?' Olivia expanded on not knowing to include being paralysed: 'I think people recognise that unless we all do our bit we're not going to recover as a nation, but a lot of people have been paralysed by the enormity of it. Not knowing where to start.'

A denial of benefit and responsibility

Finally, many felt that a barrier to restitution was that most White South Africans did not believe they were perpetrators of South Africa's unjust past, and therefore cannot be held responsible for making amends. According to 36-year-old Rose, 'People say, I wasn't an architect or a perpetrator of injustice ... so [restitution] is not my responsibility ... I didn't steal the bicycle.' Dylan added: 'People are feeling it's not really necessary, feeling they're not personally responsible.' Leo summarised succinctly:

> **Leo:** The absence of restitution comes from an inability to see or take collective responsibility for acts done in our name and for our benefit ... For many people the existence of someone like Eugene de Kock ... has allowed us to transfer the responsibility to him, abdicating our responsibility and the responsibility of our forebears ... Not seeing collective responsibility as an issue prevents many from actively making restitution themselves.

Archbishop Tutu spoke of this denial from Apartheid's beneficiaries and their failure to recognise their role in the current day impoverishment of most Black South Africans in the most painful terms:

> Apart from the hurt that it causes to those who suffered, the denial by so many White South Africans even that they benefited from Apartheid is a crippling, self-inflicted blow to their capacity to enjoy and appropriate the fruits of change. [37]

---

[37] Truth and Reconciliation Commission (2003). *Truth and Reconciliation Commission of South Africa Report* (Vol. 6). Department of Justice of the Republic of South Africa. Introduction.

He continues to say that many White South Africans 'carry a burden of guilt which would have been assuaged'[38] through participating more fully in the TRC and its recommendations for 'a social dynamic'[39] of restitution.

In the next chapters, overcoming these obstacles to restitution will be addressed, at least in part, through inviting people to think through the roles they occupy in relation to South Africa's past, whether or not they were physically present.

---

[38] Truth and Reconciliation Commission (2003), Introduction.
[39] Truth and Reconciliation Commission (1999a), p. 131.

7   Locating yourself in the conversation

What is it about the past that makes it such an untouchable subject? Why are people so reluctant to remember, or to want to examine the details of our past?[1] Why should they want to? 'I wasn't there when it happened'; 'We didn't know what was going on so how were we meant to do anything about it?'; 'We were powerless to stop it'; 'Let's just move forward; stop going on about the past?' These are four commonly encountered responses from White South Africans when asked to reflect on South Africa's past. Responses from Black South Africans are not dissimilar. In addition, many young people deny that they were affected by Apartheid: 'It didn't affect me; it affected my parents and grandparents'. Some speak of 'not knowing much about Apartheid', and many speak of 'looking to the future, not the past'.

The answer to why it is important to examine the past is that its effects remain with us. Certainly, in the South Africa of 2016, many of our problems emerge from the past. The gravid worms of Apartheid education, job reservation, superior attitudes and land policies all continue to give birth to the poverty, inequality and social ills we still see today. Past injustice exerts a huge influence on the present and therefore, before moving on, we must face up to these past injustices. If we do so, we have a far greater possibility of being able to build the kind of country we want.

This chapter describes a labelling activity undertaken with the group of people who participated in the study. My hope is that the activity can be repeated in small groups at schools, in homes, university classrooms, faith communities and the workplace. Like the two stories of the soccer field and the bicycle, it is designed to open up the conversation of what it is like to be 15 in South Africa and to have been born sometime after the end of Apartheid, what it is like to be 30 and to have been a child during Apartheid, or 50 or 70 years old and to have first-hand memories of stayaways, pencil tests, forced removals and 'White affirmative action'.

---

[1] Certainly when I did these interviews in 2014, possibly less so in 2016.

Making distinctions

When speaking of human rights violations, crime and abuse, it has become common to speak of 'victims' and 'perpetrators'. For those working in justice fields, the term 'bystander' is also commonly used. These labels, in varying forms, have been used when sensitising children to responses to bullying, thinking through the actions of people in the Holocaust, and in incidents of racial violence, amongst many other issues of injustice.[2] Preeminent Holocaust scholar Raul Hilberg[3] provides a comprehensive historical account of this victim-perpetrator-bystander triangle. Over the years, scholars have added other labels to this triangle, including 'activists', 'helpers' and 'rescuers'.[4]

What has not been added, or certainly has not become as popular as Hilberg's original triangle, is the role of those who benefited from the injustice years or generations later, or those who resisted, or who currently resist these lasting effects of injustice. What has also become clear over the years is the reluctance of people to call themselves victims – because of the connotation of helplessness; or to call themselves perpetrators – because of the lack of nuance between those who gave orders to maim, kill, exclude or dominate versus those who simply obeyed the orders.

In my teaching, especially on race and justice, I have increasingly begun to make use of distinctions beyond victim and perpetrator, or even bystander. Frequently, this has been in response to the comments with which this chapter begins, but also because, too frequently, I can't fail to notice the glazed look that comes over the faces of Black and White 19-year-old students when I begin to

---

2   Dan Bar-On (2001) The bystander in relation to the victim and the perpetrator: Today and during the Holocaust. *Social Justice Research* 14(2): 125–148; Bibb Latané and John M. Darley (1970) *The unresponsive bystander: Why doesn't he help?* New York, NY: Appleton-Century Crofts; Melvin Lerner (1975) The justice motive in social behavior. *Journal of Social Issues* 31(3): 1–19; Ervin Staub (1989) *The roots of evil: The origins of genocide and other group violence.* Cambridge, UK: Cambridge University Press; Ervin Staub (1996) Activating bystanders, helping victims, and the creation of caring. *Peace and Conflict: Journal of Peace Psychology* 2(3): 189–200.

3   Raul Hilberg (1992) *Perpetrators victims bystanders: The Jewish catastrophe, 1933–1945.* New York, NY: Aaron Asher Books.

4   Gillian Straker (2011) Beneficiaries for evermore: Reply to commentaries. *Psychoanalytic Dialogues* 21(6): 670–675.

talk about victims and perpetrators. These were the terms used in South Africa's TRC by which to distinguish people. The TRC, that began in 1996, seems to be ancient history to these young people who suffer from 'ahistoricism'– a lack of historical perspective, or more colloquially, for them 'only today exists'.

When I offer my students a few other labels to consider, such as 'beneficiary', or 'ostrich', or 'dishonoured', then eyes open, attention is diverted from smartphones, and hands shoot up, each with vocal opinions – not always in agreement with me or each other. These distinctions begin with Hilberg's triangle, but expand his definitions in each category, before adding two new terms – also expanded with synonyms.

Perpetrator

A perpetrator is someone who commits an illegal, criminal, violent or evil act. In the South African context, perpetrators of Apartheid's injustice include all those who acted to ensure subjugation and domination of Black South Africans – from the lawmakers and rulers, to the soldiers and clerks who kept its systems in place. The distinction I have increasingly made here is between those who were *architects* of Apartheid's injustice and those who were its *implementers*. It is helpful to make this distinction since it enables a response to those who want to escape culpability by saying 'I didn't set up the system … I just did what I was told.' Are both perpetrators? Surely, yes. Is their culpability equal? Arguably, no. Distinguishing between those people who actively devised a system of greed, hatred and injustice and those who did as they were told offers the opportunity for more people to locate themselves in the past. Hilberg does distinguish – using the terms 'chief perpetrator' (Adolf Hitler) and other categories including 'sadistic vulgarians' between 'those with misgivings' and 'old officers' amongst others – but not in the same way as I believe the terms architect and implementer capture the distinction.

I would therefore consider an architect of injustice as the person who designed the policies and created the environment in which injustice might occur, and those who carry 'political guilt … [by legitimating] perpetrators in their roles'.[5] Examples of perpetrators as architects of injustice in the South African context

---

5   Susanne Buckley-Zistel (2009) Transitional justice in divided societies – potentials and limits. In *5th European Consortium for Political Research General Conference*. Potsdam Universität, Germany, p. 9.

would be National Party government ministers, such as Hendrik Verwoerd – infamous for his Bantu education policy of 1953; John Vorster – the minister of police and subsequently Prime Minister; and Adriaan Vlok, minister of police under whom countless house raids, detentions, incidents of torture and deaths occurred.

A perpetrator as an implementer of injustice, on the other hand, is someone who followed orders or took the lead from others. Implementers of injustice might for example be a White conscripted soldier into the Apartheid army, a member of the security police, or those who chose to inform on struggle activists or who collaborated with the security police.[6] It may also have been those who paid unjust wages to employees, an evil act though not criminal at the time, and those who treated Black people inhumanely in other ways.

Victim

No one likes the term victim.[7] Being labelled a victim comes with associations of helplessness, a lack of agency and a position of shame. 'How did you allow yourself to get into this position?' is frequently a silent accusation – the 'blame the victim phenomenon'. In cases of domestic violence, often the term 'survivor' is preferred to the term victim, in order to remove this association. Hilberg also differentiates between types of victims in his typology and calls some victims 'leaders', others 'resisters', 'survivors' and 'collaborators' – those who went along with the Nazis (through coercion, fear, or personal gain).

The word I have begun to use alongside the word victim is that of dishonoured.[8] To have been on the receiving end of injustice, crime or an

---

6   See for example, Jacob Dlamini (2014) *Askari: a story of collaboration and betrayal in the anti-apartheid struggle*. Johannesburg, South Africa: Jacana Media.

7   Neil Ferguson, Mark Burgess, and Ian Hollywood (2010) Who are the victims? Victimhood experiences in postagreement Northern Ireland. *Political Psychology* 31(6): 857–886.

8   The issue of honour is complex. I use it to denote the honour and dignity inherent in being human. For a detailed treatment of honour see John Iliffe (2005) *Honour in African history*. Cambridge, UK: Cambridge University Press On dignity, see Michael Rosen (2012) *Dignity: Its history and meaning*. Cambridge, MA: Harvard University Press.

evil act is to have been dishonoured as a human being, to have been treated as not being worthy of dignity, respect and equality. Those who have been dishonoured by the systems, structures and actions of Apartheid include all Black South Africans, no matter their social position, whether one of the few permitted to become professionals or the masses who were educated only for servitude. This dishonour extends across generations as children inherit the physical impoverishment of their parents, missed opportunities due to poor quality education, and low levels of social and cultural capital due to Apartheid's policies.

It may also be accurate to say that those who were dishonoured may also have been 'harmed' or 'damaged', but these words are too often perceived as negative and do not help people to locate themselves in the past. Of course, perpetrators may also have been harmed or damaged in the course of committing atrocities (and thus can also be called dishonoured and victims especially if they had limited choice in their involvement). This situation is frequently encountered with those returning from conflict.

Bystander

Hilberg's description of a bystander is someone who sees an evil, criminal or violent act and does nothing to stop or change it. A bystander, according to Karl Jasper,[9] bears 'the moral guilt of those who did not act but looked on'.[10] Many bystanders see themselves as being too powerless to act, or being too insignificant to disrupt the crashing waves of injustice that were being perpetrated. In making distinctions and offering alternative descriptions, I have frequently used the terms 'silent', 'avoiding', or frequently, to laughter, ostrich – someone who buries their head in the sand to avoid what is going on around them. The ostrich label, for all its humour, seems to be the one to which people most easily relate. More about why this is so later.

---

[9] Karl Jasper distinguishes between individual and collective guilt, and proposes three further types of guilt: political guilt that legitimates the actions of perpetrators, the moral guilt of bystanders who look on and the metaphysical guilt of survivors who did nothing to stop atrocities. Jaspers' distinctions are described in Buckley-Zistel (2009).

[10] Buckley-Zistel (2009), p. 9.

Resister

For Hilberg, those who resisted injustice do not form a separate category; instead, they form a sub-group of the victim category. The problems with this are obvious – it detracts from the active position of resistance, and does not do justice to the moral significance of resisting injustice. Furthermore, it is also important in distinguishing between those who were the leaders and architects of resistance to injustice, and those who were the implementers or foot soldiers of resistance. Here again, the distinction is helpful since many may not see themselves in the same light as resisters such as Albert Luthuli, Nelson Mandela, Robert Sobukwe, Steve Biko, Ben Turok or Walter Sisulu. These are examples of people who designed ways of resisting, who led the armed struggle, devised ways of educating people in prison for their liberation, and prepared the ground for the South African transition to democracy.

Implementers of resistance to injustice may have been an Umkhonto we Sizwe foot soldier; someone who participated in a mass action campaign that aimed at making the country ungovernable and thus forcing the hand of the White government to relinquish power; someone who was a member of a civic association or a youth member of the Soweto uprising; or someone who through any action, followed leaders' orders to disrupt the injustices of Apartheid, whether by civil disobedience (such as using Whites-only amenities or refusing to be conscripted into the Apartheid army), teaching about injustice or supporting jailed resistance members. These were activists and resisters to injustice, albeit at a different level to those who designed strategies of resistance.

Beneficiary

A further category that Hilberg's triangle omits is that of beneficiary. The reason for this is that his location of actors was limited to the actual time of the Holocaust, although he does talk of 'survivors' of the Holocaust. However, a generation or two after an injustice has occurred – as is the case in South Africa now – there are numerous categories of people who have benefited as a result of Apartheid. The most obvious is to talk about having benefited from the injustice of the past, of still receiving benefit from Apartheid's policies of job reservation, differential education and the Group Areas act for example. As a White South African, you or your family are likely to have accumulated undeserved wealth from all of these policies, along with unearned privilege and a baseless sense of superiority that comes with both wealth and privilege. To be a beneficiary seems to be a passive location – you find yourself in a situation without ever having lifted a finger as a perpetrator – neither architect nor implementer. After all, you were not there at the time. For those who were there at the time, you may not have been an active perpetrator but you benefited from *doing nothing*, either financially or from escaping the violence and disruption (jail for example) that resisters endured. You may have benefited because you were ignorant or did not care to know from where your property, wealth, job and education came. But benefit you did.

You may also have been a beneficiary of resistance to injustice without having actively resisted yourself. Perhaps you were born to a family where great resistance took place, and whose values you imbibed, and whose resistance helped you to escape a sense of inferiority, or whose flight into exile meant that you received a far better education than those who were trapped in Apartheid South Africa. More recently, perhaps your family's resistance still has an effect on you now, as a young Black South African, since it may have helped conscientise you to the effects of the past on the present. More starkly, as a Black South African, you could be a beneficiary of the many programmes of redress to mitigate the past in terms of employment, education or business development opportunities. While the usefulness of this label is questionable (and does not fit my schema as neatly as the others), it nonetheless invites discussion.

Benefit may have been direct, or one may have inherited it, much like one may have inherited dishonour (or victimhood). This is especially true of these who were 'born-free' after 1994, and who are now in their twenties and younger. Many inheritors experience both the benefit of resistance and the ongoing consequences of injustice (and in some cases both simultaneously). Examples of inheritors of benefit include the social and physical capital inherited by many young White South Africans, while many young Black South Africans inherit the internal strengths of resistance, along with the affirmative action opportunities now afforded them.

Complex relationships and multiple locations

Of course making distinctions is not always easily done. There may be those who experience dishonour as recipients of unwarranted benefits. How might it feel to have wealth and privilege as a White South African only because jobs had been reserved for you, not because of any talent or merit on your part? Or how might it feel to have perpetrated violent acts against neighbours as part of a dehumanising complicity in the army, police or 'third force'?[11] How might it feel to have been the leader of a Bantustan, and to have received some privilege in return for compliance and silence? So even perpetrators may be victims, and can be dishonoured (although arguably to incomparable extents), and victims can be perpetrators.

Resisters can become perpetrators as they design strategies to stop injustice that can be judged to be human rights violations. The TRC indeed judged some actions of Umkonto cadres as human rights violations in the struggle *against* Apartheid but noted the difference between those who perpetrated human rights violations in pursuit of a just objective and those who perpetrated human rights violations in pursuit of an unjust and inhumane cause.[12] So, as complicated as these various locations are, I designed a simple labelling activity for participants to complete as part of their interviews with me. I was hoping it might deepen our conversation about the past, as well as about what needed to be done to make things good for the future.

Choosing labels

About mid-way through their interviews, participants were given a list of labels on a sheet of paper in English (see Table 7.1 for the complete list but not categorised as it is in this table) and asked: 'When thinking about the past, what labels would you give yourself? Choose from the list or add your own.'

---

[11] The third force was shown to be instigated by the South African Security Police and various other right-wing groups which aimed to prevent the end of Apartheid. Third force activity was frequently disguised as ethnic rivalry.

[12] This was one of the reasons for the final TRC report being given a lukewarm reception by the ANC government in 1997. See Truth and Reconciliation Commission (2003) *Truth and Reconciliation Commission of South Africa Report* (Vol. 6).

Table 7.1 *New language and categories for labels*

Victim	Perpetrator	Bystander	Beneficiary	Resister
• Harmed by injustice	• Architect of injustice	• Ostrich	• Beneficiary of privilege	• Rescuer
• Damaged by injustice	• Implementer of injustice	• Avoider	• Inheritor of benefit	• Architect of resistance
• Dishonoured by injustice	• Informer	• Silent	• Beneficiary of redress	• Implementer of resistance
• Inheritor of dishonour	• Collaborator		• Beneficiary of resistance	
• Dishonoured by resistance				

The interview was paused while they chose, with most people taking around five minutes to choose. They shook their heads, muttered to themselves, circled and scratched out labels, added labels,[13] then placed lines through them, and finally looked up ready to talk about their selections.

When the interview resumed they were asked, 'How easy or difficult was it for you to choose a label?', 'Which labels do you like or dislike and why?' and 'Are there any you don't understand?' This activity consistently provoked participants into engaged conversation. In terms of analysing people's responses, I wanted to know the following:

> Who chose labels from the traditional triangle of victim, perpetrator or bystander?

> What difference did it make when synonyms and broader descriptions for these words were included?

> How did people respond to the terms resister and beneficiary, along with synonyms for both terms?

> How did people's social location – in terms of race, class and age – affect their choice of labels?

---

13 Added labels included 'conscientiser about injustices', 'culpable', 'disengaged', 'forgiver of injustice', 'ignorant', 'peacemaker', 'someone who did my bit' and 'survivor of injustice'.

Who chose victim, perpetrator or bystander?

Sixteen out of 60 participants chose the actual label entitled victim, 3 chose perpetrator and 18 chose bystander. When discussing their choice of the victim label, 48-year-old Black woman and domestic worker, Nontembiso and 56-year-old Black man and struggle veteran Sipho reflected:

> **Nontembiso:** Victim, definitely victim because we were suppressed by government who is a big corporation and you on the other hand, you are a little person on the street, so there isn't much you could do to defend yourself.

> **Sipho:** Victim. It is difficult having to admit what happened to me. It still brings me sadness and sorrow when I think about it.

Nontembiso reflects a collective understanding of being a victim, Sipho a personal one.

Others were clearly conflicted, although they retained their choice of the actual word victim, like two Black male graduate students, 32-year-old Thamsanqa and 23-year-old Sizwe. Both qualified and explained their choice:

> **Thamsanqa:** Taking away that term [victim] actually takes away responsibility from the perpetrators and that's unfair.

> ***

> I don't like the meaning that the term has come to be given; that when we claim we're a victim of the past it's seen as a negative thing ... I do feel that the past affected me personally ... I never had choices. I was born into a system where I was destined to be given sub-standard education, which affects me even to this very day even though there have been opportunities later. So I will claim victim.

> **Sizwe:** I did take it – victim, but I was like I'm not sure cos it takes away my agency ... I am a victim, but then it doesn't – I don't know – it doesn't sit well. I am a victim, but I'm a victim who fights back.

> ***

> I think for me, yes, I am and I haven't been healed of the injustice or restored. Like it messed my family up. I mean, I don't want to

blame Apartheid for my father leaving my mom, but his violence is because, I think, that he used to go and work for White people, and was treated like a child, and come back home and he has to take back his manhood.

Only one White man, 34-year-old chef Robert, spoke of being a victim because he believes he is currently discriminated against in present-day South Africa:

> **Robert:** I have become a victim of current day circumstances of people of colour being favoured in certain posts … It's more like a sort of reverse racism. It's as bad as Apartheid was almost … I feel like a bit of a victim … It's not a label that I walk around with.

The three people (38-year-old Heather, 46-year-old Leo, and 48-year-old Johan) who chose the label perpetrator were all White and deeply involved in non-profit organisations working for social justice. Heather had been a child in the '80s at the height of the Apartheid struggle; Leo had been a conscientious objector and had not served as an Apartheid conscript; and Johan had been a chaplain in the army and had refused to bear arms. For them, choosing the label perpetrator was about assuming a sense of collective responsibility as Johan explains: 'I was part of the Afrikaans community that were the perpetrators of Apartheid'.

Thirty-seven-year-old graduate student Angela, while not initially choosing the label perpetrator, later describes herself as a 'recovering racist' and calls herself 'a perpetrator of racism':

> **Angela:** [US author] Toni Morrison calls racism a disease, and I kind of agree with her. And I am still racist, a perpetrator of racism, the assumptions and stereotypes are still there. Even though I pride myself on being human with everyone that is really a false pride.

Thirty-four-year-old White man and researcher Dylan, while also not choosing the 'perpetrator' label, describes some of the conflict he feels about taking collective responsibility and his understanding of the intentionality behind the label:

> **Dylan:** Was I a perpetrator of injustice in some ways? I think that I probably was a perpetrator of injustice, but unintentionally. It's probably a matter of semantics, but the term perpetrator has an intentional element to it. So I wouldn't include myself in that category.

It is clear that using the terms victim and perpetrator results in a mostly Black-White binary, although relatively few White South Africans chose the label of perpetrator.

When it came to those who chose the label bystander, these racial distinctions blur somewhat. Of the 18 people who chose bystander, 12 were White, 2 were Coloured and 4 were Black. Black and Coloured people who labelled themselves as bystanders were mainly middle generation – between ages 26 and 49. White bystanders included almost all the older generation and half of each of the younger and middle generation groups. White participants Sarah (37, teacher) and Harry (63, retired businessman) both labelled themselves bystanders and spoke of having been sheltered or removed from the realities of Apartheid:

> **Sarah:** [I chose] bystander because growing up during Apartheid it wasn't something that we ever discussed. It was just how things were. I was born into Apartheid and it just was. It wasn't anything that you argued about … Even now, bystander. I just go with the flow. I am not a great revolutionary or anything.

> **Harry:** I circled bystander … I didn't get involved. We carried on with our sport, and our jobs, and our business and our families. Only later, later, towards the end of the Apartheid era did my generation, and me, become even remotely interested in the injustices of the past.

Seventy-seven-year-old retired architect Michael described himself a little more reluctantly as a bystander: 'Let's just say I wasn't as active in making a noise about it as I probably should have been or other people were.' Most Black South Africans responded with incredulity to the label of bystander, as captured by 21-year-old Black unemployed woman Naledi, who said she 'disliked' this label:

> **Naledi:** A bystander is someone who stood and watched while things were happening. People don't stand by and watch – you fight for what you believe is right or you support what is wrong. No in-between!

Only a few Black participants and Coloured participants spoke of themselves as bystanders. None except for 32-year-old help desk assistant Nollie, who said, explained why they had chosen as they had, 'Because I have not been involved in anything that would make right what happened in the past.'

As insightful as these reflections on conventional labels are, the fact that nearly half of those in the study did not choose any of these labels as appropriate to locate themselves in the past indicate the limitations of their usefulness. If in a school, university, community or workplace environment, one was trying to talk about the past in the present and what needs to be done about it, limiting the discussion to Hilberg's triangle would allow many people to simply opt out of the discussion – because of their age, their historical population category, or because, as Dylan puts it – the absence of 'intention'. What might happen when new descriptions are added to these three categories?

Table 7.2 *The effects of using Hilberg's labels versus expanded labels*

Number of people who chose labels		
Victim	*Narrow*	*Expanded*
Black	12	19
Coloured	2	5
White	2	12
Total	**16**	**36**
Perpetrator	*Narrow*	*Expanded*
Black	0	0
Coloured	0	1
White	3	4
Total	**3**	**5**
Bystander	*Narrow*	*Expanded*
Black	4	8
Coloured	2	4
White	12	15
Total	**18**	**27**

Number of people who chose labels		
Beneficiary		Expanded
Black	–	11
Coloured	–	3
White	–	23
Total	**–**	**37**

Resister		Expanded
Black	–	8
Coloured	–	2
White	–	7
Total	**–**	**17**

Adding new language to old categories

The possibilities supplied to participants did not only include the three conventional labels of victim, perpetrator and bystander – but also various other labels that could be clustered under each of these traditional categories. As a result, this had a dramatic effect on how participants were able to see themselves, and locate themselves in the conversation.

Seeing how our humanity has been hurt

In terms of who described themselves as a victim, adding additional descriptors increased those who recognisd themselves as victims from 16 to 36 (see Table 7.2). Now, however, the descriptions included those harmed or damaged by injustice, those dishonoured by injustice or in the process of resisting injustice, and those who have inherited this dishonour. While the number of people who chose expanded victim descriptions increased from all racial groups, it is striking to note that whereas only two White people described themselves as victims, now 12 do. Some may argue that this is not a good development, but if a key to making restitution lies in understanding how all of how humanity has been damaged, and how injustice dishonours us all – perhaps this is a useful reflection for White South Africans – along with the incomparability of the loss.

For many others, though, describing yourself, as someone who had been dishonoured by past injustice was an attractive option, including those who had indicated how hard it is to call yourself a victim. Twenty-nine-year-old unemployed Black woman Luxolo explains:

> **Luxolo:** It's the word victim. It's kind of – I don't know – it puts me down so I hate that feeling. I don't like to feel like a victim … Dishonoured – it's better. It's better than victim. Dishonoured by injustice is the truth whereas victim puts you down.

Perpetrators are still hard to find

In connection with adding new descriptions to the category of perpetrator, such as 'informer' or 'collaborator' and distinguishing between architect and implementer of injustice, nothing much seems to change. Those who had already chosen the actual term 'perpetrator' also choose these other terms, with one exception. Haley describes how her failure to resist White superiority made her a 'collaborator' with Apartheid:

> **Haley:** I think that what must happen as part of restitution is [Black people] must acknowledge Apartheid was shit, but at some point admit, 'I conspired with that lie that created the world in which I now live. I'm not to blame … [but I] did make some choices and chose what to believe [about inferiority and superiority]'. And that's good news because it means … you can choose differently in the future.

Clearly, however, no one seemed to like the category of perpetrator, no matter what language is used to describe it. Why are perpetrators so hard to find? Olivia, spoke about 'the word perpetrator … it's a blood-on-your-hands kind of word … But it is what it is. So you can't really use a different word'. And Michael, in asking for clarification about the word perpetrator, showed how it is synonymous with collaborator:

> **Michael:** Perpetrator of what? Atrocities? Certainly, I can say no, then … but I circled collaborator. I did live according to a whole lot of Apartheid laws because it was the line of least resistance.

Ostrich is easy to understand

Although the bystander category was already frequently chosen, when I looked at who had chosen labels that mean bystander – such as ostrich, 'avoider' or 'silent' it became ever more popular and with a range of people. Four additional Black people chose bystander-type labels, two additional Coloured people and three additional White people. In total, those choosing bystander-type labels increased from 18 to 27 people.

Twenty-eight-year-old Black woman and finance administrator Mbali, labelled herself an ostrich. Like Nollie (who had called herself a bystander), she said it was because:

> **Mbali:** In the past when it was still Apartheid I was young and there was nothing that I could do. And now, there is nothing that I am doing to contribute to the society in a positive way so … ostrich!

She was among very few Black participants (five in total) who called themselves ostriches. Those who did so, gave the reason for their choice as not having 'a very strong opinion on … the political situation in this country' (Sindiswa, Black woman, 25, client services). Similarly, 30-year-old Donovan, a Coloured man, explained why he identified with the ostrich label:

> **Donovan:** I do know what's going on. It's just I'm an ostrich – sticking my head in the ground … I'm not in despair, but not because there aren't bad things going on … I don't get too involved, except with the things that matter … like Rebecca and my cycling. Because life's a bit short to worry about everything.

Candice (Coloured woman, 29, graduate student) called herself, 'An ostrich. Silent … you're watching but you just don't care … so you can say self-interested'. A number of White South Africans called themselves ostriches for 'putting their heads in the ground' but some had other interpretations. Harry called himself an ostrich then changed his mind:

> **Harry:** Ostrich. No. I don't think we were ostriches. I don't think we knew enough about what was happening. An ostrich effect would imply that you knew what was happening and you put your head down. But I have to say I don't think we were informed enough.

Johan called himself an ostrich because he said he gets 'tired of fighting' with the conservative White community:

> **Johan:** I don't have the energy to engage with conservative Whites … I am very good at changing the topic … 'Yo, but the rugby was good this weekend' … I'm tired of hitting my head against the wall.

As was the case with bystander, many Black participants expressed disbelief about the possibility of being an ostrich:

> **Lwethu (Black woman, 24, retail merchandiser):** You need to pick a side and stand for whatever you believe in … [rather than] being weak with no backbone.

> **Palesa (Black woman, 22, financial administrator):** How can you avoid things when you are faced with such situations daily? You can't just avoid things. You need to do something because … all races were affected. So I don't think there's such a person that avoids things like an ostrich.

Vukani (Black man, 34, finance executive) was particularly scathing when he told me that White people cannot call themselves ostriches:

> **Vukani:** It's a big topic of discussion amongst many Black people … It's funny how Apartheid ended and you suddenly can't find one White person who thought it was good [laughs]. But during Apartheid … the people who benefited from it … couldn't say no to what their leaders were implementing … When the *stem nee* [vote no] or *stem ja* [vote yes] referendum came in 1992 to end Apartheid some people did *stem nee*. Not everyone *stemmed ja* you know.

What is interesting with the expanded descriptions given to bystanders is how people chose these other labels for different reasons: For knowing and choosing to stick your head in the ground; for knowing and not doing enough; for not caring enough to do anything about injustice; for being ignorant and not caring to find out; for not listening to the news now, or accepting what was going on at face value then (as both a sheltered White South African and a Black South African living in a former Bantustan confessed). The ostrich label was particularly interesting since it elicited much discussion, debate and reflection way beyond interviews.

Adding new categories

Offering people the opportunity to label themselves as resister and beneficiary (also shown in Table 7.1) was also an important contribution beyond Hilberg's triangle. People who had not chosen labels in the other three categories now included themselves by choosing one or the other. Furthermore, the conversation about what it means to be a beneficiary or resister became animated.

Beneficiaries of privilege and redress

Eleven Black participants labelled themselves as beneficiaries, choosing labels that described being a 'beneficiary of resistance' to injustice and 'benefiting from redress' since 1994. These choices are captured by Mayaya (Black woman, 34, business executive) and Thamsanqa:

> **Thamsanqa:** I chose beneficiary of resistance first because when I saw that phrase it took me back to Crossroads. I was young and I remember the toyi-toyis and the different protests. I was too young to take part in that but then I was aware that they were fighting for me. So that one I really identify with.

> **Mayaya:** Beneficiary of resistance ... I've benefited. I was 15 in 1994. I could not even vote. The policies were drafted. And when I started university and I started my first job there were already these policies that said we have to pay special attention to women in the work place, to Black people in the work place. We have to have share schemes that benefit Black people and women and so forth.

Three out of the seven Coloured participants spoke of being a 'beneficiary of injustice'. Like Manny (Coloured man, 48, university administrator) they highlighted their relative privilege under Apartheid compared to Black South Africans:

> **Manny:** I think as a Coloured person I was a beneficiary of injustice because it's something that's not politically right to say, but Coloured people got more than what Black people got.

Almost all White participants spoke of being a beneficiary of injustice (23 out of the 26 participants), across generational boundaries. Noah (White man, 21, student) spoke of the benefit of 'having White parents who … received benefits that they might not have had, had the system been fairer' while his same age peer Jane (White woman, also a student) elaborated: 'whether it was job reservation, better schooling or just freedom of mobility … I inherited that benefit from [my parents]'. Thomas (White man, 23, recent graduate) spoke of the land he stands to inherit despite his family having received a claim against the land they own:

> **Thomas:** Beneficiary of injustice – *ja* I am one of those. My family has a farm in Northern Natal. It's safe to say technically they had a land claim [against it] and kept it. Inheritor of benefit would follow that one.

Connie (White woman, 71, non-profit administrator) reluctantly admits:

> **Connie:** I suppose I would say I'm an inheritor of benefit … I do have the benefit of property, a certain amount of money. But it wasn't through inheritance or anything, it was through hard work.

Here Connie invokes the meritocracy myth, little realising that 'we worked for what we have' means very little in the light of South African's history of job reservation. Others echoed Connie's point of view, also providing a meritocracy caveat to the label of 'beneficiary'.

A few White participants spoke of being the beneficiary of resistance to injustice, like 38-year-old non-profit worker, Heather:

> **Heather:** I like the label 'beneficiary of resistance'. I feel that it acknowledges and honours the countless people known and unknown to me that worked towards a democratic South Africa when I was too young, too afraid and too dependent on my parents to become actively involved.

Resisters, then and now

In total 17 out of the 60 participants chose a label that related to resisting – 8 Black, 2 Coloured and 7 White participants. Since there was no label that only used the word 'resister', there is no differentiation between a narrow and more expanded understanding of the term. People chose (sometimes in more than one sub category) either 'architect of resistance' (4 in total, 3 White and 1 Black), 'implementer of resistance' (12 in total, 5 Black, 1 Coloured, 6 White) or 'rescuer' (5 in total, 3 Black and 2 White).

Sipho, the MK veteran, clearly labelled himself a resister and talked a little about his experiences as a soldier. Sizwe (23, student) and Nontembiso (48, domestic worker) both told me they would have been active resisters if they were old enough (Sizwe), or lived in Gauteng instead of the Eastern Cape (Nontembiso). Gina (White woman, 69, retired retail manager) says she resisted through her vote, and through her actions at work:

> **Gina:** I didn't vote then for the Nat government. [I voted for] the United Party.
>
> ***
>
> [At work] I had 139 staff at this one branch I had to train. I couldn't say the African names and I got a girl to teach me how to pronounce these names.
>
> ***
>
> We went into Soweto without a permit ... Thank goodness, the police didn't stop us. And we went to the wedding [of a staff member] and we came out.
>
> ***
>
> When they had the unrest in Soweto ... [the staff] wanted to sleep on blankets in the store. And I said: "No, I'm going to get mattresses plus bedding". I hired it for every one of them.
>
> **Interviewer:** Why did they have to sleep in the shop?
>
> **Gina:** Because they could not go home. They would have been killed if it had been known they'd come from work.
>
> **Interviewer:** Do you know why they were told to stay away from work?
>
> **Gina:** No.
>
> **Interviewer:** The liberation movements had called for people to stay away from work so that White people could see that without Black people the country can't function.
>
> **Gina:** But some Black people actually went to work because they needed to work to earn money. And I fed them, clothed them, gave them toothpaste, gave them everything they needed.

What Gina failed to notice in both of her accounts of resistance was the fact that the United Party, while ostensibly against Apartheid as a system, still supported White minority rule. Furthermore, in supporting her staff with mattresses and food, she was in fact, not supporting the struggle to bring down Apartheid.

Ricky (Coloured man, 66, small business owner) used the story of refusing to obey the hand-painted sign denying him access to a Whites-only toilet at work as his example of resistance, while Leo (White man, 46, non-profit organisation director), labelled himself both an architect of resistance and an implementer of resistance. For him, resistance was about then and now. With regard to then – the years of Apartheid – he regards his conscientious objector status as a modest form of implementing resistance against the government's policies of conscription. Now, in his role as the director of a non-profit organisation with a firm focus on strategising to redress past injustices, he considers himself an architect of resistance. He commented: 'architect of resistance to injustice … I'd love for that to be more and more true for me'.

Like Leo, a number of people, spoke of being current resisters – too young (or too oblivious) to resist the injustice of Apartheid in the '80s, they see themselves as playing a role in redress and in ensuring that injustices are ended. So Sizwe speaks about being 'a victim who fights back' and adds the label 'a conscientiser about injustices' to his list, while Jane speaks of resisting contemporary gender injustices. Mayaya describes how in her current job she resists 'in my small way' through ensuring equal pay for men and women, Black and White.

Peter, a White 38-year-old business owner, continued Mayaya's theme of doing small things in your sphere of influence to resist injustice and explained why he circled the 'implementer of resistance' label:

> **Peter:** Any time that you go and vote, you are implementing a form of resistance to injustice … The way that I go about my business. I run it really well. I don't do anything that's corrupt or unjust. I pay my taxes. I feel like I'm setting a good example … showing that I'm resisting some of the current injustices.
>
> ***
>
> You could say that those things are not big things and it's not like I'm going out on the weekends and involved in active programmes, but I genuinely believe that if all South Africans made an effort to

be just in their little sphere ... collectively it would have a great, positive impact.

Analysing difference by race, class and generation

As I analysed *who* chose which labels, I was very interested to see if there were any trends or patterns regarding the proportion of label-type each group chose – by race, age and by class. Since this was designed as an interactive activity to encourage dialogue, I do not have the rigorous quantitative data I need to do a thorough analysis. However, is it possible to draw any conclusions from the fact that 60 people selected 202 labels to describe how they located themselves as actors in relation to South Africa's past? Some of these conclusions are simple, others more complex.

There were both expected and unexpected differences by race. Not surprisingly, Black participants chose more victim labels than any other label category. A little more surprising is that the second highest number of labels they chose was that of beneficiary; both as being a beneficiary of resistance to injustice and a beneficiary of redress. Again not surprisingly, but quite gratifyingly, White participants chose more beneficiary labels than any other labels. However, that quite so many would also call themselves victims (in the expanded definition) is somewhat unexpected. By choosing the dishonoured label, White people are reflecting their recognition of how Apartheid damaged their humanity. Coloured participants predominantly chose an equal proportion of bystander and resister labels.

In connection with generational differences, while there were no clear patterns as was the case with race, there were some interesting findings. Those over the age of 50 saw themselves least as victims or resisters, mostly as beneficiaries and bystanders – and none saw themselves as perpetrators. Those between 36 and 50 saw themselves mainly as resisters. Young participants saw themselves mostly as both victims and beneficiaries.

For the sake of analysis, I divided participants into categories: middle class if they were employed in a professional job or were students and likely to get professional jobs; working class if their jobs were un- or semi-skilled; and those who were unemployed. Middle-class respondents were most likely to see themselves as beneficiaries; working class as bystanders; and those who are unemployed as victims. However, Coloured middle-class participants were more likely to choose victim labels than Coloured working class participants. Black working-class participants were twice more likely to call themselves victims than Black middle-class participants. The explanation for this is likely to be the positive impact of affirmative action on Black professionals that is not being felt as extensively by Coloured professionals. The benefit of social grants is likely most appreciated by the unemployed, while Black working-class participants are likely to be experiencing what has become known as 'the working poor' phenomenon[14] characterised by labour unrest, poor working conditions, and low wages (frequently arising from outsourcing and labour brokering). Testing these tentative observations in a nationally representative sample would be extremely interesting.

What does choosing labels achieve?

The choosing labels activity elicited great discussion during the interview and beyond. Besides the data it generated, how useful might such a labelling activity be in everyday conversations about restitution, and in educational efforts aimed at bringing about everyday restitution?

More recognition, less opting out

People were able to locate themselves more easily than if the activity was limited to only three or even five categories. Offering people the opportunity to add their own labels increased this participation even further – although only half did so. Only one participant (Andiswa, Black woman, 25, call centre) said no labels applied to her. She argued that labels forced you to remain focused on the past and did not help you to move on:

> **Andiswa:** I'm not saying I've forgotten. I haven't forgotten, but fighting and opening old wounds the whole time is not going to help anybody. It's not getting anybody anywhere. There are new things which are happening now which we need to focus on.

---

14 See Hein Marais (2011) *South Africa pushed to the limit*. Cape Town, South Africa: UCT Press.

Sipho (the veteran, now gardener), who had called himself both a resister and a victim and whose story I recounted in Chapter 3, had the opposite view – talking about the past was helpful and necessary:

> **Sipho:** It's very difficult to talk about the Apartheid era because it brings so much pain … I hear people talk about the struggle and you can tell from the way they speak about it that they know nothing about it, the pain we went through … It was difficult having to admit what happened to me; it still brings me sadness and sorrow when I think about it … I don't mind [talking] even though you have opened old wounds that haven't properly healed.

In the main, if I had limited labels to Hilberg's triangle, only half of the participants would have been able to locate themselves in the conversation about injustice, and subsequently have the kind of meaningful discussion that ensued.

Complicated labels result in nuanced discussion

The second outcome of the labels activity was that it resulted in nuanced conversation – partly because the labels themselves were complicated. When I asked the people whom I interviewed to give me some feedback about what it was like to choose labels – was it easy or difficult, was the language too difficult to understand, a few told me it took a little thinking to get their head around some of the labels. Olivia told me, 'These resistance to injustice ones were difficult too – like I couldn't just read it and go "oh, that's what you mean". I had to spend time thinking about it.' Despite these difficulties – people came to understand – and to see, as we discussed what each label might mean. That participants had to think was precisely the point of the activity. As Candice put it – it is because the terms victim, perpetrator are so 'simplistic' that the conversation usually ends: 'If you're a perpetrator that's all you did. That's all we remember – you're the bad guy. If you're a victim, you're the sad guy. If you're the bystander you just didn't do anything.' A wide array of labels coupled with nuanced positions ensured deeper conversations.

Provoking emotional responses

The activity also provoked emotional responses, perhaps best summed up by Angela: 'Some of them make me uncomfortable, but that is as it should be.' People reacted strongly to 'victim', as Luxolo did, but also Naledi:

Naledi: I don't want to call myself a victim at all ... though my mother is probably a victim of the past, definitely ... Things that were due to her, positions that were due to her, she could not get purely because she's a Black woman. But for myself I do not like that description at all.

Graham (White man, 29, retail marketer) said, 'I disliked the labels which accuse me of creating the injustice and unfairly benefiting from the situation, as the prior history of the country was out of my control' – referring to the perpetrator labels. Another White respondent, 23-year-old Thomas, took issue with the conventional victim, perpetrator, and bystander labels and felt that his generation was too far removed from Apartheid to be able to relate to them. He felt that the label architect of injustice should only and 'quite strongly be reserved for the people who actively put the whole system of Apartheid together'.

Some people found it easy to choose labels, others quite difficult. Noah reflected that while the act of choosing labels was 'fairly easy ... but not so easy acknowledging them'. Echoing this, Vukani asserted, 'I think it was fairly easy if you're honest about what you went through.'

Coming to see – gaining new insight

The most gratifying part of the exercise was watching people come to see, and gain new insights from the activity. Sindiswa, who had initially said she did not have an 'opinion on ... the political situation in this country' later noted the intergenerational transmission of injustice: 'You don't have to have been living in that particular time to suffer the consequences of what was going on.' This idea was expanded on by Olivia (Coloured woman, 41, non-profit) who in Chapter 4, is reported to have spoken of 'inheriting victimhood' and how the effects of dishonour are intergenerational: 'My father was dishonoured and as a result I inherited or have lived under that dishonour ... my siblings and I are still having to carry him financially.'

Speaking of the label 'inheritor of dishonour', Portia (Black woman, 26, financial services) said, 'It's really unfair and it just shows the impact that our past has on all the generations.' Patrice (Black man, 60, teacher) said the label architect of injustice reminded him of the intentionality of Apartheid injustices: 'Once a person is designing things for injustice it means that person is not fair ... he hates other people.'

Rose (White woman, 36, part-time lecturer) speaking of the label dishonoured by injustice reflected on how meaningful it was to consider yourself a victim – dishonoured by the unearned privilege her skin colour has given her:

> **Rose:** I'd love to stand up and be proud and say 'Look what I've achieved [in my career]'. But I can't do that because of ill-gotten gains – you know. I understand … it came to me on the back of poor Black people having to suffer and sacrifice.

She was joined by Angela who commented eloquently on the same label:

> **Angela:** Dishonoured by injustice – this is more complex, but I think in a system which is based on dehumanising the other, the person doing the dehumanising is also dehumanised. Not to the same extent, not with the same effect, but there is a cost, a shutting off of possibility, of self.

Categories are fluid, no longer racialised

The most important part of the activity, besides the conversation it generated, both during the interview and subsequently, was the way in which the participants continued to mull over various categories and reflect on how multiple labels applied, or did not apply. How they changed their minds, or added new locations. For many, the victim category was de-stigmatised due to new language – speaking of dishonour. White people were able to speak of victimhood as dishonour – since victim was uncomfortable and felt 'awkward' since they had gained materially but had been robbed of dignity through unearned privilege. The damaged label was controversial but provocative – resulting in deeper conversations. The perpetrator category was clearly unpopular but also provoked deep conversations about why this is the case – even with the roles of architect and implementer distinguished.

A new discussion about benefit was also possible – as a beneficiary of injustice (with its unearned privilege, unfounded sense of superiority and material wealth) but also the benefits of resistance and redress. Mayaya, the 34-year-old Black woman business executive related how she had benefited from affirmative action policies and talked eloquently and more broadly about being a beneficiary of resistance to injustice:

> **Mayaya:** I've had the benefit of access to positions that I know my father would never have had access to. So I've inherited what they fought for without really being involved because I was never there, I was a child.

Clearly, this category (along with others – 'dishonoured' mainly) also serves to de-racialise labels. No longer are beneficiaries only White. Nor are resisters only Black. In addition, opportunities for current day resisters come to the fore, as Sizwe, Jane, Mayaya and Peter all described earlier.

Finally, the category of bystander – one which many chose – took on new meaning. It is no longer so morally neutral. Doing nothing is unbelievable! Since so many chose ostrich – Black, White and Coloured – it became a focal topic of conversation. The humour it evoked helped people choose it freely (unlike the 'blood on your hands' word – perpetrator), and talk easily about it while also reflecting deeply on the somewhat awkward implications of doing nothing, or being an avoider. This was no more evident than in Donovan's case.

Debate, reflection and the possibility of shifting positions

Donovan, with whom this chapter began, is a 30-year-old Coloured man, who manages a cycling shop and is himself a competitive cyclist. When asked to choose labels that reflect how he is located in relation to the past he chose only two, that of bystander and ostrich. Donovan made it clear, as reported earlier, that being an ostrich was an intentional choice since 'racism won't be abolished in our lifetime' and that 'there are enough people trying to do something about it. I'll rather just live my life'. When I interviewed Donovan he was engaged to be married to a White woman he had met at school in 1997 when they were both 13 years old, in the early years of South Africa's new democracy. After telling me he was an intentional ostrich and a bystander, I pushed him a little further. I asked him how he was going to help his children deal with racism in the future, to which he replied:

> **Donovan:** I guess then we try and teach them to cope. Try and teach them to not let it affect them. I can't ever remember being taught by my parents how to handle [racism] … It was just something that you learned to deal with as you grow up, because when you're young you don't actually notice it. It's only as you get older that you start to see that you are different from someone else.

Donovan's comment about seeing 'that you are different' provoked further conversation. Eventually he said:

> **Donovan:** [The past] affects your mind-set to some degree – your confidence, to some degree. Because if you meet someone of a different colour – and I'm referring to the lighter colour – you automatically think they're looking down on you ... So that messes with your head a little bit. Especially when I started working ... a lot of the customers are White, more well-off people. So I get a lot of that [racism] ... the way someone will talk to me ... I'm the only Coloured rider that rides downhill ... A lot of the guys that race are Afrikaans ... So I'll see a bit of cockiness, maybe, from them looking at me. But to me I've got to prove it in my riding. That's all I've got to do.

The insight that Donovan came to after choosing labels and then talking about them was how he was also a victim, someone who was harmed and dishonoured by the injustices of racism. Experiencing racism at school, at work from customers but 'not my boss', and from the Afrikaans guys he cycles with, 'from them looking at me'. He says he copes with it by being a really good cyclist proving his worth 'in my riding'. He also told me how Rebecca's parents were against their dating because he is Coloured, and how they used to 'burst in' when he and Rebecca were at school dances or at the mall watching a movie. But Donovan also speaks of the benefit he has inherited due to those who resisted the injustice of the past:

> **Donovan:** I've been able to vote in the last three elections ... I went to primary school in [a Coloured area] ... then I went to [a former White high school] with Rebecca.

The biggest benefit Donovan and Rebecca acknowledge is how they would not have been able to date and get married, and that their kids won't have to go through what they went through if they want to marry someone of another colour. 'Our kids will have more opportunity than us or than my parents', he told me, and Rebecca added:

> **Rebecca:** Racism actually is carried on and passed on from parents to children. They get taught that it's bad, it's wrong. So we'll teach our kids: 'If you want to date a Black person, or a Chinese person, or a green alien that comes from Mars, you're most welcome to'. Our kids will treat everyone equally.

In the course of our interview, Donovan moved from being an ostrich and a bystander to being a victim and a beneficiary. He accumulated labels as we talked. Clearly, he had not had many conversations like this. He concluded by saying: 'You chose a very difficult subject that I had to talk about'. But he was smiling by then, not frowning, as he was when he arrived for the interview, having forgotten how Google defined 'restitution'.

We are all involved – then and now

This chapter has shown how important it is to move beyond conventional thinking around labels. In particular, it has moved beyond Hilberg's triangle of victim, bystander and perpetrator by adding new descriptions to these terms that offer more nuanced understandings of each. It also added two new categories – to make a pentangle of locations – that of resister and beneficiary – and made new distinctions regarding the nature of the benefit and the magnitude of the role in resisting (see Figure 7.1). By allowing participants to add their own labels, the conversation was opened up even further.

The main aim of this activity was to deepen discussion, and this the activity facilitated. It also allowed more people to relate to the past, and locate themselves in the past. Its basic argument was that in order to address the past, in meaningful ways, one needs to intentionally locate oneself in relationship to it.

Figure 7.1 *Pentangle of actors in injustice*

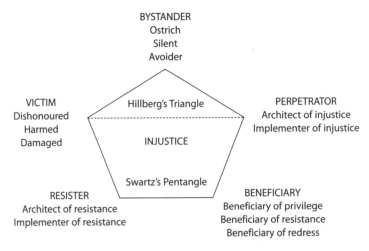

This chapter has also shown that a more nuanced conversation about *benefit* is overdue; that current resistance is worth pursing, since so much still needs to be addressed; and that many more people identify with the label of 'dishonour' rather than 'victim'. Many respondents also showed how an initial choice might become more nuanced and complicated when followed by discussion, and that simple binaries tend to polarise debates or prevent these conversations. Instead, the choosing labels activity has the potential to diffuse simple accusations of guilt and blame along strictly racial lines. Such an approach can be aligned with Iris Marion Young's view that 'disagreements over the question of guilt, one-sided accusations ... further hardens the conflict lines'.[15] In the context of a country such as South Africa, which is still deeply divided along racial lines corresponding to the legacy of Apartheid, this more social understanding of responsibility invites everyone to the conversation as part of making things good again. It also invokes Alistair McIntyre's notion of 'continuums of community'[16] that invite us to take responsibility for the dehumanising actions of others, along with the moral obligation to contribute to their rehumanising.

---

[15] Buckley-Zistel (2009), p. 9.
[16] Alasdair MacIntyre (1981) *After virtue: A study in moral theory.* London, UK: Duckworth.

8 Restoring our humanity

Joining the conversation about how we fit into South Africa's past is the first step to being fully human in South Africa. Our country is filled with stories of violent crime, deep-seated racism and callousness to which many of us have become immune. Taking a panga to a neighbour from somewhere else in Africa, a farmer dragging a worker behind a car, a man hiring someone to shoot his wife, a nine-year-old being abducted, raped and then set alight, shooting a policeman who stops to help a car stranded on the side of the road, abandoning a new-born in a gutter, and punching an elderly person in an old age home. These are the stories, and many others beside, that have made headlines in the past year or so. They do not reflect well on the state of our humanity.

Neither do the stories already recounted by the Black participants in this study about what it is like to be Black in South Africa. At their core, theirs were stories of being humiliated, belittled and dishonoured by Apartheid's injustices – both then and now. Mayaya's father belittled by a young White policeman 'no older than a boy', struggling to get her children enrolled in a private school, and being taken for the administrator rather than the director she is at business meetings. Vukani, a finance executive, being refused service at a bar and being held up outside his own home by the armed response services because he is an anomaly – a Black man living in a White suburb. Welile being called 'a kaffir' by a White Afrikaans-speaking man for not being able to locate goat's milk in an upscale supermarket where he worked, and concluding that 'you still know if you're Black you're Black'. Zethu's son being called a baboon at school and having to resort to physical violence to end this ridicule, and Haley speaking of Black people defaulting to inferiority, White people to superiority.

Then there are also Sibu's accounts of being thought of as a thief, burglar or hijacker just because he is Black, and noting how Black people feel they have constantly to prove themselves through what they buy and wear, 'to show you are good enough'. Sizwe, reflecting on 'how my mom reveres White people' which made him fear White people when he was a child, and then growing up to be incredibly angry at them, including at university: 'the way [White] lecturers speak to you and look at you, they think you are stupid because you don't look and speak like them'. Fundiswa, a contract cleaner, speaking of her constant struggles with unfair treatment and racism at work, and explaining how she feels seeing her unemployed father 'pushing a trolley and … collecting dirty stuff'. Luxolo revealing how being chronically unemployed has eroded her confidence, her sense of 'being someone', and how Apartheid has made Black people 'feel smaller than other people'. These experiences are surely evidence of how effective Apartheid was in eroding our humanity, in creating the conditions in which people could be dishonoured and belittled by other human beings.

I also related stories from White South Africans about how Apartheid had left them feeling ashamed and guilty on the one hand, and arrogant and superior on the other. Rose's shame at being assumed to be complicit when someone starts telling racist jokes, and at always being deferred to by older Black people (and younger ones too) as 'the White madam' even though she is only in her mid-thirties. Thomas's guilt at being jarred by the sight of White beggars and White homeless people, having come to see Black begging and Black homelessness as 'normal'. David, Angela and Heather's shame at always being deemed as 'valued', 'on top of the pile' and 'the masters'. Noah's guilt 'for being White' and the fear that 'people resent me because of the colour of my skin and my wealth', and Sandy's shame at 'White people for what they allowed'. And of course, the realisation that what we have so much of is not because we were so good, or so skilled, but because an entire system conspired on our behalf to give us 'the best jobs … loans … houses … nice cars. And we weren't even clever' as Harry put it, succinctly defining unearned, undeserved privilege.

Once we are immersed in a conversation about the past, about where we stood then and where we stand now, it becomes easy to see how we have all been dishonoured by Apartheid. The core of the matter is the way in which our humanity has been eroded. The next step, if we are intentionally to pursue a project of restitution, is to understand what it means to be human, and what acts and attitudes can contribute to restoring our humanity.

Losing our humanity

When I asked participants directly whether we were losing our humanity, many agreed. Sizwe (Black man, 23, student) said, 'We've lost our humanity on different levels ... we need counselling as a country'. Harry (White man, 63, retired business executive) described the overall effects of Apartheid:

> **Harry:** One must be very aware of what Apartheid meant. The laws, rules, passbooks, where you can sit, and what bus you can catch ... If you think what Apartheid actually did to families. So you talk about humanity – we had miners ... who were separated from their wives and children for months and years ... I still don't believe we've recovered from all of that.

Many described what losing our humanity means: paying people 'slave wages' (Ricky, Coloured man, 66, small business owner), people being corrupt and being 'just for themselves' (Welile, Black man, 24, sales rep), and believing 'that certain races are inferior to others' (Jane, White woman, 21, student). According to Fundiswa (Black woman, 26, contract cleaner) and Sibu (Black woman, 27, auxiliary social worker), further examples are ongoing violence, even amongst children, and refusing to help people in need:

> **Fundiswa:** Maybe you see someone outside asking you for help. You don't even care what situation brought them there. You will just look at them and then you will walk away. You don't even try to help them or something. So there's no humanity at all.

> **Sibu:** I was watching a documentary about a gang in Khayelitsha of ten-year-olds who were stabbing and killing each other ... They have lost their humanity because a normal human being will never –.

Leo, a 46-year-old White man working as the director of a non-profit organisation, recognises the current levels of violence, crime, aggression and rape in South Africa as an expression of our wounded humanity and links it to Apartheid:

> **Leo:** Our humanity has been collectively and individually broken. Apartheid didn't simply make some people poorer: it challenged their very identity for generations and that will have consequences. This damage exists in all sectors of South African society, not simply those who were oppressed during Apartheid.

Understanding, explaining and recognising this damage or woundedness is a critical first step.

Chris, the 34-year-old White chef, whose views were frequently conservative, rather eloquently described how Apartheid may not have 'destroyed our humanity, but it was like losing a limb ... there are permanent scars or damage'.

If not a complete loss of our humanity, these accounts all point towards deep damage to it. How then do we restore this humanity? In the next chapter, I report on the very many practical suggestions that participants came up with for making good where we can't make things right. I want to relate just one story of re-humanising among many others told to me by Johan, the 48-year-old non-profit organisation director. The story concerned a White lawyer who experienced a humanising event at the hands of some Black South Africans. Let's call the man, Fred. Fred was a lawyer in the Apartheid army, and then settled in a rural town 100 km outside of Cape Town. He became well known as someone who would legally 'represent right wing people'. One day, shortly after democracy, he was travelling with his family when his car broke down, in the middle of nowhere. When he opened the boot of the car to change the tyre he discovered the spare wheel was also flat. He realised: 'Okay, I'm in a big predicament. I'm on this very desolate road and I'm in trouble.' He got out of his car and waited. A White person stopped and asked if they could help him, but since he had no spare tyre he said he would wait with his car, but would be grateful if they could drive his family to the nearest town so they could arrange help. They did so.

Still he waited. An hour later, a mini-bus taxi 'filled with Black people and a Black driver' arrived and he immediately thought that they might be a threat to him; he clutched a wheel spanner behind his back, expecting the worst if the taxi stopped. It did, and the driver asked if he needed help. 'No, I am waiting for somebody to come and help me', was Fred's reply. Silently he thought: 'If they're going to give me any problems at least I've got something to defend myself with'. An hour later, the same taxi came back having unloaded his passengers, and again the driver asked: 'Are you sure that somebody's going to come and help you?' and Fred said, 'Yes, I'm sure. You don't need to worry'. But nobody came, and when the taxi, at the end of the day, arrived for the third time and stopped, the driver said: 'Well, we know you don't want to make use of our help, but here's some food. We thought you must be hungry after a whole day of waiting'. Fred said that hit him between the eyes. He became very emotional and started to cry. The taxi driver got out of his vehicle and embraced Fred. This had a huge impact on Fred's life journey. Fred is now involved in local government and is a champion of 'housing projects to promote integration' in a very divided town in which he still lives and works.

Remembering the past is important to restoring our humanity

As important as individual re-humanising stories are, the key to retrieving our humanity is for there to be a groundswell of remembering the extent of the harm done, so that we can continually make amends, and stop ourselves from repeating the acts and attitudes that led us there in the first place. Amnesia about the past serves no one. There is no magic in forgetting in order to move on. Rather, remembering and acting together in a 'social dynamic', as Desmond Tutu reminds us, is what is now needed. Our amnesia keeps in place the view that White South Africans have worked for what they have. It also allows us to fool ourselves into believing that the road to success, especially for young Black and White South Africans, is the same. It allows us to forget that while the course is similar, there are many more obstacles for Black South Africans than White South Africans. These obstacles include the financial capital, social capital, cultural and symbolic capital that many White South Africans take for granted. To forget is to make us blind. To remember enables us to see clearly the obstacles, and work together to make the road navigable for all.

This amnesia is not only limited to White South Africans; some Black South Africans who are too young to remember the past, display similar blind spots, while others choose to forget it. Naledi, a 21-year unemployed Black woman states: 'I think going back to the past is holding us back from moving forward because if we don't move on we will be holding onto unnecessary grudges.' Luxolo sums up well when she says that 'Most of the people ... just want to forget about it, but they can't' – the circumstances of their lives do not allow for forgetting. Acknowledging and resolving the past seems to be a better way forward, as Noah (21, White man, student) and Sibu argued:

> **Noah:** Whites need to acknowledge that they have benefited enormously from Apartheid and that even though there is no longer a systematic advantage for Whites, there is a need for

rebalancing, given the economic and educational advantages they received.

Sibu: There are still scars and wounds that are infected by the bacteria of the past, and still need to be cleaned and bandaged so that we can move on.

Moving on will only be possible once we've resolved the past, and restitution is a key aspect of this resolution. Moving on without making good is 'doing us all a little bit of a disservice, because I don't think we're ready to just move on' (Cara, 21, White student). Welile articulates it well when he says:

Welile: I didn't even know the meaning of the word "restitution". It's not a word that is commonly used. The only thing is reconciliation. Let's forget about the cost. Let's just continue and live as one. But how do you continue to live as one while the White man still owns everything that they owned before? For me I feel like that's just Apartheid continuing, but now it's friendly Apartheid. [laughs]

As reported earlier, Welile described clearly why many suppress the past, despite the pain and anger they feel:

Welile: If it wasn't for White people, Black people would have had a better education, better jobs … People are afraid of raising their voices, people are afraid of talking about their feelings … If you say something now, chances are you're going to hurt someone … So I feel like before we can move on we need to open these platforms for people to say how they feel. Where what you say is not going to be held against you.

Welile is not alone in his sentiments and is joined in his explanation by two Black men, Sipho, the 56-year-old veteran who now works as a gardener, and Thamsanqa, a 32-year-old graduate student:

Sipho: If the country tells us that we need to forgive then you must forgive even though your heart is not in it, because you might be accused of not wanting this democracy … If the majority want to forgive and move on then let it be … If that's what government says should happen then we have no other choice but to do it. Even though I was almost thrown off a cliff by security police, I have to forget and move on. We are a rainbow nation now. If I don't support that, I might be accused of treason. So I need to move on even though I still carry the pain.

Thamsanqa: Most importantly, I feel we're refusing to be honest about the past. To acknowledge what really, really happened. We're too quick to claim change. We're only 1% of the way to undoing the injustices of the past and a lot of people are saying: "Let's move on". And when you articulate those ideas, that we're still unequal and still feel oppressed as a Black person, its taboo.

The problem with forgetting or suppressing is that no healing can occur. It becomes impossible to move on, impossible to compete on equal terms, impossible to have the life we all want.

Forgiveness

South Africa is an incredibly religious country; the most recent survey puts the figure at 85%[1] and so it is not surprising that the concept of forgiveness is centre stage when it comes to dealing with the past. My respondents were no different. Many spoke of both forgiving, and forgiving and forgetting, although they acknowledged that the latter was difficult – and for some unnecessary:

Siphosethu (29, Black man, retail floor coordinator): As South Africans we should forgive and forget. Yes, what happened was terrible but we can't do anything about it. We should carry on with our lives.

Michael (78, White man, retired architect): I agree that it is easy to forgive but impossible to forget, especially if one has been on the receiving end of prejudice and racism.

For 67-year-old Ted, and 46-year-old Leo, both White men and non-profit organisation directors, seeking forgiveness is the key to restitution. According to Ted, asking for forgiveness achieves two things – it speaks for your community thereby showing group repentance, and it acknowledges that the impact of the past remains:

---

[1]   80% are Christian, 5% adhere to Islam, Hinduism or African Traditional Religion and 15% have either no religion or their religion is undetermined according to the 2001 Statistics South Africa Census, the last time religion was included.

Ted: [Restitution] is aided by asking for forgiveness, by acknowledging that the impact of the past is still with us … Admission of wrong seems to me to require a request for forgiveness … People speak about it as something that has been life-changing for them – that some White person has asked for forgiveness, and they say to me that heals me in my relationship with other White people … So in a sense I'm speaking for my community.

Leo talked about a deeper level of 'saying sorry', one accompanied by actions of repentance:

Leo: Talking about forgiveness puts the onus on the victim to move without necessarily requiring anything of the perpetrator. There is a deeper need for White people to learn how to say sorry, to repent in meaningful and appropriate ways.

Johan (White man, 48, non-profit organisation) calls this 'doing sorry' rather than merely 'saying sorry'.

Forty-eight-year-old Nontembiso, who is a domestic worker, sums up most eloquently the dilemma faced by Black South Africans when it comes to forgiving, forgetting, moving on and resolving the past:

Nontembiso: Yes, the past did happen – where we lost our lands and resources, but we were told to forgive and we did. However, we still had concerns about the things we lost and how we were going to get them back … We have forgiven but we don't know how to move forward: whether to forget everything and move on with our lives, or before we move on let's have a talk on how we will be compensated for things our grandfathers lost due to the system at the time. We have forgiven but we didn't forget.

Thirty-four-year-old Nobuntu, a Black woman business executive, adds, 'As time passes, even beneficiaries forget their privilege', which is why remembering has such a critical role to play in making good in South Africa. I hope these comments from participants show that amnesia, far from helping us, keeps us from experiencing a new dynamic in South Africa. By forgetting, we only experience a fragile peace, rather than an enduring one.

Lessons from the Truth and Reconciliation Commission

The TRC was one of the chief mechanisms that addressed our amnesia and our damaged humanity. During the human rights violations (HRV) hearings, it forced us to confront stories of how those who resisted Apartheid (including children and young people)[2] were hunted, jailed, tortured and killed by the security police and army. The TRC went to extraordinary lengths to find out details of where loved ones were buried, and attempted to return their remains, so that families could bury their loved ones with dignity and honour. Reports are filled with stories of the way in which HRV hearings helped victims and perpetrators regain their humanity. Nomvuyo Cynthia Ngewu, whose 25-year-old son Christopher Piet was shot 25 times by security police in the chilling 'Gugulethu Seven' incident, spoke of how she saw the TRC process of reconciliation:

> If I am understanding it correctly … if it means this perpetrator, this man who has killed Christopher Piet, if it means he becomes human again … so that I, so that all of us, get our humanity back … then I agree, then I support it all.[3]

***

> We do not want to return the evil that perpetrators committed to the nation. We want to demonstrate humaneness towards them, so that they in turn may restore their own humanity.[4]

She did, however, ask that her son and others who gave their lives in the struggle be remembered: 'What I would ask is [for] something – a memory that will be held for them, even if it's just a crèche or a building or a school that could be named after – after our children.'[5]

---

2   Pamela Reynolds (2012) *War in Worcester: Youth and the Apartheid state*. Bronx, NY: Fordham University Press.

3   Yasmin Sooka (2000) South Africa's human spirit: An oral memoir of the truth and reconciliation commission – We should not forget.

4   Truth and Reconciliation Commission (1999b) *Truth and Reconciliation Commission of South Africa Report* (Vol. 5). London, UK: Macmillan, p. 366.

5   South African Department of Justice (1996) Truth and Reconciliation Commission Day 2 – 23 April 1996 – Case No: CT/00100 Christopher Piet (son).

During the TRC, Brian Gcina Mkhize, a former Inkatha Freedom Party hit squad commander, also spoke of the need for the many IFP and ANC 'foot soldiers' who committed human rights violations to be given the opportunity to 'become human again':

> The foot soldiers who carried out these activities ... We need counselling because this affects you mentally, psychologically ... Nobody has come forth to suggest how we can get this counselling ... how we can become human again.[6]

Although very few stories emerged of White perpetrators of human rights violations told by perpetrators themselves, one does stand out from the Amnesty hearings. Eugene de Kock,[7] a commander of an Apartheid police hit squad based at Vlakplaas, just outside Pretoria, was notorious for the callous killing of numerous anti-Apartheid activists and then braaing (barbequing) nonchalantly afterwards. De Kock was humanised, not so much by relating stories of political motivation and ideological blindness, as might be expected, but rather in the story about him written by Pumla Gobodo-Madikizela,[8] one of the commissioners. De Kock did not receive amnesty and was sentenced to 212 years imprisonment. In prison, he repented of his actions and his racism and took several other young White right wing extremists[9] under his care and helped them recant their ideologies. He was released on parole in 2015.

---

6 Truth and Reconciliation Commission (1999), p. 366.
7 Anemari Jansen (2015) *Eugene de Kock: Assassin for the state*. Cape Town, South Africa: Tafelberg.
8 See Pumla Gobodo-Madikizela (2003) *A human being died that night: A story of forgiveness* (Claremont, South Africa: David Philip), for a story that relates De Kock's role but also their interaction over the extended period she spent interviewing him.
9 Stefaans Coetzee was one of these right-wingers with whom the Restitution Foundation has subsequently engaged in victim-offender dialogues. He was a perpetrator of the Worcester Christmas bombings that killed four people and gravely injured 67 in a grocery store on 24 December 1996. He was 18 at the time. Pumla Gobodo-Madikizela has subsequently produced a documentary about Coetzee's attempts at seeking forgiveness entitled *Black Christmas* (2016) and the responses he received from the community.

There is currently a spate of books[10] that tell the stories of Apartheid's White foot soldiers, written by those who were conscripts in South Africa's infamous 'Border Wars'. These stories lay bare the heart of darkness and stripped humanity of many young White men, who are now in their fifties and older.

Antjie Krog, in a speech given at a meeting of the Restitution Foundation in 2010, spoke of how victims forgave perpetrators because of the way in which they 'understood themselves to be interconnected to the perpetrators':

> People forgave in the hope that perpetrators would change so that
> their humaneness would be shared, bringing about the healing
> of the victims. This action with the imperative it places on the
> perpetrator was completely misunderstood especially by White
> perpetrators and beneficiaries. Many perpetrators expressed
> surprise by a forgiveness extended without them even asking for it.
> To them it did not mean that they should reach out to the victims
> and try to correct the wrongs they did, for them it meant that they
> could continue their lives as unperturbed as before.

Memorialising

It is clear that remembering and memorialising must play a critical role in post-conflict societies. To remember is to recognise harm done, and the consequences of that harm. It is to admit that some harm is so heinous that it is a crime against all our humanity[11] – treating some human beings as better, or worse, than others. Furthermore, 'the point of memories, then, is less to tell

---

10 Gary Baines (2014) *South Africa's 'Border War': Contested narratives and conflicting memories*. London, UK: Bloomsbury; Gary Baines and Peter Vale (2008) *Beyond the Border War: New perspectives on Southern Africa's late-Cold War conflicts*. Pretoria, South Africa: Unisa Press; Karen Batley (2007) *A secret burden: Memories of the Border War by South African soldiers who fought in it*. Johannesburg, South Africa: Jonathan Ball; Andrew Feinstein (2011) *Battle scarred: Hidden costs of the Border War*. Cape Town, South Africa: Tafelberg; Jannie Geldenhuys (2009) *At the front: A general's account of South Africa's border war*. Jeppestown, South Africa: Jonathan Ball.

11 Truth and Reconciliation Commission (1999a) *Truth and Reconciliation Commission of South Africa Report* (Vol. 1). London, UK: Macmillan, pp. 94–102.

us what 'exactly' happened, than what it felt like to experience an event'.[12] To do restitution, to make good, we must see the past clearly.

All over the world, there are examples of how memories have been written in stone – there are many Holocaust museums and memorials, and street names that were renamed after struggle heroes. In addition to the physical memorials are the symbolic memorials – the dates that remember victory over oppression, and that include national holidays honouring uprisings, as well as memory recovery workshops such as Northern Ireland's Ardoyne oral histories commemoration project, or South Africa's healing of memories workshop run by the Anglican Church, or even laws passed to ensure remembrance, such as the Spanish Law of Historical Memory that aimed to end 'amnesia' about Spain's civil war (see Chapter 6). It has been shown that these memorials and laws have the effect of exposing atrocities, human rights violations and the untruths crafted by injustice, and so make such actions vital for social and political change.[13] They are an important element in restitution.

Memory projects prevent us from forgetting our past – something we are prone to do – illustrated most vividly by those interviewed in this study who either refused to see or had distorted vision about the effects of the past in the present. Visiting the Apartheid Museum in Johannesburg, or the District Six museum, the Slave Lodge or Robben Island in Cape Town, reading the writings of Sol Plaatje, Robert Sobukwe, Steve Biko, Nelson Mandela and recent histories of South Africa are all ways in which we can practice restitution by active remembering. Such 'dangerous memories'[14] are 'disruptive because they call for a solidarity with others on the basis of common human suffering ... [they force us to] remember events of the past that question our

---

12 Michalinos Zembylas and Zvi Bekerman (2008) Education and the dangerous memories of historical trauma: Narratives of pain, narratives of hope. *Curriculum Inquiry* 38(2): 129.

13 Martha Minow (2000) The hope for healing: What can truth commissions do? In Robert I. Rotberg and Dennis Thompson (eds) *Truth v justice: The morality of truth commissions.* Princeton, NJ: Princeton University Press; Claire Moon (2009) Healing past violence: Traumatic assumptions and therapeutic interventions in war and reconciliation, *Journal of Human Rights* 8(1): 71–91; Margaret Walker (2010) Truth telling as reparations, *Metaphilosophy* 41(4): 525–545.

14 Zembylas and Bekerman (2008).

consciences and assumed horizons'; they allow for memories that are at once 'challenging, critical, and hopeful'. This kind of remembering helps restore our connectedness and helps foster our humanity, and pushes us further along the trajectory towards wholeness.

This understanding of connectedness is what we frequently call *ubuntu*[15] in South Africa. In 1985, at his investiture as Archbishop of Cape Town, Desmond Tutu paraphrased its meaning as follows: a person is someone who *recognises* the humanity of others. An African understanding of humanity is one of personhood bestowed by another. It is worth trying to understand this concept of personhood, and how it may be restored.

What is personhood and how has it been damaged by injustice?

Debates around personhood have long existed, especially about contentious social issues such as slavery, cognitive impairment, animal rights, capital punishment, abortion and euthanasia. Definitions abound, and are usually closely related to a particular religious or political stance on one or other of these issues. In the context of injustice, in which the domination of one group over another is a crime against *humanity*,[16] the idea of personhood takes on special importance. What exactly does it mean to be human, to be a person? Can our humanity or personhood be damaged or lost? This calls for a deep understanding of what we mean by personhood.

Personhood can be viewed from various perspectives: psychological, philosophical, anthropological, theological or biological. For the purpose of this study, I draw on the works of US sociologist Christian Smith and African scholars Kwame Gyekye and Francis Nyamnjoh to provide a multi-

---

[15] Ubuntu is the isiXhosa or isiZulu word meaning 'humanity' or 'humanness', although it is often the phrase *umuntu ngumntu ngabantu* translated as 'a person is a person through other people' which better summarises the philosophy. It is the South African (and African) notion of social harmony, being for the other, and respecting our shared humanity. See Thaddeus Metz and Joseph Gaie (2010) The African ethic of Ubuntu/Botho: Implications for research on morality. *Journal of Moral Education* 39(3): 273–290.

[16] Truth and Reconciliation Commission (1999a) *Truth and Reconciliation Commission of South Africa Report* (Vol. 1), p. 94.

disciplinary understanding, before turning to the work on the subject by Frantz Fanon and Nancy Fraser to inform a plan of action.

What is a person?

For Christian Smith, healthy people are formed through healthy relationships. He argues that personhood is 'emergent';[17] whole and integrated people come into existence as they relate, interact and are connected within specific environmental conditions, as well as to systems and structures.[18] People cannot simply be reduced to the sum of their parts; they are formed based on social connectedness. In order for a person to be healthy – this connectedness requires an environment that is conducive to psychosocial, emotional, economic and political connectedness. Seeing a person as *emergent, connected* and in a *conducive environment,*[19] Smith captures the paradox between individual agency, group dependence and environmental influence, and how all operate together to allow us to be fully human.

Where any of these three elements are damaged, one's personhood will be damaged. Smith further argues that qualities such as self-awareness and moral commitment alone are not the central defining features of our humanity; rather these elements need to operate within relationships of social connectedness. Human beings are thus self-aware, group-aware, and morally aware beings that function healthily as others treat us in the same way, thereby allowing our personhood to emerge and to fulfil this potential, as the environment and structures around us permit. Smith's treatise *What Is A Person?* is a recent one, and its focus on being human in community dissolves much of the distinction between African and Western ideas of what it means to be human.

---

[17] Christian Smith (2010) *What is a person?: Rethinking humanity, social life, and the moral good from the person up.* Chicago, IL: University of Chicago Press, p. 38.

[18] Smith (2010), p. 36.

[19] Smith offers the following complex definition of what it means to be a person: 'By person I mean a conscious, reflexive, embodied, self-transcending center of subjective experience, durable identity, moral commitment, and social communication who – as the efficient cause of his or her own responsible actions and interactions – exercises complex capacities for agency and intersubjectivity [social relationships] in order to develop and sustain his or her own incommunicable self in loving relationships with other personal selves and with the nonpersonal world.' Smith (2010), p. 61.

Emergent and connected personhood

Cameroonian anthropologist Francis Nyamnjoh[20] also blurs this individual-group distinction when he argues that individuals must be able to achieve *'self*-fulfilment' within a *'collective* framework'. People must have the means to be fully human in themselves and within the community to which they belong. Ghanaian philosopher Kwame Gyekye speaks of three features of personhood.[21] Like Nyamnjoh and Smith, he stipulates that community *defines* the individual; that personhood is *acquired* (or emergent), not bestowed at birth; and that personhood is something at which an individual could *fail*. For Gyekye, 'African personhood is evidence of the responsibility one has toward others.'[22]

Nyamnjoh and Gyekye demonstrate very clearly the African philosophy of *ubuntu* in their descriptions of personhood, with its emphasis on social connectedness and social harmony.[23] If our personhood depends on these emerging relationships and connectedness, and on people bestowing humanity on each other, it follows that personhood can be lost by ruptured relationships, disconnectedness and failure to treat people as spiritually and morally equal. It makes a healthy humanity an obvious goal of a national project of restitution where such disconnectedness and rupture between individual, group and environment has occurred.

Fanon on re-humanising, dignity, sovereignty and land

Frantz Fanon, the Martinique/French psychiatrist-turned-Algerian-revolutionary, shows clearly how this rupture has occurred through colonisation, racism and other forms of domination. In the wake of the brutal decolonising experiences of the 1950s in Africa, Fanon offers a contemporary and postcolonial understanding of personhood and human dignity as he asks for people to

---

[20] Francis Nyamnjoh (2004) Reconciling 'the rhetoric of rights' with competing notions of personhood and agency in Botswana. In H Englund and F Nyamnjoh (eds) *Rights and the politics of recognition in Africa*. London, UK: Zed Books, p. 38.

[21] Kwame Gyekye (1997) *Tradition and modernity: philosophical reflections on the African experience*. Oxford, UK: Oxford University Press.

[22] Kwame Gyekye (1984) The Akan Concept of a Person. In R Wright (ed.) *African Philosophy: An Introduction*. Lanham, MD: University Press of America, p. 199.

[23] Metz and Gaie (2010).

'reconsider the question of ... all humanity, whose connections must be increased ... whose messages must be re-humanised'.[24] Fanon stated his mission as helping 'human beings to co-create systems of human encounters that are non-oppressive, reciprocally beneficial, and mutually nurturing of human development'[25] in the midst of colonialism. For Fanon, colonisation resulted in 'a systematic negation of the other person and a furious determination to deny the other person all attributes of humanity'.[26] This stripping of human dignity removes the right to 'self-willed and self-chosen, co-created modes of living and being'.[27]. Domination is therefore contrary to an understanding of human dignity since it is predicated on spiritual and moral *inequality*. This inequality is in turn held in place by what has come to be called 'structural violence'; not merely physical violence or oppression, but the indirect ways in which institutions and systems are designed to operate so that they 'without the use of overt force, compel people to live in conditions of abjection, helplessness and wretchedness'.[28]

Ultimately, domination results in excluding some and including others. Winston Langley[29] superbly summarises Fanon on this matter:

> [This] construction of the 'other' ... makes him or her an instrument of another's will, belittles and demeans him or her being, causes him or her to betray friends, to betray oneself, to doubt one's worth ... This, to Fanon, is *violence against personhood, against one's identity as a human being, against human dignity* ... Domination and oppressive power ... denies a basic human need ... to experience reciprocal recognition, to have others affirm our being as humans.

Fanon's call is for those who are dominated to regain their personhood, not by emulating their captors, 'catching up' or aspiring to their systems and ways of life, but in maintaining their 'rhythms' and 'collective' ways of life. He speaks of living in community rather than in a stretched-out caravan, 'hardly see[ing]

---

[24] Frantz Fanon (1963) *The wretched of the earth.* New York, NY: Grove Press, p. 314.

[25] Winston Langley (2007) Fanon: Violence and the search for human dignity. *Human Architecture: Journal of the Sociology of Self-Knowledge* 5(3): 2.

[26] Fanon (1963), p. 250.

[27] Langley (2007), p. 2.

[28] Langley (2007), p. 3.

[29] Langley (2007), pp. 2–3.

those who precede it; and men who no longer recognize each other ... and talk to each other less and less'. Living in such a way, Fanon argues, will result in the 'tearing apart of his functions and the crumbling away of his unity ... differentiations, the stratification, and the bloodthirsty tensions ... on the immense scale of humanity ... racial hatreds, slavery, exploitation, and above all the bloodless genocide'.[30] By bloodless genocide, Fanon again refers to the way people internalise external oppressions, believing what oppressors say about them, and thus also losing their humanity.[31]

Fanon offers further insight into how personhood may be restored. One of the means he advocates is through the restoration of dignity, the other through insisting on equality or sovereignty – in fact for Fanon 'dignity and sovereignty were exact equivalents'.[32] Fanon believed the only means to achieve this in 1950s Africa was through violent revolution. Independence (by whatever means) for him was 'moral compensation to colonized peoples, and ... established their dignity.'[33]

He further explains that not only will revolution bring about equality and dignity but it will result in the 'redistribution of wealth', a question to which 'humanity must reply ... or be shaken to pieces by it.'[34] Fanon is clear about the relationship between equality, dignity and wealth. He asserts that dignity takes priority over physical means – whether bread or land, although the three are integrally related:

> For a colonized people the most essential value ... [is] land: the land which will bring them bread and, above all, dignity ... The well-known principle that all men are equal will be illustrated in the colonies from the moment that the native claims that he is the equal of the settler.[35]

***

---

[30] Fanon (1963), pp. 314–5.
[31] This is another version of symbolic violence, although Fanon never used the term in his writings.
[32] Fanon (1963), p. 198.
[33] Fanon (1963), p. 81.
[34] Fanon (1963), p. 98.
[35] Fanon (1963), p. 44.

Hunger with dignity is preferable to bread eaten in slavery …
Colonialism is incapable of procuring for the colonized peoples the
material conditions which might make them forget their concern
for dignity.[36]

Finally, for Fanon restoring the personhood of the colonised was about
reclaiming their history, related both to memory and belonging, or the full
citizenship of equals:

> The native intellectual … discovered that there was nothing to be
> ashamed of in the past, but rather dignity, glory, and solemnity. The
> claim to a national culture in the past … rehabilitate[s] that nation
> and serve[s] as a justification for the hope of a future national culture
> … [In contrast] colonialism is not simply content to impose its
> rule upon the present and the future … is not satisfied merely with
> holding a people in its grip and emptying the native's brain of all
> form and content. By a kind of perverted logic, it turns to the past of
> the oppressed people, and distorts, disfigures, and destroys it.[37]

Fraser on recognition, representation and redistribution

This memory of what was lost is also a key feature of Nancy Fraser's[38]
understanding of justice after atrocities. Fraser describes the elements of
recognition, redistribution and representation in her schema. For justice to be
effected there must be recognition, both of the past and also of the dignity of
the individual. There must be redistribution of wealth and of status. The third
element in her three-part definition of personhood concerns representation.
Representation concerns not only the ways in which people are represented,
i.e., fairly, respectfully and sufficiently (for example, in the media), no matter
their race, religion, culture or sexual orientation, but also that they are offered
democratic voice and freedom to organise in order to realise desirable group
outcomes and rights (for example, the right for homosexual couples to legally
marry, and for women to receive equal pay in the workplace).

---

36 Fanon (1963), p. 208.
37 Fanon (1963), p. 210.
38 Nancy Fraser and Axel Honneth (2003) *Redistribution or recognition? A political-
   philosophical exchange*. London, UK: Verso.

Elements of the restitution of personhood

In Chapter 6, I looked at the various ways in which restitution has been defined and redefined. In the law, restitution concerns itself with restoring to its original condition, compensating or making reparations, satisfying the injured party, and stripping the perpetrator of unjust benefit. Sometimes it makes allowances for rehabilitating the offender, as in the case of restorative justice programmes. I showed that the law and scholars in general, have long seen restitution as encompassing other aspects of restoration beyond legal, land or other economic remedies, and embraced regret, apologies, acts of remembrance and other symbolic acts, alongside restoring civil, political and property rights. What is clear is that restoring things to their original state is seldom possible and that instead our aim should be to make good what was damaged by injustice – since what was lost cannot be remedied through financial compensation alone. To do so involves paying attention to the emotional, psychological, philosophical, theological and symbolic elements along with physical and economic elements. Furthermore, dialogue and interaction are needed if all concerned are to understand these other aspects of restitution. This approach also offers a more relational interaction between those dishonoured by injustice and those complicit in it. It is also a forward-looking idea of restitution, and speaks about a voluntary moral obligation rather than a legal penalty. John Braithwaite's view of the multiple 'dimensions of restoration' captures this wider definition of restitution excellently:

> Restoring property loss, restoring injury, restoring a sense of
> security, restoring dignity, restoring a sense of empowerment,
> restoring deliberative democracy, restoring harmony based on a
> feeling that justice has been done, and restoring social support. [39]

Grouping these facets under three headings – dignity, belonging and opportunity – is not the only way a response may be categorised, but it does follow Frantz Fanon's and Nancy Fraser's understanding of how justice is achieved. Together these three elements form what I have called the restitution of personhood. Relating dignity, belonging and opportunity to our sense of humanity and selfhood in community demonstrates the many

---

[39] John Braithwaite (1999) Restorative justice: Assessing optimistic and pessimistic accounts. *Crime and justice* 25: 1–127.

possibilities available to individuals, civil society and communities, and institutions to concretely and strategically contribute to the restitution project of making good – by delineating domains in which action can be taken. Figure 8.1 summarises these elements, which will be considered in turn, along with responses by study participants to each element and examples from the literature of actions taken in each domain and by each kind of actor – individual, community or institutional.

Figure 8.1 *Elements of the restitution of personhood*

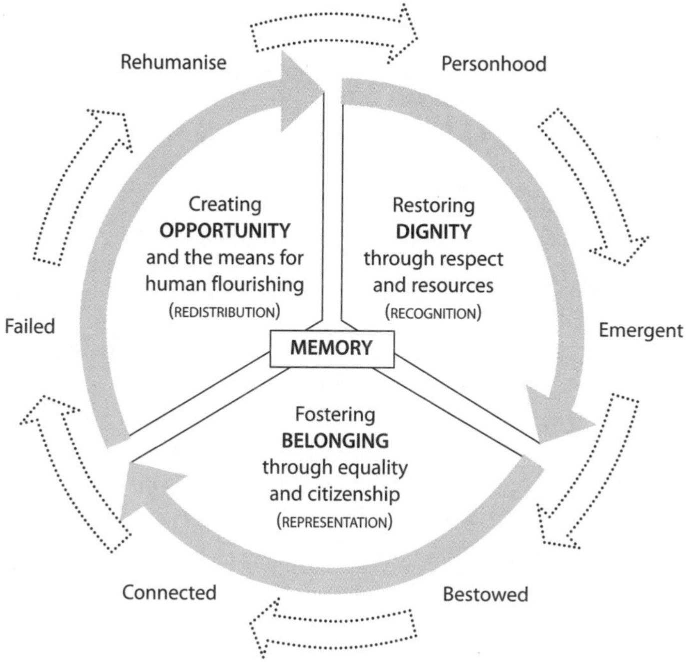

Source: Author

Restoring dignity

Given the context of having been drafted at the end of a dehumanising global conflict, it is not surprising that the first sentences of both the preamble to, and the first article of, the Universal Declaration of Human Rights[40] concern the dignity to which human beings are entitled:

> All human beings are born free and equal in dignity and rights.

***

> The inherent dignity and the equal and inalienable rights of all members of the human family is the foundation of freedom, justice and peace in the world.

The remainder of the declaration speaks to all the possible ways in which this dignity can be assaulted. Without exception, injustice, conflict and domination deny people each of the rights found in the declaration, whether rights to health, education, life, shelter, enjoyment of culture, love and marriage, ownership and work. In the case of South Africa, racism as a form of domination causes multiple effects, from mental health problems[41] to impoverishment, intentional under-education, and 'learned helplessness'.[42] To strip someone of their dignity is to deny them their basic right of humanity and equality.

In contemporary society, structural efforts to restore dignity include the constitutional rights of dignity and equality being enshrined in law. In the 1960s, social and civic groups embarked on mass campaigns and social movements to help those who were on the receiving end of oppression to counter these physical and psychological effects and address loss of dignity. Amongst these were the Black Consciousness movement in South Africa, the Black Theology and Liberation Theology movements in Latin America, and the Civil Rights movement in the USA. But what about at the individual level?

Multiple accounts of the loss of dignity experienced by individuals such as Sizwe, Welile, Luxolo, Fundiswa, Ricky, Mayaya and Vukani were related in

---

40 United Nations (1948) *Universal Declaration of Human Rights*. New York, NY: United Nations.

41 Dawn Szymanski and Destin Stewart (2010) Racism and sexism as correlates of African American women's psychological distress. *Sex Role* 63(3): 226–238.

42 Martin Pierre, James Mahalik, and Malcolm Woodland (2002) The effects of racism, African self-consciousness and psychological functioning on black masculinity: A historical and social adaptation framework. *Journal of African American Men* 6(2): 33.

Chapters 3 and 4. For some, these experiences of indignity were experienced during the years of Apartheid rule in South Africa, but for many others these experiences remain an everyday and continuing occurrence. Without being prompted to speak of dignity, many of those I interviewed spoke about it readily and frequently; sometimes in relation to the effect of the past on the present, sometimes in relation to what is needed to make good for past injustice. People spoke about how restoring dignity would include new ways of treating those who were previously treated as inferior; offering sincere apologies and asking for forgiveness; and getting to know people and building new relationships across lines of previous racial divisions.

Ted speaks of 'how hard it is to find one another' across racial lines in the first place, but if this can be done, then any acts of restitution need to be done in relationship:

> **Ted:** If I can only get to know you as a person … have a sense that in a dignified way I can do something to help you and that it can be done in a way that does not undermine your dignity but actually, if anything, enhances your dignity.

Twenty-six-year-old Max (Black man, finance administrator) spoke of how we confer dignity on people based on their wealth, or absence of it:

> **Max:** If I meet someone who sleeps on the streets, I need to understand that they have value … People have value, whether they have money or not. Money is not their value, if we can understand [this] … it might bring back the consciousness that we are all human.

Forty-one-year-old Olivia (Coloured woman, non-profit organisation) emphasised how our preconceived ideas of each other prevent us from seeing each other as having equal dignity:

> **Olivia:** There has got to be a fresh approach to how we see each other. We've become so tainted by our past that when we look at the Black person across the street we have an image of them before we've even met them … To see the other person you've got to have a connection with them.

All three reflect Fraser's understanding that dignity depends on recognising the other as equal and of equal value, and of coming to appreciate this dignity in relationship with each other. This may sound like a simple task, but given our past ideological and remaining geographical separation in South Africa, it remains a mammoth task requiring intentional effort. While it is almost impossible to talk of dignity without intrinsic equality, it is also worth considering equality on its own as a central element of personhood.

Fostering belonging, equality and citizenship

Equality encompasses political, legal and social elements. It is especially pursued in connection with race, gender, class, sexual orientation and geographical origin (urban/rural, immigrant/national). To be equal to others implies that a person is entitled to the same sense of belonging, citizenship and value as all others. Equality is a simple notion to define, but one which in the aftermath of South Africa's unequal past, remains difficult to achieve.

After the advent of democracy in South Africa, the main means of achieving equality on a structural level was through the overturning of all the Apartheid legislation that enforced inequality (see Appendix 4). Chief among these were the repeal of laws that limited where people could live and who they could marry or be intimate with; that differentiated between the quality of education given to Black and White children; that reserved jobs, universities and public facilities for Whites; that forced Black people off their land, and into Bantustans; and that denied Black people the right to mobilise politically and to vote. In the place of these laws, a new constitution was written that guaranteed equality for all, and outlawed the treatment of people unequally based on their race, sex, sexual orientation or religion.

However, legislative equality is not (and has never been) a guarantee of lived equality. At a civic society or community level, non-profit organisations such as Equal Education, Section 27, Ses'khona Peoples' Rights Movement, Abahlali baseMjondolo and the #RhodesMustFall collective have all played a role in ensuring actual equality – especially in connection with access to education, socio-economic rights, dignified sanitation, land and housing, and abolishing institutional racism on university campuses, respectively.

At an individual level, action that can be taken to ensure equal treatment for all might include relinquishing privilege when offered based on skin colour or educational level, and refusing special treatment at shopping malls, airports and even government departments because you are White – the converse rarely applies. The other is facilitating access to spheres of life that historically have been the preserve of the privileged.

Luke (White man, 37, businessman) offered a helpful example of how, along with the owner of a local surf school, teaching Black street children to surf may seem like a small example of encouraging equality on an individual level, but it creates hope for further belonging. He explained.

> **Luke:** It's not a full restitution package, but there's lots of evidence that if you can take Black street kids surfing that there's lots of joy and meaning ... There are a growing number of stories of guys who have got themselves into a new community in which they then have a whole bunch of associated benefits ... an opportunity for employment ... a step up in the community.

As was the case when participants spoke about dignity, many spoke about how fostering equality comes from engaging with people. Hillary (White woman, 21, student) spoke about having frank discussions with those whose life experiences you have had no exposure to:

> **Hillary:** Speaking to that elderly woman in the middle of Philippi who doesn't have access to healthcare or speaking to a lesbian teenager in a township about how her encounters differ significantly from mine, makes you realise ... these are individual human beings ... that we really are all equal. So ensuring those conversations happen.

Thamsanqa pointed out that these discussions remain unequal because our interactions frequently force Black South Africans to speak English, not their mother tongue:

> **Thamsanqa:** I cannot express myself fully in English. So part of me will always be lost in translation, because the person I'm interacting with doesn't understand my world ... I'd feel acknowledged as a human fully when I can have a full-on engagement with a White person without having to struggle through English.

Thamsanqa's point concerns power. In the act of pursuing equality, White people frequently wield disproportionate amounts of it. Furthermore, moral equality without the sense of belonging and equality that comes with equal access to economic means has a somewhat hollow ring. It is one of the reasons why South Africa struggles with social cohesion. Without socio-economic equality,[43] or at least the opportunity to aspire to such equality, social cohesion is an empty platitude. 'No social cohesion without restitution' is a mantra I have frequently used – to polarised responses.

To be a citizen and belong to a nation requires that each person has access to and experiences a conglomeration of rights and responsibilities. Apartheid then, and injustice now, result in people being denied access to basic rights of equality: the means to earn a living, to own a home, or pursue the career of their choice. These rights have been legally, and therefore also structurally, restored. However, accessing these rights remains difficult. This can be put down to poverty and the capital required to access the benefits of equal opportunities. There is also no protection against incidents of racism, sexism, xenophobia and homophobia. These problems need to be addressed in order for the people of South Africa to enjoy full equality, equal citizenship and the feeling of fully belonging after the injustices of the past.

This dispossession of citizenship is seen in the lives of various participants, from Ricky who does not own his own property and relies on his children to support him, to Luxolo who at 29 remains unemployed and lives in a backyard shack, to Haley's financial loss due to the Group Areas act, amongst many other accounts already related. Contrast this to the experiences of the following young White South Africans: Angela received her own apartment while studying at university, Cara whose parents gave her a Mercedes Benz to drive while she was a student, Peter whose family helped him to start a business after he completed medical school and decided that being a medical doctor was not for him. These examples illustrate the different experiences of equality and citizenship in South Africa, based on the injustices of the past.

Sizwe and Welile offered a blunt summary in relation to equality and inequality in connection with physical resources of wealth and opportunity:

> **Sizwe:** 'Apartheid is over. Let's move on.' But we can't just talk. I can't eat freedom. I don't eat reconciliation, you get it? … They preach this message: 'We're liberal, we're equal,' but I'm not. Do you

---

43 Sharlene Swartz, James Hamilton Harding, and Ariane De Lannoy (2012) Ikasi style and the quiet violence of dreams: A critique of youth belonging in post-Apartheid South Africa. *Comparative Education* 48(1): 27–40.

know how hard some of us have to work either at school or in life in general?'

Welile: The White men ... they've just taken everything. Now they own everything. It's theirs. Now they say: 'Okay, we've taken enough so now you can come and take.' But if you were eating from a dish with someone and they ate, they're done, they leave the bowls there. Then they say: 'All of you come, eat.' What am I going to get? There's nothing in that dish already, and how many of us need to share from what is left?

Creating opportunity, means and wealth

In the first chapter, I mentioned the newly elected democratic government of South Africa's three main ways (besides repealing Apartheid laws and drafting a new Constitution) to enact restitution for the past. These are economic empowerment (Black ownership, employment and procurement affirmative action), land restitution, and the Truth and Reconciliation Commission. All three were aimed at returning to those dishonoured and dispossessed by Apartheid 'a sense of empowerment ... [and] social support'.[44] It is notable that two of these three measures were economic in nature.[45] Government restitution aimed to change the economic conditions in which Black South Africans lived. Economic restitution is also the kind of restitution with which we are most familiar – financial compensation for property loss, gain-stripping, wealth redistribution and punitive payments.

Detractors of financial restitution frequently argue against 'entitlement' or 'hand-outs', and argue that people 'should work for what they have', usually followed by 'as I did'.[46] Few proponents of these views stop to recognise the insidious way in which Apartheid, especially through the vehicle of job reservation, stripped people of access to opportunities for decent work, and that those for whom jobs

---

[44] Braithwaite (1999).

[45] The TRC did pay reparations to victims but these were largely symbolic and only reached a very few victims of Apartheid's atrocities.

[46] Sally Matthews (2010) Differing interpretations of reconciliation in South Africa: A discussion of the home for all campaign. *Transformation: Critical Perspectives on Southern Africa* 74(1): 1–22.

were reserved, regardless of skills or 'cleverness' (as Harry pointedly remarked earlier), cannot be said to have earned what they now possess. This is the myth of meritocracy I referred to in the previous chapter.

A similar, and more contemporary argument, concerns the universally bemoaned current state of education in South Africa. Poor quality, low retention and inferior outcomes deprive people of access to opportunity. Children from township schools invariably fare less well at university than those from the privileged (suburban or private) education system.[47] Those who complain about the current state of education frequently forget that a divided education system with binary outcomes – of inferiority and superiority – were the intentional aims of the Apartheid system. It was overwhelmingly successful – and the fact that 22 years later it is still not fixed is more about its evil genius than about the present government's inefficiencies. That said, education is a structural good that must form part of the restitution of personhood if opportunity and wealth are to be possible for all in South Africa.

To talk about returning 'opportunity' rather than only redistributing 'land' or 'wealth' is to place emphasis on the way in which restitution is not an end-product or handout. Recall the complaint of Dylan who had, when I interviewed him, recently completed a doctorate: that while he understands White privilege, he finds it difficult not to be able to take some credit for his own achievements and effort. In my thinking, social restitution is neither an act of charity to deserving beneficiaries, nor is it a simple handout. White South Africans, having received preferential access to education, land and work, still had to study, farm, build, and develop skills and do their jobs. Many did so with great Protestant zeal, thereby amassing great wealth.[48] Restitution is aimed at restoring personhood and focuses on opportunity, since its aim is to level the playing field, to allow people equal opportunity to build wealth, to acquire assets, and to own homes.

---

47   A Bhana, S Swartz, S Taylor et al. (2011) Education and skills development. In Bongani Magongo and Mphela Motimele (eds) *South African youth context: The young generation*. Midrand, South Africa: National Youth Development Agency.
48   See Max Weber (2002) *The protestant ethic and the spirit of capitalism: and other writings*. Johannesburg, South Africa: Penguin.

The following are examples of the restitution of opportunity. At the level of group involvement, there can be corporate social investment in education or community upliftment; commercial banks could provide loans to those who were deemed 'non-creditworthy' due to being undocumented or lacking credit history as a result of Apartheid impoverishment. All forms of social assistance to new Black farmers and those new to the labour market are other examples of the restitution of means.

On an individual level, numerous examples exist of how personal wealth, gained ostensibly by legitimate means yet only possible through repressive laws, might be redistributed. One might make a personal choice for one's biological children not to be sole inheritors of personal property, but instead to divide property between biological children and others who were dispossessed by injustice. Another might be the intentional investment in education for children of employees at the same level as for those of one's own family members, or committed involvement in non-profit activities that uplift communities. This will be discussed further in Chapter 9.

In Chapter 4, I related Ricky's experience of repeatedly hitting career ceilings due to his racial classification as a Coloured man, as well as Welile's experience of discovering his inferior schooling when he reached university. Both had strong opinions about how financial wealth and dignity are related: for Ricky through work, for Welile through ownership:

> **Ricky:** This charity thing, it's not what we need. We need to give people dignity. He needs to earn that money.

> **Welile:** The land … We are not going to get it back, you know … Now you're free. Now you can go study. You can open your own mine … live in Camps Bay … but, you know, there's no money.

Many more participants made direct connections between physical resources such as housing, education and human dignity:

> **Dylan (34, White man, doctoral student):** In the public discourse we think that making the recognition part right without the economic part is enough … [but] people haven't had the resources to be dignified, and they have been ignored, made to feel like second-class citizens.

Patrice (60, Black man, teacher): The only way to restore human dignity is to empower people, allow them to have education ... so that they know their rights. And they know what they are supposed to do in order to become proper human beings.

Thamsanqa (32, Black man, researcher): By taking land and opportunities away, you're taking dignity and humanity away.

Manny (48, Coloured man, university administrator): Things like housing does something for the dignity of people. Those things, amongst others, will add to us restoring human dignity.

A number made the connection between opportunity and restoring someone's humanity:

Mayaya (34, Black woman, business executive): For me it's not taking things from this person and giving them to that person. Just give people equal opportunity. Everybody. Equal opportunity, equal access, you know.

Nobuntu (34, Black woman, retail executive): Making opportunities available and helping people heal. This is not necessarily the role of the government but other human beings in society.

Graham (29, White man, marketing): Providing equal opportunity to everyone. Humanity lies not only in the previously disadvantaged but in White, Black and all South Africans.

Graham's comment however, contains within it a barb – equal opportunity is not the same as opportunity for those who have borne the brunt of injustice. Equal opportunity is not restitution; restitution takes into account how people arrived at their current day circumstances.

Changing mindsets

In 1968, Martin Luther King preached a landmark sermon at the National Cathedral in Washington, DC in which he addressed the problematic concept of equal opportunity for all.[49] He called this 'bootstrapping philosophy' –

---

49 Martin Luther King (1968) Remaining Awake Through a Great Revolution. National Cathedral, Washington, DC: Congressional Record, 9 April.

asking people to pull themselves up by their bootstraps with little regard to the fact that they may not be wearing boots at all. It is a commonly held view that makes the restitution of personhood such a difficult task, and one that requires a change in how we see; a change in what many respondents in this study called 'mindsets'.

King addressed this 'over-reliance on the bootstrap philosophy' and challenged the views of those who believe it:

> [Some say] if the Negro is to rise out of poverty, if the Negro is to rise out of the slum conditions, if he is to rise out of discrimination and segregation, he must do it all by himself. And so they say the Negro must lift himself by his own bootstraps.

King then goes on to describe how in 1863 when Negro slaves were emancipated they were 'not given any land to make that freedom meaningful'. In addition, he continues, those who hold to this bootstrapping philosophy,

> Never stop to realize that no other ethnic group has been a slave on American soil ... that the nation made the Black man's color a stigma ... They never stop to realize the debt that they owe a people who were kept in slavery two hundred and forty-four years ... It simply said, 'You're free,' and it left him there penniless, illiterate, not knowing what to do.

In contrast, King describes what was done for new White immigrants upon their arrival in the US, 'giving away millions of acres of land in the West and the Midwest'. He argues that the government 'was willing to undergird its White peasants from Europe with an economic floor ... but failed to do anything for the Black man'. Not only did it give them land:

> It built land-grant colleges to teach them how to farm ... provided county agents to further their expertise in farming ... provided low interest rates so that they could mechanize their farms ... [and provided] federal subsidies.

***

> And these are so often the very people who tell Negroes that they must lift themselves by their own bootstraps. It's all right to tell a man to lift himself by his own bootstraps, but it is a cruel

jest to say to a bootless man that he ought to lift himself by his own bootstraps.

The parallels with South Africa's history are obvious. Personhood in the South African context has been damaged because people were not able to pursue lives in which they were socially connected; people were prevented from freely associating, forming intimate bonds of love and community – in short, they were prevented from bestowing humanity on each other. Furthermore, they were robbed of a national sense of belonging – one group was unable to acquire the means for human thriving, the other group was unfairly and lavishly endowed with these means.

Undoubtedly, Apartheid resulted in multiple rips of our social fabric and our humanity. However, it seems as if we are not irreparably damaged. Stories abound, although they are seldom found in the newspapers, that illustrate this: a repentant Apartheid killer helping a young White supremacist reform his thinking and change his life; a taxi driver and Apartheid lawyer embracing because of an act of kindness; and a mother of a son shot 25 times, not wanting revenge, but reconciliation and a school named in his honour.

What is needed to restore our humanity is neither unknowable nor impossible. Restoring dignity is intricately intertwined with the availability of opportunities to create wealth and restore belonging. Recognising injustice and threats to our humanity is important. However, we need to move beyond this recognition to find ways to implement a redistribution of wealth and a reallocation of respect. In the next chapter, we look at examples that people in this study suggested of how we might do so in practice.

PART 4

A TIME TO ACT

9 Everyday actions for individuals and groups

Although I have yet to travel in Ethiopia, I have long been fascinated by the country, its history, architecture and geography. The Danakil Depression is one such feature that intrigues me. It is one of the lowest and hottest places on earth, with temperatures reaching up to 50°C. Located on the border between Ethiopia, Eritrea and Djibouti, it forms a natural basin into which the great Awash River flows, but never leaves. Instead, it dries up to form a chain of salt lakes, never reaching the Indian Ocean. During the Cold War, the Danakil Depression, due to its remoteness, functioned as a natural incoming satellite dish for the CIA. The CIA was able to listen in to various communications flitting across the globe without their listening being discovered, nor were they able to transmit messages. Both these features have implications for a restitution project.

This book has set out a case for social restitution, which is distinguished from legal restitution by being voluntary rather than mandatory, and is based on a sense of moral responsibility instead of legal liability for past injustice. Social restitution is forward-looking, aimed at building another kind of country, different from our present reality, in which our damaged humanity is restored. For it to succeed, Black and White South Africans need to recognise the effects of the past that are still present, and be motivated to address the challenges of opportunity, dignity and belonging, creating something for everyone rather than having a skewed distribution of resources based on race, perpetuated across generations. Social restitution invites Black and White South Africans to take action together, in dialogue with each other.

One apprehension I have for this book is that it will fail to be a catalyst for such action: lots of talking, theorising, activities and stories but with little practical action. A little like the Danakil Depression: lots of inflows with no output, many messages received but none relayed. This chapter therefore addresses the concern that we might recognise injustice, even locate ourselves meaningfully in it, but still remain unengaged, passive, overwhelmed and immobilised. To counter this fear, this chapter records how the 60 people in the study generated a number of ideas that have the potential for further discussion and implementation, and that could generate other equally useful or better ideas for social restitution in South Africa. It does not reflect the *process* of social restitution, since this depends on a dialogue between groups of Black and White South Africans, deciding together what is possible (and which I address in Chapter 10).

What it does is to offer possibilities for everyday acts of social restitution. Inspired by antiracist scholar Philomena Essed,[1] who speaks of the *everyday* acts of antiracism in response to everyday acts of racism, social restitution is ultimately about everyday action. Everyday restitution is also not a panacea for addressing every challenge of poverty, inequality and damaged humanity with which South Africa contends. But it has the potential to make a significant practical and symbolic contribution.

Those who participated in this study put forward a raft of ideas for what should and could be done to change the status quo in South Africa. Not all fit the criteria of social restitution. Many ideas were aimed at government: asking for better and more efficient service delivery to the poor, with the leaking holes of corruption plugged. However, there were a number of ideas for how individuals and groups can *act alongside* government and other institutional programmes of structural restitution focused on education, land, employment and services that can be considered social restitution. The actions civil society could take, as individuals or as communities, generated a wide range of ideas. I report in this chapter on both categories (see Table 9.1). I note the aspect of personhood that is targeted (dignity, belonging, or opportunity) or whether the act of remembering is addressed. I also indicate when there are clear patterns, who put forward ideas: were they young or older, Black or White, working class or university educated? I also note the 'restitution language' (as Zethu suggested in Chapter 6) that is addressed: is it about 'saying sorry', about 'doing sorry' or about material 'giving'?

---

[1] Philomena Essed (1991) *Understanding everyday racism: An interdisciplinary theory.* Newbury Park, CA: Sage.

Table 9.1 *Categories of ideas for social restitution*

Acting alongside government and other institutions	Opportunities for groups and individual initiatives
Infrastructure and services	*Develop common purpose*
• A restitution tax to eradicate the bucket toilet system	• Treat people with *ubuntu*
• Upgrading townships through cross-subsidising the upkeep of the suburbs	• Challenge single stories and social perceptions
• Accountability to end corruption	• Learn a local language
Education	*Uplift communities*
• Bursaries	• Join boards of community organisations
• Strengthening teaching in township schools	• Financially support community organisations
• De- and recolourising schools	• Get practically involved on the ground
• Tutorials in communities	*Dissolve social boundaries*
Land and wealth redistribution	• Organise events across previous divides
• National referendum on land reform	• Through property choices
• Restitutionary finances: debt, wages, loans and compensation	• Through youth community service
• A salary increase moratorium for high earners	*Use faith spaces to bring people together*
Employment	• Address racial divisions in the church
• Offering training for people in affirmative action positions	• Integrate through partnership
• Offering stakes in business, employing more people	• Teach about racism, equality and restitution
• Work experience and mentorship programmes recognised as part of BEE	*Engage in dialogue*
• Local business fund and focus	• About race, privilege and symbolic violence
	• Learn our, and other African, history
	• Develop children's stories to explain the past
	Mentoring
	• Mentoring programme for young people
	• Mentoring people in business
	• Sharing inheritances and assets
	• Changing your will
	• Sharing holiday homes and swimming pools

Acting alongside government and other institutions to accelerate structural transformation

These areas included providing improved infrastructure and services for the poor; rooting out corruption among government officials and enabling better political participation; fixing education quality, access and completion rates; redistributing land and wealth; and ensuring access to work and opportunities for people previously denied these.

Infrastructure and services

Here, one of the major themes participants highlighted concerned the *urgency* needed to improve service delivery (houses, toilets, healthcare and increased social grant payments) and to develop South Africa's infrastructure so that it is able to facilitate economic growth and serve all of its people instead of just 10% of the population, as was the case under Apartheid. Forty-eight-year-old contract cleaner worker Lyanda summarised what is needed: 'The past can be forgotten if essential services are given to people, such as houses and jobs. White people and government should pay back and provide houses and better services'. Fifty-six-year-old Umkhonto veteran Sipho noted that government needs to focus especially on rural areas: 'There are still a lot of things we don't have ... government has done a lot of good but we still have a long way to go, like in the rural areas there hasn't been enough progress'. Overall, there seemed to be a consensus that any action that individuals or communities took to ensure faster, more efficient services for Black South Africans comprised useful and needed social restitution. Ideas in this category addressed dignity and belonging, and spoke the restitution language of doing sorry and material giving.

A restitution tax to eradicate the bucket toilet system

Two specific ideas were put forward by two White men: Luke, a 36-year-old businessman, and Johan, a 48-year-old non-profit organisation director. Johan advocated a special, but voluntary, restitution tax to be levied on White South Africans, which could be used to eradicate the bucket toilet system throughout the country in one concerted effort. In order for the money to be well used, it might be managed separately from government's usual budgets, and may need a strong civil society-state partnership. Others raised the idea of a wealth tax, but not for a specific purpose, as Johan did. Key questions were how it should be collected, by whom, and what to spend it on. Ted suggested a referendum to decide on what to spend it.

Upgrading townships through cross-subsidising the upkeep of the suburbs

Luke's idea concerned cross-subsidising the upgrade of townships through scaling down services to the suburbs. He proposed that municipalities charge suburbanites the same amount of money as they currently pay but only provide half the number of services for their contribution. Services such as fixing potholes, trimming verges and trees, and the upkeep of parks should become residents' responsibilities. They could either mobilise volunteers from the neighbourhood to do these jobs or hire people as part of neighbourhood or residents' associations. Municipal workers who were assigned to suburbs could then be deployed to townships to accelerate the upgrade of these living environments. Luke called this 'Model C-ing the upkeep of the suburbs', referring to a similar system in operation in suburban schools, where government subsidies are kept to a minimum and parents pay for additional resources and services they want in their school. Luke believes that many White South Africans would be 'happy with that redistribution ... happy that the government doesn't provide me as a wealthy, White, middle-class South African with lots of benefits', especially if this 'aggressive cross-subsidisation' is spent on upgrading services 'for those without'. He recounted a story where this was tried in a small coastal town, but ran into problems:

> **Luke:** The community got together and said: 'Let's start collecting R100 per family that signs up for this thing and the retirees in the community will start volunteering their labour'. They started trying to fix potholes and do flower beds around town ... And they were stopped from doing it because they were told it was government's job to do these things. That for me is just bizarre ... I think that's a way for me to be involved in restitution – to take responsibility for some of those things myself.

So while municipalities need to be invited into the dialogue to make this possible, so do middle-class Black South Africans living in the suburbs. This act of voluntary restitution would have to have the agreement of both parties. Luke also suggested that retired White people could be invited to volunteer in municipal offices, not replacing existing workers, but enhancing their capacity for service delivery.

Accountability to end corruption

While a number of people had ideas about how to end corruption, the overall feeling was that anything done by White South Africans to ensure politicians deliver on their promises and do so without corruption is an act of restitution. Comments on corruption came mostly from older White and young Black participants. Concrete ideas included ensuring public officials are appointed on merit, not as 'payback for the struggle' or as 'jobs for friends'; lobbying for the strengthening of public institutions like the courts and Public Protector's office; addressing tender fraud by returning to recommended fees' tables for professional services; holding public officials responsible to comply with the expenditure rules and limits in the Ministerial Handbook or from Treasury; and bringing their expertise to bear on formulating policy changes. Here, discussion is needed to ensure that these acts by White South Africans who start NGOs, lead campaigns or propose new policies, come from a motive to improve the lives of those impoverished by Apartheid, rather than to cast aspersions on 'an incompetent Black government', as a number of participants sadly commented. Ensuring better service delivery through specific actions is a noble act of social restitution, but maligning government officials for general incompetence is inexcusable.

Education quality, access and completion

For many, fixing education was the most important act of restitution to be made, as Olivia, a 41-year-old Coloured woman, who runs an educational non-profit organisation, explained:

> **Olivia:** I think that there are lots of acts of restitution that we can do, but ... the thing that's going to make the biggest difference quickly is if people invest their time into education for young previously disadvantaged kids because that's going to put them on a different path.

Mayaya, a 34-year-old Black woman and corporate executive, spoke with tears, about education providing 'a crack of light', as experienced first-hand in her own life, and her gratitude for her parents' sacrifices to ensure she got an education that has resulted in her current success.

Ideas for social restitution in education centred on equalising education quality, improving completion rates, and ensuring greater access and pass rates for young Black people at university level. Clearly, this is a mammoth task in the restitution arsenal of what needs to be done. For many, addressing education was about doing and giving in equal measure. Ideas were offered by more Black participants than White ones, and generally by the middle generation, with very few ideas generated by those over 50.

Bursaries

A frequent suggestion was that White South Africans pay for the education of Black young people at school or at university. For example, a domestic worker's child, children in their faith community, someone whom they know from work, or by contributing to education and bursary funds for Black youth. Sizwe (Black man, 23, graduate student) passionately advocated for White people to 'stop being guilty ... I don't eat your guilt. Do something tangible ... find one Black person that you can help at school or through varsity'. Young Black woman and retail merchandiser Lwethu reflected the views of many others of her generation: 'If I was President I would like to make education free, and stop this division between the so-called Model C schools and township schools'. Access to quality education has long been a desire of Black South Africans. The #FeesMustFall movement that began in 2015 has served to place it centre stage.

Strengthening teaching in township schools

A number of people proposed that this might be done by inspiring young people of the highest calibre to choose to teach in township schools,[2] and encouraging experienced teachers to share their skills with township schools. A related idea was put forward by Ted (White man, 67, leadership non-profit) who asked, 'What if some of the older generation of professional and committed White teachers were to be asked to go ... and be *advisers or coaches* to a new generation of teachers in the townships?'

De- and recolourising schools

While the obvious answer to improving education quality was to have every school run like former Model C schools (that operate almost like private schools), the amount of money needed to make this possible was prohibitive. Many Black South Africans therefore remain excluded from a top-rate education. Noting this, Dylan and Leo offered two ideas for how schools might be decolourised and recolourised. Dylan asked, 'What do you think would happen to township schools if you bussed White kids in?' He answered

---

[2] There are a number of these programmes in existence in, for example, the US, such as *Teach for America* and *Teach First* with varying results.

his own question by saying that White suburban parents are likely to bring all their resources, whether financial or social, to bear on these schools to ensure their children get a good education. Adding just ten White kids to each township school could have interesting effects on education quality.

Leo (White man, 46, non-profit organisation director) advocated a related idea, this time one of recolouring Model C schools in less wealthy suburbs. 'Choose a school that engages your children in the life of South Africa, not just the White bubble. Actively participate in governing bodies and school PTAs to build these values.' Currently, what is happening is that as Black youth enrol at former White and Coloured schools, White parents tend to send their children to private schools, or 'better' government schools (the phenomenon known globally as 'White flight', and one that also occurs in residential areas). An act of restitution would be for White parents to stop this practice, to keep or re-enrol their children in these neighbourhood schools, and to offer their skills and resources to ensure high standards, so that both Black and White children benefit.

Tutorials in communities

A further idea was to provide remedial education while we wait for education quality to improve. This might include NGOs offering tutoring programmes or homework clubs, individually tutoring children from township schools in maths and English, possibly even as a family project; and offering catch-up programmes for those already in the workplace who have been on the receiving end of poor education. Haley, the 42-year-old Coloured priest, challenged: 'If you are a White family and your kids are in high school, take your child once a week to go and tutor four or five Black kids in whatever subject they are best at … it will be good for everyone on many levels.'

Education is clearly a critical area in which social restitution must and can happen. Quality education serves to restore dignity, reiterates a sense of belonging and provides opportunities for young people to access employment and livelihoods in the future.

Land and wealth redistribution

The issue of redistribution of land and wealth came up frequently. Twenty-five-year-old Sindiswa, a Black woman who works in client services, summed up the feeling of many when she said: 'The nation's financial gains should be shared equally among the rich and the poor. We as the poor, we also want the financial gains of the freedom we currently have in South Africa.' Here she referred particularly to the issue of Black ownership of businesses, and was adamant that it should not only be 'the elites' who benefited from these government policies. Most participants recognised government's lead in redistributing wealth, but wanted more urgency, for it to be 'more aggressive … targets need to be higher' and for its outcomes to benefit more people as 21-year-old White student Cara declared. These views were shared by Black and White participants, with twice as many White South Africans as Black South Africans flagging this area of restitution.

National referendum on land reform

Thirty-eight-year-old White development worker Heather suggested a national referendum on land reform: 'I think that referendums should be held regarding the national feeling towards land reform and on what action should be taken by government to put this right on a national scale.' She added that she believed government was too cautious in land reform because they misjudged the response from landowners, who would probably be relieved to participate in a planned programme for making things right, rather than face the spectre of 'land grabs'.

Restitutionary finances: debt, wages, loans and compensation

A number of ideas were offered around restitutionary financial relief for the poor. This included civil society-led compensation for victims of Apartheid; debt forgiveness for victims of Apartheid; and low or interest free loans to start businesses or acquire property. A number of White participants spoke of paying not just decent wages to domestic workers and gardeners, but 'restitutionary wages'. This might best be done through a smartphone app that could help employers decide what kind of wage they are paying, or would like to pay: a minimum wage, a generous wage, or a restitutionary wage, and what to factor in when deciding (number of dependents, wealth of suburb, travel distance, main breadwinner, etc).

A salary increase moratorium for high earners

While a number of people spoke of limiting the ratio[3] between the highest and lowest earners in a company or institution, Ricky had a novel idea regarding a 'salary increase holiday' for White high income earners:

> **Ricky:** If the top earners ... could take a salary increase holiday for five years, then receive their increases again ... If the money that would have been due to them every year is then filtered into the salaries of the lower earners ... with the proviso that more productivity, better attendance and improved work is expected from them.

Ricky's idea is fantastic. As is the case in Model C-ing the upkeep of the suburbs, Black high-income earners need to be involved in deciding how best this is done.

The redistribution of resources in all its various forms was central to participants' discussions about restitution. A number of participants echoed Frantz Fanon's call to tackle 'the question ... of the redistribution of wealth' along with his warning that failure to do so will result in being 'shaken to pieces by it.'[4] Thamsanqa, the 32-year-old Black graduate student, said that he believed that 'a lot of White people feel their wealth threatened whenever you talk about restitution' while Leo said White people fear redistribution because 'they are trapped in their gilded cages ... of high standards of living ... terrified of "lowering the standards". They [are]... unable to make meaningful justice decisions for fear of losing out on their entitlements'.

The breath of fresh air in these conversations was that none of the participants was opposed to a redistribution of land or wealth – and twice as many White respondents spoke positively of redistribution compared to Black participants. The current government may be guilty of treading too carefully on the matter of redistribution of land and wealth. As Heather explained, people might in fact be relieved to contribute through such planned redistribution.

---

3   It has been suggested that the wage difference between highest and lowest paid employees be limited to a twenty-fold difference by various civil society groupings. Businesses and other institutions have yet to agree.

4   Frantz Fanon (1963) *The wretched of the earth*. New York, NY: Grove Press, p. 98.

Redistributing land and wealth addressed all three elements of the restitution of personhood: dignity, belonging and opportunity.

Accessing work opportunities

In this category, ideas were predominantly related to implementing existing policies of affirmative action and employment equity as well as finding ways of creating jobs. Black and White participants, in almost equal numbers, spoke of how groups and individuals could join government in making restitution for the past in this area. Far more tertiary-educated participants offered ideas of how this might work, and far more in the middle generations, rather than younger or older participants. These ideas address the element of opportunity in the definition of personhood most clearly, although many spoke of how work provides dignity, and contributes to a sense of belonging to a collective and accessing the full rights of a citizen.

Offering training for people in affirmative action positions

From a *dignity* point of view, a number of people noted the need for those who are given affirmative action positions to be adequately trained, for their own sake and the sake of the business or institution in which they are employed. Some spoke of how many Black South Africans feel inadequate when 'thrown in at the deep end', and how many never advance because their employees do not develop their potential. Mayaya explained how too many Black and Coloured people are made to languish in low-level positions: 'I've met ladies like that at my previous employer. Fifteen years – same job ... Why is it okay for the management to watch this woman languish? She's good at her job.' An act of social restitution may be to provide voluntary training for people in these circumstances on a one-to-one basis, or to start an NGO to work alongside businesses to do so. Care would be needed not to stigmatise employers or employees in these circumstances.

Offering stakes in business, employing more people

Ricky suggested that the practice of offering people a stake in the businesses they have helped to build is becoming more common and widespread. He talked about an example of a garage owner his father knew who empowered all of his staff through ownership. 'He did it with petrol jockeys ... and his sales went up'. Ricky also spoke of shortening the workweek for senior executives, reducing their pay by 20%, giving them a three-day weekend, and using the freed-up capital to employ more people.

Work experience and mentorship programmes recognised as part of BEE

Peter, the 38-year-old White business owner, spoke about the complexities of BEE. He spoke of his frustration at not being able to do business with government since he does not qualify based on ownership (both he and his partner are White). He has considered 'fronting' but does not believe this to be ethical. If he were allowed to do business with government, his business would grow and his capacity to employ young Black people would also increase. His idea for social restitution by young White business owners in his position is to lobby government to insert alternative ways to obtain BEE points. These could include the number of young Black employees a business has, the internship and mentorship programmes running for these workers, and the placements for work experience offered. All of these were also separately mentioned as important components of social restitution for White business owners.

Local business fund and focus

Two related ideas for increasing financial viability of Black business owners included a civil society fund for Black entrepreneurs (even at street or neighbourhood level) and a focus on local businesses. Some explanation is needed for both. Since South Africa remains geographically divided, predominately White suburbanites are unlikely to know a large group of Black South Africans who are in the process of starting up, or owning a small business. This idea will only work if there are suburban-township community partnerships. White people could then invest in small local Black-owned businesses, both by providing start-up capital for ventures such as garden services or a recycling business, and in using services and buying their goods. These might include buying your fresh produce from township vendors rather than large supermarkets, and using township-based services such as plumbers, carpenters, electricians, and painters.

Opportunities for groups and individuals to take the initiative

The remaining ideas, of which there were many, could be classified as actions of social restitution in which civil society could take the initiative. These include actions that could be taken, and attitudes that could be displayed by individuals and groups of people. I've divided these into seven categories to make for easier reading, but there are unavoidable overlaps.

Developing a common purpose

A number of ideas were offered that could be categorised as developing a common purpose, developing a sense of social solidarity or *ubuntu* across racial boundaries. These ideas primarily addressed people's sense of dignity and belonging. Its advocates were overwhelmingly Black, with secondary education or less, and belonged to the middle generations. Cara summed up the importance of having a common purpose: 'This idea that what you're doing is an investment for others'.

Treat people with ubuntu

Suggestions for how this might be done included, 'Everybody in South Africa must make an effort to make things right ... it is important to work together' (Patrice, Black man, 60, teacher); 'Be big enough to help anybody, not think more of yourself because you are in a "better" race, class or whatever' (Robyn, Coloured woman, 33, administrator) and 'We need to just go back to the basics of *ubuntu*' (Welile, Black man, 24, sales representative). Others had more specific ideas, such as getting to know the homeless person who collects recycling in your street and making him or her a cup of coffee, as Haley suggested, or 'stop putting each other down ... stop being so evil and vindictive towards each other', as Siphosethu (Black man, 29, retail floor coordinator) proposed.

Challenge single stories and social perceptions

This idea of 'not putting people down' was reflected in a number of conversations about how we need to change the nature of our public conversations. Mzwakhe, Dylan and Ted – all men, one Black, the other two

White, and aged 29, 34 and 67, respectively – had similar views. Their idea centred on encouraging the media to share the progress we have made in connection with transformation, and to show the agency of people across race groups in doing so. Dylan lamented how the media sensationalises the negative, and since White people 'are not party to a lot of South African life' because they do not work in government, this is a recipe for disaster – they never receive any counterpoint to their negativity. Positive changes in South Africa, Mzwakhe suggested, should take the form similar to the 'loveLife campaigns … through sport activities, billboards, and on TV'. We should be 'sharing the status of all races in terms of relationships, financial stability and transformation'.

Dylan and I, and Rose and I discussed at length how we might change the tone of suburban dinner party conversations, where it has become a sport to criticise the government, bemoan corruption and 'complain about potholes'. Instead, what is needed are constant challenges not to tell the 'the single story', but to relate accounts of progress in the civil service, gains made in stamping out corruption, the stories of *efficiencies* in municipalities, and how far we've actually come since Apartheid. If we fail to do this, too few people will want to join acts of social restitution. As I described at length in Chapter 2, perceptions of government corruption, for example, are a key reason why White people do not want to be part of restitution. People need a vision of how close we are, and what little effort it might take to reap the benefits of a truly transformed South Africa. Perhaps we need a national campaign for improved dinner party conversation, characterised by 'no whinging' and 'no single stories'.

Learn a local language

A few people mentioned that if White South Africans made a concerted effort to learn an indigenous language, even if only at the conversational level, this would greatly contribute to a sense of shared purpose. White South Africans also need to make an effort to learn how to pronounce indigenous names, and refrain from mocking Black people who speak English as a second or third language. A Tweet by celebrity Siv Ngesi[5] summed it up well: 'Dear White person, I dislike Zuma but you making fun of his English, distracts me from disliking him to checking you for your White privilege.' White South Africans show a lack of respect by doing both: mispronouncing indigenous language names or words, and then mocking those who speak English as a second or third language for their pronunciation.

Young White student Noah argued that learning 'another South African language serves to create a better platform for engagement and shows a willingness to communicate'. While it was surprising that so few advocated learning an indigenous language, it was one of the indicators that many gave when asked how we will know when we've done enough about the past: 'More White people will be speaking isiXhosa and isiZulu.' Furthermore, if a White South African asked someone to teach them an indigenous language, they might also help that person with advanced English language skills, such as those a student might need for academic writing, or a young graduate for making business presentations. This issue mainly addresses the belonging element of personhood, it also falls into the category of doing something tangible, although symbolic.

Uplift communities and support those who do

Over 20 ideas for addressing the past centred on uplifting communities and supporting existing organisations that do so. While this was a clear area for involvement by individuals and groups of people, some suggested that government has a role to play in creating enabling environments (through coordination, research and scaling up good models of practice). This category of ideas addressed all three features of personhood – belonging, dignity and opportunity – and came from twice as many Black people as White people,[6] twice

---

[5] This Tweet was made on 1st April 2016, in the wake of the Constitutional Court judgement which found that President Jacob Zuma had breached the Constitution and had to adhere to the Public Protector's findings to repay a portion of the expenses for upgrading his private residence. The entire country seemed to take to Twitter to express their dismay at the President. Some mocked the way he spoke and his difficulty in reading numbers.

[6] Note this is the opposite to ideas for redistribution itself, where twice as many White participants than Black participants flagged redistribution as a desirable restitutionary action.

as many university-educated people than high-school educated, and twice as many middle generation participants as those younger or older. Ideas included general ones such as increasing the capacity of community organisations though financial giving, joining boards and offering skills, and volunteering your time.

Get practically involved on the ground

Non-governmental and community-based organisations abound in South Africa, and so do opportunities for involvement. Many suggested that getting involved in an NGO or CBO was a good way to begin restitution. Many of these organisations deal with housing, health, education and job creation – all important elements of community upliftment that addresses the legacy of the past. In addition, some mentioned becoming involved with NGOs that dealt with 'things like beautifying and greening the townships' (Manny, Coloured man, 48, university administrator) in an effort to restore dignity to people's lives. For 36-year-old part-time lecturer Rose, who saw high levels of crime in townships as one of the 'legacies of the violence and deprivation of the past', tackling crime through 'community policing' was an important part of restitution and restoring personhood.

Financially support community organisations

A number of people suggested that people could decide to give a proportion of their income to community organisations:

> **Haley:** Families who have benefited from Apartheid should decide together to give away 50 or 60% of what they have to NGOs working for restitution. When it comes to employment creation, and education, and housing … there are plenty of NGOs who are doing good work and who can do a lot more if they had some of your money to help them.

For Jane (White woman, 21, student), this could include contributing to something like the Five Plus Project, started by UCT academics, who challenged people to give away 5% of their taxable income to organisations that sought to alleviate poverty and inequality.

The main feature in participants' responses was the sense that through NGOs, Black and White, rich and poor, could work together to fight a common enemy, as Max, a 26-year-old Black financial administrator observed:

Max: What if we are all fighting the same enemy which is poverty – Black folk, White folk, fighting the same enemy. I think in communities we will be able to do good … getting the people on the ground involved, the government contributing, the private sector contributing towards activities.

Join boards of community organisations

Leo had a further specific suggestion to make, namely that of joining the board of an 'on-the-ground movement with very little access to funds' and offering skills and finances to that organisation.

Dylan made an important point regarding the need for community upliftment to go beyond 'a blanket catch-all for what gets through the cracks in the system':

Dylan: I think South Africa's just brimming with civil society organisations … there are lots of individuals doing their individual thing and leaving their own little individual legacy … If all of those people worked together to create a systemic intervention I think it would be much more effective.

His point was that that community upliftment too frequently happens in silos 'providing services that the government doesn't have capacity to provide' with scant regard to how each effort can contribute to structural change. So 'instead of mending the roof, you just make an efficient puddle collection scheme'. Instead, having talented people use their skills to coordinate efforts, so that every small initiative has bigger impacts, was one way in which people could make meaningful restitution though community upliftment.

Many participants made the point that community upliftment should not be something done *for* the poor but *with* the poor. It also needs to transcend the Black-White divide by ensuring that Black professionals become increasingly involved in NGOs as volunteers – a role long played by White people.

Dissolving social boundaries

The notion of working together was a recurrent theme in participants' ideas for social restitution. A number of people made suggestions that could be called efforts to remove the social boundaries that keep White and Black South Africans apart: geography, class, and culture. While dismantling some of the spatial boundaries will require government assistance, participants came up with four ideas for everyday restitution that contributes towards dissolving social boundaries. These ideas all reflect the belonging element of personhood.

Organise events across previous divides

A number of people suggested we do things intentionally across racial divides that we might not have thought of before. Sizwe spoke of peaceful protests, finding a common issue and working on it together 'so it's not a Black issue or a White issue but an *our* issue'. Sibu mentioned a walk to Parliament that had been arranged one Easter by the Archbishop of Cape Town. She was delighted when she saw 'there was a Black person there, there was a White person, there was a Coloured, there was an Indian. They were holding hands … to achieve a common goal … to make South Africa a better place'. For others like Harry, sport is a means to achieve this common goal, it gives us the opportunity to develop national pride, and offers 'an opportunity for everybody to communicate across racial lines'. For others, the idea of visiting people in their homes across racial divides will also contribute to appreciating people's cultures, and help people 'realise the disparities caused by Apartheid' and make 'Whites more able to, or increase their willingness to "do sorry"'.

Through property choices

Some participants spoke of White people making intentional choices about where they lived. So for example, instead of perpetuating the 'White flight' phenomenon referred to in relation to schools, what was needed was for White South Africans to remain in communities into which Black people moved. The result would be that property prices would remain stable and those people who had social connections in the community would be able to extend its benefits to those who were newly arrived.

The reverse idea, of White people choosing to purchase property in Black, Coloured and Indian communities, was also mentioned – but some raised the problem of 'gentrification' that also accompanies such action. Poor people, frequently Black, get pushed out of areas because property prices increase. Angela recommended that property developers should intentionally embark on mixed priced housing when building new properties to encourage social class and racial integration. There was not much optimism when it came to geographical integration. Throughout interviews, however, people spoke of how very little contact we have with each other, and that if we were ever going 'to live together' we would need structural intervention.

Through youth community service

Rose put forward an idea around community service for school leavers that, among many other benefits, would contribute towards dissolving social boundaries. She explained:

> **Rose:** We've got a big problem with unemployment – especially among the youth. School leavers need to do community service and they need to do it outside their community … So if you live in the suburbs then you must do some community service in a township or a rural area – and live in the community for a year, hosted by a family. If you've had a good education you must go and read to primary school children for a year and there must be a stipend. If you matriculate from a township school, you should go and work as a lab assistant in a suburban school, where you can learn skills and be better prepared for university.

While this might best be done on a structural level, she said, as is the case for those who graduate from the health professions, there is nothing to stop civil society institutions from promoting such an idea – *a restitution or social cohesion* gap year – especially since the UK has abolished the idea of working holidays, which were popular amongst young White South Africans.

Harnessing faith spaces to bring people together

Almost two-thirds of those who participated in this study said they attended religious services, mainly church, either weekly or monthly. It was not surprising therefore that a number had recommendations about how faith communities could address the past. Three ideas stood out, mainly from middle generation White people, but covering all elements of the restitution of personhood – dignity, opportunity, belonging, and memory.

Address racial divisions in the church

The first was that churches need to address the issue of racial divisions in the church, at institutional and local levels. Sadly, there are still some church denominations where historically Black, Coloured and White groupings of the same denomination exist. These churches should take intentional steps to unify. They should also ensure that there is an equitable redistribution of the land they own, invariably skewed along racial lines.

Integrate through partnership

Churches are spaces in which integration and living together across social boundaries could be practised, although few churches are currently racially diverse. Because of South Africa's ongoing spatial separation, Sunday morning services remain among the most racially divided hours in South Africa's social life. Churches need to take intentional steps to integrate – encouraging White people to attend services, *serve* and *give* in Black communities, and inviting and *welcoming* Black people into White churches, including into positions of *leadership* so that churches transform culturally. Middle generation White couple Sandy and Peter, both committed church members, reflect on their own church situation, its potential and current reality:

> Peter: The church has got a great role to play because the church has a culture of bringing people together from different backgrounds into forums where we talk about things.
>
> Sandy: This [Black] lady said she loves the church that we're in … So she invited her Black friends and when they came they were like: 'It's lovely, but there's no Black people'.

Teach about racism, equality and restitution

Heather, a White woman, picked up on the third idea, that churches should be teaching about and doing restitution, when she said: 'Churches should consider how to share land, share resources, staff, etc. and should be preaching about restitution much more'. Churches could also teach about race and racism, since equality is a key feature of Christian theology, although there were times when it was not practised. They are ideal spaces in which to convene dialogues and discussions on the topic.

Restitution is an integral part of Christian theology, in the Old Testament as well as in the Gospels. Jesus teaches forgiveness but also repentance, and advocates that his followers 'produce fruit in keeping with repentance'[7] of which restitution is a clear example. Jesus also gives restitution directions about what should be done with money obtained unjustly in the account of Zacchaeus,[8] the tax collector. A number of participants spoke strongly about how the church errs with a focus on forgiveness ('saying sorry') rather than an equal focus on repentance ('doing sorry'), frequently failing to advocate practical ways in which restitution may be made 'through properties and other resources being distributed' according to Leo. Haley, the priest, suggested that the church should teach about its historical role in entrenching Apartheid, as well as the many ways in which it brought about Apartheid's demise, including the faith origins of the Black Consciousness movement, and the activism of many Christian-motivated heroes of the struggle, such as Desmond Tutu and Frank Chikane. Johan added: 'Churches should be taking a lead in restitution and for the most part we have not.' The real loss here is that churches and faith communities have enormous audiences of generous and good-willed people, who frequently give and volunteer in ways that make significant differences to their communities – as acts of charity, but which can so easily be transformed into acts of restitution.

Engaging in dialogue about the past in the present

By far most of the ideas that were proposed could be termed 'dialogue' along with the social and informal contact necessary to achieve this. This category of restitutionary action was equally divided between what individuals can do and what groups can do, with government being enjoined to make such dialogues part of the antiracist education and citizenship education curricula in schools. Suggestions in this category came from equal numbers of Black and White participants, although almost no ideas for dialogue were advocated by those over 50. About twice as many ideas came from participants with tertiary education than those with secondary education or less.

Ideas for dialogue largely addressed issues of dignity and belonging, along with remembering the past. A few related to opportunities, such as developing

---

7 Luke 3: 8 (Holy Bible, New International Version).
8 Luke 19: 1–10 (Holy Bible, New International Version).

empathy for people affected by the past, as Palesa, a young Black finance administrator noted: 'Think and talk about what could have affected certain people, and not just think that people are lazy ... because they didn't have certain things that the others have'.

The purpose of dialogue, according to respondents, was multi-faceted. It was to find each other, creating 'initiatives', as Ted described it, 'where folk from disadvantaged backgrounds are meeting with those from advantaged backgrounds and exploring ways in which resources can be shared'. Many, like Jane, wanted 'spaces for people to meet and recognise each other's humanity', while Sibu talked about how dialogue could foster trust between racial groups: 'We need to work together and be transparent ... so that I can trust you, you can trust me. And then I can understand your motives, and you don't have to be scared about my motives.'

About race, privilege, symbolic violence and restitution

With regard to these discussions, the notion of 'White privilege' and 'symbolic violence' was mentioned a few times, mainly by the students in the study who, like Sizwe, lamented the too few spaces that existed where race could be openly and honestly discussed: 'People are wounded ... I think it's a disease, as a White person, to think you're superior ... As a Black person, to think you're inferior ... We must talk blatantly and bluntly about race. Have discussions'. Cara concluded, 'Perhaps the most meaningful thing you can do is make everyone understand restitution and the importance of it'.

Learn our, and other African, history

Besides discussions on privilege, race and prejudice that could take place in all kinds of institutions – churches, schools, the workplace and universities were suggested – we need to be intentional about recounting the TRC's findings and learning African history. Sandy, the 38-year-old White part-time teacher, observed: 'It's very beneficial for White people to hear Black people's stories and ... genuine experience of prejudices today, where there's still a legacy of pain ... It can open your eyes to where you are actually still showing prejudice.'

Develop children's stories to explain the past

Sandy and I had an extended conversation about how we needed children's stories that could explain South Africa's past; that would help Black and White kids grow up knowledgeable, empathetic and keen to act to ensure equality and dignity for their peers.

While dialogue across racial divides was a popular suggestion, a number of Black participants also advocated for spaces where Black people can first talk together among themselves, develop a strong voice and then engage in dialogue with others. Mbali, a 28-year-old Black financial administrator echoed Steve Biko in this connection, when she said: 'we need places for Black people to learn ... to voice their opinions ... to know more about their situations, and to know ideas on how to solve their problems lie with them'.

The majority felt that dialogues could ultimately bring people together across social boundaries, not merely for the sake of outward social cohesion, but for meaningful engagement. These dialogues have the potential to increase social solidarity and shared decision-making about what actions are necessary to end the status quo. Luke summed this up well when he said that these dialogues could help us 'walk in someone else's shoes ... to understand'. Given our ongoing geographical separation, these opportunities and spaces will be difficult to create, but they are possible and necessary.

Mentoring and skills need to flow from those who have

Mentoring and skills sharing have the potential to address each of the aspects of the restitution of personhood, with a special emphasis on opportunity – sharing skills that will enable people, especially young people, to access economic and life opportunities. Advocates of mentoring and skills sharing were mostly tertiary educated, middle generation participants, and came from Black and White participants.

Mentoring programme for young people

Specific ideas included establishing a large-scale mentoring programme for young people, and fostering, or adopting Black children without family to care for them, formally or informally. For David (White man, 43, doctor), an informal approach meant 'not extracting them out of their contexts but journeying with them in the midst of their contexts ... exposing them to other realities and future possibilities.'

Nollie and Sibu, young Black women, made a strong case for mentoring and skills sharing across racial and class divides:

> **Sibu:** Because the rich people have got the money, they've got the resources ... I don't want your millions. I just want you to teach me the skills ... I'm staying in a shack. How do I build a house for myself and look after it? How do I make a vegetable garden so that I can pick and cook my own food ... If those who have resources can make their resources available to those who don't have, I think things will be different.

> **Nollie:** The more something is done, the more it opens people's minds. They'll be able to get out of that whole shell, and do something and be something.

Mentoring people in business and leadership

Businessman Luke spoke, with regret, about not having Black business people to mentor since his social circles are predominantly White – and transferring business skills to others is what he feels he can contribute to the project of restitution. Ted warned that any mentoring needed to be sensitively done so that any sense of paternalism is avoided: 'I don't have a problem with White people mentoring Black people, but they've really got to be prepared to play a low-key role out of the public eye'. A few people spoke about choosing careers that served those affected by South Africa's past, such as rural development, non-profits or teaching in rural areas, as another way of sharing skills. Mentoring and sharing skills is a long-term 'doing-sorry' form of restitution.

Sharing inheritances

The issue of inherited wealth in South Africa is an elephant in the room. If, as has been repeatedly argued, and with which most participants agreed, that what White South Africans inherit from their parents is an unjust inheritance, then, surely White people have a responsibility to use it to make good. However, what one does with inherited wealth already received, or still to come, came up only rarely with participants, often in response to a pointed question. Peter, who stands to inherit one-third of about R12 million from his parents, responded by saying:

> **Peter:** I've never thought about that question at all. Now that you raise it, I think there could be a case for saying that for the current generation inheriting things from the previous generation – a portion of that should be used wisely in the process of restitution. But until you've raised the question today, I've never even considered that as being a viable thing.

Peter continued to say how he would like to see such a sharing of inheritances done:

> **Peter:** I would not be happy if it became another tax that goes to buy BMWs and fancy homes for the political elite. That is going to make me more angry. It's not going to make me want to restitute anything. So if it were administered by a body – something like the Public Protector ... if there were a restitution body that was strongly independent of politics – and if I could genuinely see that they were using that money well for purposes of re-educating etc, I would then feel that that money's gone to a good cause.

Heather, a 38-year-old White woman who also stands to inherit a share of a large sum from property her parents own, was thoughtful about the responsibility of her inherited wealth:

> **Heather:** If there were an organised programme that could help me and my siblings consider how to turn the inheritance ... into a practical help for another community ... so that beneficiaries of the opportunity to receive land knew that it came from willing participants in restitution, I think that this could restore some dignity to us all.

The key in inheritance-sharing is that it is an act of social restitution if it is voluntary. Currently the state takes 25% of all inherited wealth and redistributes this in services, often to the poor. Many wealthy South Africans, however, have grown extremely skilled in avoiding inheritance tax through legal means, without a thought for the intergenerational perpetuation of wealth. So how could what White South Africans do with their inheritances become part of a significant programme of restitution?

Changing your will

The key question to be asked is how institutionalised such inheritance-sharing as an act of making good needs to be. Heather's request for 'an organised programme' is not a requirement for sharing an inheritance. She may have to discuss how best to do it with her siblings. She may also need to think about modifying her will to reflect her wishes not to leave her share to her immediate family, or to leave only part to her family and another part to a trust, a non-profit, or to others with whom she has developed a relationship built on restitution. But she also raised another issue, of wanting the recipient to know that this was a voluntary act of restitution. This could be achieved through formal or informal means. A letter that accompanies one's bequest to be read at the time of reading your will, or as Peter would prefer, a civil society fund to which White South Africans could leave a significant part of their assets. The truth is that most White South Africans do not need a financial inheritance from their parents to succeed.

Haley, whose story I related in detail in Chapters 3 and 4 – including the material cost to her of Apartheid, calculated only on the loss of property – spoke about calculating the way in which Apartheid had enriched and impoverished average families in South Africa. She strongly endorsed the idea of sharing inheritances:

> **Haley:** If your kids have been given the benefit of your Whiteness already, don't leave your money to them … Give your grandchildren your love … but don't give them your money … [It] is unhelpful for your grandchildren and for you, and for this country. We've got to rethink inheritance … You only have what you have as an inheritance because you were White … Give it back!

This issue of what White South Africans do with their assets when they die is one worth igniting a national conversation about on its own. Included in that discussion might be the issue of our gilded cages that might prevent us from sharing, and leaving perhaps half of one's assets to family, the other to a non-profit organisation, or to an individual with whom you have a restitutionary relationship.

Sharing holiday homes and swimming pools

In a similar vein, Leo added that those who owned holiday homes should think about 'offering them for use to people who don't have the opportunity for holidays, or selling inherited holiday homes and helping a [Black] family to purchase property'. The same could be said of luxury cars, swimming pools, and all the other accoutrements of modern White South African life. Sharing seems the least that should be done.

The challenge of turning ideas into reality

If White South Africans are to embark on a journey of social restitution, I believe that three things need to be in place: people need a simple plan to follow, they need the goodwill of a group of Black South Africans who will walk this journey with them, and they need to be motivated and inspired by leaders, preferably White leaders, to do so.

Ted spoke of how leaders are often at 'the frontlines of changing cultures', and argued that White leaders need to 'prepare other White people to make restitution, and need to ensure that any acts of restitution are done with humility'. He noted that there was a conspicuous absence of White leaders speaking out on the issue of restitution, whether in business, politics or in faith communities. The problem with this is an age-old one. When 'the community of the aggrieved' – those who have been wronged – make suggestions for action, it can frequently be dismissed as being self-interested, for example, when women call for gender equality, or a group of gay men and women advocate gay marriage. It becomes very powerful when allies advocate on behalf of other groups: when White people campaign against institutional racism, or when the able bodied insist on accessible shopping malls and office blocks. Not because they believe that the group is incapable or powerless, but because allies add another layer to the call. They tacitly say, 'This action is right and just and I have nothing to benefit from advocating that it be done.'

I also believe that White South Africans who wish to embark on a journey of restitution need the goodwill of a group of Black South Africans to walk the journey with them, to ensure that what begins as restitution does not turn into 'charity', or 'philanthropy' or 'development'; and that power is reined in so that White South Africans do not default to their usual place of superiority, believing themselves to know what to do, and what others want or need.

Discussing ideas together and asking people to say what they think will be an appropriate restitutionary response, but will not be easy or comfortable. But it is what is needed.

Finally, what is needed is a simple, not complicated plan. Let me offer a lesson learnt from my own experience of recycling in Italy. I wrote a great deal of this book while on sabbatical for three months in a small Sardinian village surrounded by the most stunning cliffs and azure blue sea. The village had resisted recycling for many years, but had embarked on it in the year of my visit. To help people understand the system, the town officials issued a four-page colour brochure with instructions. There were eight different types of recycling: big household items, small household items, electronic waste, kitchen waste for composting, glass, paper, cardboard and plastic. Recycling was collected seven days a week with two different types collected each day in different combinations; kitchen waste was collected every day. Waste had to be put out in three different coloured bins, with varying permutations per bin. Two kinds of bags were to be used, with kitchen waste only acceptable in biodegradable bags. In addition, there were different time-slots for collection allocated to each part of the village and the surrounding beach cottages. If this wasn't difficult enough, wild boars rampaged through the village late at night and in the early morning, tearing apart bags and knocking over bins in search of food. Bags that were ripped when the recycling trucks came by were left uncollected, and were subsequently attacked by ferocious ants.

Not surprisingly, the recycling programme was a disaster. People began by getting up early each morning to put out their recycling, then stood guard to protect it from the wild boars and ants. They soon tired of this, and reverted to putting out the rubbish the night before and took their chances with the boar, that had a field day! Those who got the combination wrong – bins, bags, types – and many did, were denied collection, and fell prey to the boars and ants. Soon this veritable paradise was unsightly. After a few weeks of living there, I noticed something else. Many people stopped even *trying* to get it right. It was just too complicated. Instead, they dumped their garbage unsorted, on road verges, down cliffs and even in hotel parking lots. The village conversation also changed: the usual banter about the weather and the happy Italian obsession with food was replaced with anger and blame – towards the recycling company, the town council, the European Union and 'eco-warriors' in general. A noble ideal had turned into an implementation nightmare. The plan was simply too complicated.

Writing about restitution, and having the Danakil Depression metaphor of inputs without outputs in my mind, the parallels were obvious. Ideas for restitution need to be straightforward and easy to implement. People need to see it as fulfilling a larger, long-term noble purpose, as well as being of immediate benefit to them and their children. Detractors need to be answered, and attitudes are as important as actions, so that the atmosphere of an entire community is not soured. This is the challenge of the final chapter: to bring together the big ideas of this book and to outline a practical process for social restitution.

10 Telling new stories through social restitution

I began this book by relating how, in 1988, it took someone spitting on my shoes in Switzerland for me to see the enormity of Apartheid and my personal complicity in its injustice. Nearly ten years later, and almost twenty years ago, on 19th December 1997, I signed the TRC's *Register of Reconciliation*. In my entry I wrote of what it was like to grow up White in South Africa, slipping in and out of consciousness about Apartheid's effects on my own and others' lives, and how sorry, angry, disappointed and resolved I now am. Sorry for the past; angry for not knowing and not caring to know; disappointed in myself for not doing enough, and in people I looked up to for not helping me see and do better; but resolved now to do better. I pledged to 'continually hold the past as a road map for our future ... to work for a different South Africa in the vocation I have chosen'. So how have I done?

I spend a lot of my time thinking and reading about restitution and justice, especially for the young people in South Africa. I speak and write almost exclusively on these topics. I volunteer my time with an NGO focused on restitution. But what attitudes of restitution have I adopted and what actions have I implemented? Let me mention the three areas I am focused on: mentoring, property and listening. I do so not to hold myself as a standard, I am far from that, but because sharing my personal restitution strategy follows on from the ideas for action presented in the previous chapter and might trigger other everyday actions for readers. I am also interested in feedback on these actions, since I decided on them in isolation, and not in dialogue, as I advocate in this book.

The first action is that of mentoring young people as an intentional strategy of restitution. Over the past nine years, I have slowly increased the number of young Black South Africans with whom I meet on a regular basis. Some are students, others unemployed, others work in un- or semiskilled jobs, and some have professional jobs. I meet some once a month, and others probably once every two or three months. We meet one-on-one, either at my home, over coffee at Exclusive Books in Cavendish Square, over lunch near my office in Cape Town, in the *shisa nyama*[1] in Langa, on walks on Table Mountain, or on occasional trips to the beach. I offer them the capitals I have at my disposal: the social capital of introductions to people who might help with skills, study or work; the cultural capital that makes the rules of the game explicit – how to navigate the Department of Education when you need a matric certificate, how to deal with the police, unruly uncles, title deeds for township houses, techniques for interviews, how to get a promotion, how never to take 'No' for an answer; the financial capital needed for school fees, university fees, the cost of bail when needed, lawyers' fees, doctors bills, and for new Christmas clothes, birthday celebrations, holidays, and sometimes, for groceries and haircuts.

I share these freely because I understand that I have them in abundance due to the privilege my Whiteness has conferred on me. I hope they make a difference to these young people as they navigate life's tough streets in post-Apartheid South Africa, where many still remain second-class citizens, sometimes at the hands of fellow Black South Africans. They tell me they find our interactions useful, and many no longer rely on me to back them up when having to deal with institutions and bureaucracy. We also have many lengthy discussions and debates about South Africa, about restitution, about how things came to be as they are.

I have a total of 14 young people in my life, and with each one I have a different relationship. Some I have introduced to other friends of mine, and mentoring relationships have developed from those introductions. I am clear about why I am making this effort – it is an act of restitution, not charity – and they are all aware of my motives. As a result, I treat them like family, never giving up on the relationship because they ask too much, or disappoint me. I never feel 'burnt' when money is not used the way I had hoped it would be, plans not followed, or when friendship is not reciprocated. This is, after all, not about me.

I have also received much from them. I have learned to spend much more time listening than what my ingrained privilege and 'default to superiority' would naturally have led me to do. They teach me to speak isiXhosa, criticise

---

[1]   A township butcher turned 'braai' (barbeque) eatery.

my wasteful expenditure of money (which sometimes shames me into making better choices), and offer me insights into aspects of South African life I would never have experienced. My life is hugely enriched. I feel part of something larger than the remoteness my skin colour confers. My social analysis is enriched by their perspectives (and my work is better for it). I have a new sense of belonging in South Africa. My humanity feels somewhat restored.

The second concerns property. I bought a house in the suburbs five years ago, now worth R3 million. Over the years, I have made my house available to many of these young people with whom I have this mentoring relationship: it offers a quiet place to live when writing matric, a way to escape the craziness of township life, a haven when newly released from prison, when a new baby arrives, or to save money in the few months before entering university. I have also adjusted my will so that my family are not the sole inheritors of my property. Instead, they will share it with two young people with whom I am especially close. At the same time, I am making sure that my heirs have the necessary life skills to make good use of a million rand inheritance. My motive here is simple: inheritance perpetuates inequality and injustice in South Africa across generations. My circumstances being what they are, I want to play a small role in preventing that. I have an obligation to my family, but they will be fine with only one-third of an inheritance. For my other heirs and their families, this inheritance could make an enormous difference, even some time into the future.

The third area of restitution I am attempting, not very well, I'm afraid – is to check the innate confidence and sense of superiority that my privileged upbringing has brought. I make conscious efforts to listen more carefully to the contributions Black South Africans make, at work, in the NGO I'm involved with, in everyday life. This is probably the least successful, and most difficult of all three of my acts of restitution.

These acts of social restitution cost me around 20% of my monthly salary and around the same proportion of my time in a month. I notice it, but it doesn't hurt. Not nearly as much as the debating and pleading I engage in with friends and extended family, and in all sorts of academic and public contexts, where restitution is not a popular topic. Never allowing racist utterances to go unchecked; always having to offer alternative explanations for 'our useless Black government'; and pointing out unearned privilege and wasteful lifestyles. This is the part that costs.

To my mind, these three actions of restitution are modest. I still get to enjoy the benefits of a beautiful house now; I enjoy the benefits of a well-paying job; drive a smart three-year-old Toyota; and travel internationally for work and leisure. My life is not crippled by social restitution. In fact, the opposite is true; it is enhanced. I experience the satisfaction of making good, even if I wonder if it's enough.

Arriving at social restitution

This book is the result of a combination of my experience as a White South African, my academic thinking and reading, and the conversations I have had with the participants in this study, as well as with many others over a period of 12 years. Reflecting on our experiences of the past and how it has affected us, the kind of country we want to live in and on what might happen if we did nothing further to address the past injustices are crucial starting points when it comes to thinking about restitution. But so too are locating ourselves in the past – no matter how old we are now, or whether we were active or passive participants in the events of the past. Using two simple stories, of a stolen bicycle and an unequal soccer field, as allegories for what has happened in South Africa over its years of colonialism and Apartheid, I have tried to offer a new view of restitution: one based paradoxically on voluntary participation along with a sense of moral obligation, one that addresses injustice in previous generations, that questions the sufficiency of merely levelling the playing field, and that begins to name what 'the bicycle' really is – land, health, dignity, confidence and opportunity among many possibilities.

The ultimate aim of restitution is structural change – the institutionalisation of equal access and just and fair practices to rectify the injustices of the past. Legal restitution, still being pursued through the courts and through legislation, is nowhere near complete and must continue. However, social restitution, the acts that individuals and groups can and need to take, and the attitudes they need to adopt in order to make good for South Africa's past history of injustice, colonisation and Apartheid, is also a key part of structural change. Institutional, government-led and legal processes are never going to be enough on their own. Everyday people need to get involved, sometimes alongside these initiatives, sometimes independently of them, in actions aimed at restoring dignity, equality, a sense of belonging, to change our amnesia about the past and to eradicate shameful current inequalities. Through these acts of social restitution that address racism, housing, poverty, education, respect, and privilege, among others, social restitution can help all South Africans become fully human again. We may never be able to make things right, to return things to how they were before our experience of injustice, but social restitution has the potential to contribute, in some measure, to shaping another country in which life is good for all. So how might we embark upon a journey of social restitution? This comprises the final section of the book, steps and criteria for an active and critical process.

Criteria for critical active social restitution

The ideas that participants have come up with for social restitution and the theories I have drawn on throughout the book (summarised in Appendix 1) allow me to propose a process of critical and active social restitution. I therefore define critical active social restitution as the acts and attitudes of individuals and groups towards making good in spaces where injustice has occurred, based on principles of community, solidarity, dignity, dialogue, understanding the past and collective agency, in order to restore all of our humanity. Such a concept offers opportunities for engagement by everyday people in everyday acts, and it does so through the use of new language, new concepts and new questions with which we may evaluate our efforts at restitution. Emerging from these ideas are ten criteria (see Table 10.1) for social restitution that can also be described as a process for practical action. Appendix 3 translates these criteria into a week by week guide, which I refer to as the *10–10–10 Restitution Dialogues,* where 10–10–10 stands for 10 people, 10 weeks, 10 conversations.

Table 10.1 *Criteria for critical active social restitution*

- Operates in a diverse group based on dialogue
- Articulates a common vision for South Africa
- Recognises the effects of past injustice on the present
- Incorporates a broad understanding of restitution
- Understands the difference between charity and restitution
- Locates all participants in the conversation about injustice
- Aims to restore personhood
- Discusses multiple ideas for practical action
- Embraces the attitudes necessary for an emancipatory project
- Includes strategies for overcoming inaction

Operates in a diverse group based on dialogue

The starting point for a process of social restitution is to gather a group of 10 diverse people, unlike ourselves. This is because of the central principle of our interconnectedness as people, and that restitution must be accompanied by a process of listening and mutual engagement. Social restitution therefore requires both relationship and dialogue in order to meets its goals. Recall Zethu's parallel between love and restitution: how we each have preferred ways of giving and receiving love (the so called 'five love languages' of Gary Chapman[2]) and that different kinds of restitution may be required for different individuals or groups of people. Writing in the '70s, Steve Biko warned of the dark side of dialogue, how it can be used to make one group feel better, instead of leading to action:

> Black-White circles are almost always a creation of White liberals ... they call a few 'intelligent and articulate' Blacks to 'come around for tea at home', where all present ask each other the same old hackneyed question 'how can we bring about change in South Africa?' The more such tea-parties one calls the ... freer he shall feel from the guilt that harnesses and binds his conscience. Hence he moves around his White circles – Whites-only hotels, beaches, restaurants and cinemas – with a lighter load, feeling that he is not like the rest of the others. Yet at the back of his mind is a constant reminder that he is quite comfortable as things stand and therefore should not bother about change.[3]

Nonetheless, how we come to know which action will have the effect we hope for is only likely to take place within a group of people, involving both those hoping to make restitution and those who will receive it, and in the context of relationship and dialogue. This criterion of dialogue-in-relationship (or 'no restitution without consultation') is no easy task, for three reasons. First, we remain socially divided across former boundaries and so finding a diverse community of practice will take serious intent. Second, we have to overcome the (not unfounded) fear of many Black South Africans who may not want

---

2   Gary Chapman (1992) *The five love languages*. Chicago, IL: Northfield Publishers.
3   Steve Biko and Aelred Stubbs (1978) *I write what I like*. London, UK: Bowerdean Press, p. 22.

to engage in yet more 'dialogue' that is not accompanied by action. Third, such a consultative approach will be very difficult for those who suffer from a superiority complex; it will take much effort for White South Africans not to presume (yet again) that they know best what Black South Africans need in terms of restitution. These challenges are not insurmountable, but they take intentional effort. Once your group is convened (Step 1: *Establish a diverse group and have a conversation*), you could answer the following questions:

(1) Who are we, and why are we here?
(2) What are we each going to have to do to make this group work?
(3) How will feelings of superiority and inferiority affect our conversation, and what can we do to overcome it in this group?
(4) What has been done so far to address the injustices of the past?
(5) What do you think will happen to South Africa if nothing more is done about the past?

Articulates a common vision for South Africa

The second step in a process of social restitution is to discuss current perceptions of South Africa, and the kind of country we are hoping for within this group of diverse people. The participants in this study shared a common vision of a South Africa where race is no longer the chief determinant of our lives, where all are truly equal and where poverty is a thing of the past. However, given South Africa's history of injustice and suffering, there can be no certainty that all will share such an optimistic outlook. Our ultimate actions of social restitution need to reflect this vision: non-racial, democratic, equal, just, peaceful, and where 'the weak are protected and none go hungry or poor'.[4] A key criterion for social restitution, therefore, is to ask whether the activities we have in mind reflects this common vision for South Africa. Speaking about what brings both hope and despair offers us an opportunity to develop a shared vision, and for asking why we are so far away from realising this vision. At a second meeting of the group (Step 2: *Discuss how you see South Africa*), the following questions could be asked:

(1) What are the things in our country that make us despair, and what brings us hope?

---

4   Commonly attributed to Alan Paton.

(2) In the future, what kind of South Africa do we want to be living in?

(3) How far away are we from this vision of the future, and why is this so?

Recognises the effects of past injustice on the present

South Africans remain somewhat divided about what should be done to address the past. Our experience of change since democracy in 1994 has been different depending on where we were located during Apartheid. We also have different sources of information about the past and about present realities, based on what we read or who we talk to, and that frequently distorts our vision. This is especially true when it comes to issues of corruption and inefficiencies in our current government; many use these failures in government to excuse themselves from involvement in nation building. Furthermore, we are divided about seeing the past as an explanation for our current situation, and for using it as an excuse for not exercising agency in changing our circumstances.

What is in no doubt are the painful ways in which the past remains present in the lives of Black South Africans: through the demeaning and dehumanising effects and experiences of racism; the realisation and consequences of having received an intentionally inferior education, and continually having to 'play catch up'; the lurking sense of inferiority (and assumed superiority by White people) with which Black people still have to contend; senses of alienation; opportunity ceilings in the workplace; and the financial costs incurred through forced removals and subsequent low land values compared to White suburban properties.

White South Africans too are damaged by their involvement in past injustice. From having few friendships across racial divides, to feelings of shame for their complicity and ongoing privilege, to fear and sometimes anger (for many reasons), White South Africans are not unaffected by the past. A third step in social restitution therefore is the need to acknowledge how the past remains present in the lives of South Africans today. These effects need to be made explicit to all involved in a process of social restitution, along with ensuring that everyone understands why we need to look back before we are able to simply move on and forget the past. A third meeting of the group to consider social restitution (Step 3: *Talk about the effects of past injustice on the present*) might discuss questions such as:

(1) How has each of us been affected by South Africa's past history of injustice?
(2) In what ways does the past still affect you today?
(3) Why is remembering the past important?

Incorporates a broad understanding of restitution

Conventional restitution consists of a legally binding court order that compensates people for what was lost, returns rights, and ensures no one benefits unjustly from the past. Sometimes legal restitution also seeks to rehabilitate perpetrators. After conflict, these programmes of restitution are frequently enacted by transitional or new governments. A broader understanding of restitution talks about restitution as a project for the future rather than punishment for the past, and places emphasis on it being both a voluntary act and a moral obligation for individuals and groups of people.

By using the two analogies of the soccer game and the stolen bicycle, which reflect the possibilities of what needs to be done after injustice has occurred, the discussion of restitution can be better understood. People in this study came to understand social restitution as acts carried out towards making things good again when restoring them is out of reach; and that possible contributions to be made by individuals and groups consisted of both symbolic acts aimed at remembering and helping us all to become human, as well as actions leading to financial and material redress. Therefore, a further criterion for social restitution is a broader understanding of restitution, one that firmly gives individuals and groups a critical role to perform, defines its aims in terms of moral obligation and social solidarity or connectedness, and openly discusses what keeps people from pursuing restitution, including leaving it to government, denying responsibility, just wanting to move on, or fearing a loss of wealth. A fourth group meeting (Step 4: *Discuss the meaning of restitution and its potential*) could discuss the following questions:

(1) What does the term 'restitution' mean to you?
(2) How do you respond to the two analogies of a stolen bicycle and an unlevel soccer field that try to describe what has happened in South Africa?
(3) What kind of things still need to be done to make restitution for the past?

Understands the difference between charity and restitution

Related to the necessity for a dialogue about what action is restitutionary in nature, is the criterion regarding the difference between charity and restitution. Charity remains a noble action, and is necessary in South Africa. However, distinguishing social restitution as a moral obligation in the light of actions for which one is culpable, whether directly or indirectly through generational benefit and privilege, is critical. Here again, Biko helps us to understand:

> The native is so starved for anything, anything at all that will turn him into a human being, any bone of humanity flung to him, that his hunger is incoercible, and these poor scraps of charity may, here and there, overwhelm him. His consciousness is so precarious and dim that it is affected by the slightest spark of kindliness.[5]

So while this is certainly no longer the case in South Africa in 2016, we need to guard against any remaining vestiges of it. We also need to ensure that we don't land in a situation where White people 'educate' Black people about how they should resist 'White charity' and only accept White restitution. What is necessary, as a further criterion for social restitution, is that those on the receiving end of restitution understand the act for what it is: not charity that originates out of empathy and largesse, the obligation of those who have, but the moral obligation of those who have perpetrated injustice or have unduly benefited from injustice.

In the words of US political commentator Bill Moyers, 'Charity provides crumbs from the table, justice offers a place at the table'; and those of an Aboriginal activist group from Queensland, Australia, 'If you have come here to help me [charity], you are wasting our time. But if you have come because your liberation is bound up with mine, then let us work together [restitution]'.[6] Furthermore, at its starkest, social restitution is 'gain-stripping', rehabilitating the perpetrator, and rehumanising both parties – something that charity never does. Restitution aims to leave people's dignity intact; it must not change their character from

---

5   Frantz Fanon (1963) *The wretched of the earth.* New York, NY: Grove Press, p. 140.
6   The speech as given by Lilla Watson in 1985 to the United Nations Decade for Women Conference in Nairobi, Kenya.

active 'struggle hero' to 'subjugated', as Moeletsi Mbeki[7] argues many actions of redress do. Social restitution must explicitly distinguish between what is an act of charity and what is an act of restitution. The next group dialogue (Step 5: *Discuss the difference between charity and restitution*) might ask the following questions in order to cover this fifth requirement of social restitution:

(1) What is the difference between charity and restitution, and why is this difference important?
(2) What examples of restitution could we as a group consider doing?
(3) How are these actions different to charity?

Locates all participants in the conversation about injustice

It is important for everyone to be able to locate themselves in a conversation about injustice. Doing so offers an opportunity to reflect, not only on how the past has affected us but on the extent of our moral obligation to mitigate its effects. These roles become increasingly complicated as time passes, and those who were directly involved in conflict are replaced with children who now experience the consequences of oppression or privilege resulting from the injustice. The conventional triangle of perpetrator-victim-bystander is inadequate for engaging people across multiple generations about the past, especially when both Black and White South Africans are so eager to forget and move on.

A more complex pentangle helps us to locate ourselves better. These five locations, with richer descriptions of each location, help us to overcome simple binaries of blame and benefit based only on race. The labels used are victim (dishonoured, harmed); perpetrator (architect, implementer); resister (architect, implementer); bystander (ostrich, silent, avoider); and beneficiary (of privilege, of redress, of resistance). In the context of a country such as South Africa, which is still deeply divided along racial lines corresponding to the legacy of Apartheid, this approach allows individuals to locate themselves without alienating themselves from a national process of healing.

This sixth criterion for social restitution therefore requires that each participant locate themselves in the past, often straddling various locations, in order to grow in their understanding of what their moral duty now is. A group meeting

---

7 Moeletsi Mbeki (2009) *Architects of poverty: Why African capitalism needs changing.* Johannesburg, South Africa: Picador Africa.

for the sixth time (Step 6: *Locate all participants in the conversation about injustice*) might conduct the 'labels' activity (see Figure 7.1) and discuss the questions that follow:

(1) How would you label yourself with regard to the past?
(2) How is this exercise helpful or unhelpful, and which labels are easy or difficult to talk about?
(3) How should the role of people calling themselves victims, perpetrators, bystanders, resisters and beneficiaries differ in restitution?
(4) How should Black and White South Africans' roles in restitution differ?

Aims to restore personhood

Our sense of humanity or personhood, rooted in the African ethic of *ubuntu*, is an inherently social concept. We make each other human in the way we treat one another. Clearly, in South Africa's history, the way we have treated each other, and the way we resisted this treatment, has damaged our humanity. We live with the consequences in multiple ways. Social restitution has the potential to restore our humanity and should be done in solidarity with others for *all* our benefit. Strategies for restoring personhood comprise remembering past injustices, working towards restoring human dignity, fostering active senses of belonging (including citizenship and equality), and implementing projects to bring about material and psychological flourishing, including the ability to take advantage of opportunities for work and wealth creation or wealth redistribution. In fact, it has been shown that in societies where ideas of personhood are seen to be connected and collective, efforts at redistributing wealth are greater.[8]

A seventh criterion for social restitution ensures that the action we have in mind addresses this collective understanding of what it means to be human, remembers how the past has impacted on the current state of our humanity,

---

[8] James Ferguson (2015) *Give a man a fish: Reflections on the new politics of distribution.* Durham, NC: Duke University Press; Wolfgang Merkel (2009) Towards a renewed concept of social justice. In O Cramme and P Diamond (eds) *Social justice in the Global Age.* Cambridge, UK: Cambridge University Press.

and contributes to rehumanising each other – through providing new opportunities for dignity, belonging and redistributing wealth. In dialogue groups meeting for the seventh time (Step 7: *Discuss ideas for action to restore our damaged humanity*), questions for discussion begin to take on a more practical nature and ask:

(1) What acts of restitution could we implement in each of the areas of remembering, restoring dignity, offering opportunity, and fostering belonging?

(2) What are our practical plans for each of these actions?

(3) What happens if we can't agree on what must be done?

Discusses multiple ideas for practical action

People have many ideas for how individuals and groups might engage in social restitution, either alongside government programmes of job creation, service delivery and wealth redistribution or as purely civil society-led initiatives. These ideas include small- and large-scale actions: mentoring, building friendships across racial divides, learning an indigenous language, sharing inheritances, challenging single stories of doom and gloom about South Africa, taking salary increase holidays, engaging in dialogue about the past, or starting a national programme of community service for school leavers across social boundaries. While some have been tried elsewhere and have failed dismally, it is the creativity of everyday people that is to be applauded. Imagine how much more could be done, in terms of generating ideas, if people took time to meet together intentionally to have these kinds of discussions.

If a myriad of ideas are generated in dialogue with people different to us, and discussed and debated, we as South Africans could certainly address the socioeconomic and symbolic restitution needed to become the country we envision. In the eighth meeting of a group talking about social restitution (Step 8: *Make a plan for implementing and evaluating your ideas*), the following questions could be asked in order to ensure the implementation of restitution plans:

(1) How are we going to implement our plans, and by when?

(2) How will we know when we have reached our goals for restitution, in this group, in South Africa?

(3) Do we need to take a break in meeting to talk until we have
    done something concrete in terms of social restitution?
(4) When will we next meet?

Embraces the attitudes necessary for an emancipatory project

This book has tried to show that it is not only the acts of restitution that matter
but also the goals we envisage, and the manner in which, or attitudes with
which, we go about achieving them. A number of important attitudes have
emerged: *openness to seeing* and being persuaded by people's stories, rather
than committed to our own perspectives, is one. This is especially clear when
it comes to the 'bootstrapping' and meritocracy arguments – that people don't
need handouts, they need to work for what they get. I hope people's stories
of tenacity against great odds have dispelled these myths. The human virtue
of *grace* (or generosity) is a second attitude needed from all involved: from
those to whom restitution is extended, no matter how clumsy the effort, or
how frequently the dialogue collapses before it is translated into action, as well
as for those who see more clearly than others, those who regress to distorted
ways of seeing or who refuse to see at all. It is only through grace that we have
any chance of White South Africans coming to see, and through grace that
we can ask for ever more patience from Black South Africans for our faltering
efforts. *Humility* is another attitude of restitution: one that is needed if we are
ever to be able to ask for help in our efforts at restitution, if we are ever to truly
hear from those to whom we are offering it, and if our apologies and remorse
are ever going to ring true.

So much has already been asked of Black South Africans, and so to ask
for grace is no small request. As early as 1984, Desmond Tutu was calling
upon Black people all over the world to 'Be nice to Whites, they need you to
rediscover their humanity.'[9] This still applies. On the other hand, so little has
been asked of White South Africans that a request for humility and openness
to new ways of seeing should be no big thing. The ninth criterion for critical
active social restitution is thus to ensure that the attitudes of grace, humility
and openness accompany the journey. Each has an important role to play in

---

9   Flora Lewis, Foreign Affairs; honoring the Peace Crusade, *New York Times*,
     19 October 1984.

making good. In meeting for the ninth time (Step 9: *Discuss attitudes needed for restitution and obstacles that might arise*), dialogue groups might ask the following questions about attitudes for, and obstacles to restitution, as well as begin to record their own lessons for the process of social restitution:

(1) What attitudes do we need to have, and work on in this group, in order to make progress in restitution?

(2) What gets in the way of people making restitution?

(3) What lessons are we learning so far when it comes to restitution?

Includes strategies for overcoming inaction

If social restitution depends on knowing about past injustice, seeing its effects, feeling or experiencing responsibility or pain as a result, knowing what to do, then this book has addressed these components in great detail. It has made arguments for new ways of seeing, has countered objections to meritocracy and corruption, and made it difficult to shift blame to past generations alone. Instead, it has provided practical, everyday ideas for action that can be taken, and has offered ten steps for implementing and evaluating our efforts. However, there is no substitute for learning as you do.

Consequently, becoming part of a small, diverse community with which you begin a journey of social restitution is the best way to overcome inaction, or for failing to act on good intentions. These groups could be at school or in a partnership between two schools to ensure diversity; it could be on a university campus, in your workplace, in your mosque or church, in a local NGO, or at a club: golf, soccer, tennis, book, supper, gym or wine club – again possibly in partnership between two clubs to ensure diversity. The key is a diverse group, time for reflective discussion and action over at least 10 weeks, and with openness to a longer engagement, if that's what emerges from the process. A professional facilitator is not needed, merely a list of questions (see Appendix 3 for a week-by-week guide), and a willingness to listen and speak as appropriate. These questions have the potential to begin a conversation about issues that are not often discussed in South Africa, and it is unlikely that you will run out of things to talk about in two hours. These 10 criteria, or steps for critical active social restitution, therefore include a built-in strategy for overcoming inaction: an intentional step by step process. The first step is to decide to do *something* about this hard, noisy, restless word 'restitution'. In the final meeting of your *10–10–10 Restitution Dialogue* group (Step 10: *Make plans for an ongoing project*) it will be time to tell some new stories about ways in which you have managed to carry out restitution and to plan for what should come next:

(1) What new stories can we begin to tell about restitution in South Africa?

(2) How do we want to continue after this meeting?

Conclusion

In this book, I have described the notion of social restitution that has emerged during the course of this study. After considerable reflection, I have suggested acts and attitudes of individuals and groups that could be implemented towards making good in spaces where injustice has occurred, based on principles of community solidarity, dignity, dialogue and understanding the past in order to restore all our humanity. These actions may take the form of small symbolic deeds done with humility, and received with grace, along with large-scale projects that address the material needs of Black South Africans, as an act of restitution rather than as welfare or charity.

In short and simple terms, my theory of change has been Know-See-Feel-Locate-Act: that knowing about injustice and its effects, seeing or experiencing it first hand, feeling what it might be like to be in such a situation, and recognising your own role in the injustice is enough to cause people to act (or at least desire to act) against injustice. To help in this final step it is important that people have groups in which to talk about their actions, and to hold them accountable to implement principled actions, come up with good practical ideas on which to act, and to motivate them to overcome inaction, or to persevere in the face of fatigue. I am aware that such a framework omits other serious questions, such as the gap between knowing and acting, between values and behaviour, between intention and agency,[10] and that this gap is widened by the absence of structural scaffolds on, through and around

---

10 Augusto Blasi (1980) Bridging moral cognition and moral action: A critical review of the literature. *Psychological Bulletin* 88(1): 1–45.

which action might occur.[11] What stands between recognition and restitution? How is it that some recognise injustice, yet remain disengaged, passive and immobilised? What drives those who act to do so? How far does new language and new concepts go to bridging this gap? These are all questions that will need further investigation.

The one thing that I hope this book has made clear, both from people's stories of how the past affects the present and their many ideas for how this can be changed, is how little it would take to change the future. The ideas listed in Chapter 9 show this. Ideas such as writing children's stories about the past; offering time, skills and money to local community organisations; talking about the past in groups across social boundaries and developing these diverse relationships; paying generous wages to domestic workers; cultivating respect in the workplace; interrupting the transgenerational inheritance of poverty through sharing your children's inheritances or not accepting your parents' bequests; paying education fees; mentoring young people across divides and setting up cross-cultural community service programmes for school leavers; volunteering time to local municipalities and looking after your own neighbourhood; rebutting media perceptions; and improving dinner party conversations focused on single stories about our country going to the dogs. These are just some of many examples.

These ideas of social restitution offer a refreshing opportunity and reflective possibilities for dialogue and a more relational interaction between those dishonoured by injustice and those complicit in it. In this way the issue of restitution should not leave us angry or jubilant depending on where we are located in relation to the past. Instead, it has the potential to show how we all have a role to play in building the future we want for ourselves and our children across the divisions of the past. We need to remember that Black South Africans have always asked for so little, and have always been willing to welcome White South Africans' least efforts. In researching and writing this book the same has been true. Black South Africans were always more eager to ask the government to fix the things that others had broken, or they

---

11 Zvi Bekerman and Michalinos Zembylas (2010) Fearful symmetry: Palestinian and Jewish teachers confront contested narratives in integrated bilingual education. *Teaching and Teacher Education* 26(3): 507–515.

have made suggestions about how they themselves could fix the past instead of asking for wholesale redistribution of wealth. This is the opposite of the accusations of 'entitlement' bandied about at White dinner parties. So this book is ultimately an invitation to Black and White South Africans to make another effort at making things good, so that we can see another country in each other's eyes; eyes filled with the dignity of equality, the hope of opportunity and the calmness of belonging – fully human again.

Appendix 1
Methods and theories: Some scholarly notes

In order to ensure that the book is not cluttered with too much detail, I here set out some of the methodological details and choices I have made, as well as the theories that have guided and shaped my thinking and analysis. These theories I set out systematically and show how they are interwoven and how they helped me to arrive at some of the ideas and recommendations I make in the book. I also offer some ideas for a future agenda in which social restitution might apply in different contexts and to other forms of injustice. The methodology section offers greater insight into who was interviewed, why they were chosen, some ethical reflections on interviewing people known to researchers, and how research can be a transformative process.

Whose stories am I telling and how?

The stories, comments and views that are accounted for in this book come from a range of South Africans. Table A1.1 summarises these basic characteristics of the group of people interviewed. The sample was made up of 60 people: 34 female and 26 male. Each was interviewed for just over an hour – the shortest interview was 35 minutes, the longest two hours.

According to Apartheid's racial categories, 26 were White, 27 were Black and 7 were Coloured. The youngest was 21 and the oldest 80. When I speak about respondent ages I called them 'young' if they were between 21 and 25, 'middle' if they were between 26 and 35, 'older middle' if they were between 36 and 49 (although I frequently collapse the latter two categories into 'middle generations'), and 'older' if they were 50 and over. Half were from the Western Cape, a quarter from the Eastern Cape and the other quarter from Gauteng, KwaZulu-Natal and Free State.

In general, those who agreed to being interviewed were well known to researchers. I conducted two-thirds of the interviews myself and was helped by three young research assistants who had themselves been interviewed

Table A1.1 *Characteristics of the group of people interviewed*

Category	Description	No. of people
Race	Black	27
	Coloured	7
	White	26
Sex	Female	34
	Male	26
Age	21–25 ('Young')	12
	26–35 ('Middle')	21
	36–49 ('Older middle')	17
	Over 50 ('Older')	10
Education	Secondary or less	29
	Tertiary	31
Occupation	Unemployed	2
	Employed unskilled	4
	Employed general	26
	Employed professional	18
	Student	10
Property	Township – house or shack	13
	Suburban – rented	23
	Suburban – owned	19
	Suburban – multiple properties owned	5
Last election	Voted	48
	Did not vote	12
Religious attendance	Never or rarely	19
	Weekly	16
	Monthly	25
Geography	Western Cape	30
	Eastern Cape	15
	Gauteng	11
	KwaZulu-Natal	3
	Free State	1

by me. Respondents fell into various socio-economic groups according to their education, place of residence (suburbs/townships/rural) and property ownership. In terms of education, there was an even split between those with university education and those with only high school education. From the point of view of political engagement, nearly three-quarters of participants had voted in the most recent national elections. Of the 48 who had voted, there was an even spread of those who had voted for the DA, the ANC and the EFF. Although the interviews took place between May and August 2014, it took me until April 2016 to complete the book.

A social constructivist research approach

On a technical note, the study adopts a *social constructivist* approach[1] to knowledge production in which knowledge is assembled between researcher and participants; knowledge is neither *mine*, nor *theirs* but *ours*. In the course of the interviews, we discussed various topics according to prepared questions (see Table A1.2), although the conversation was allowed to flow freely. Time was allowed for participants to think, ponder, return to initial answers and revise what was said.

Table A1.2 *Questions asked of people interviewed*

What are the things in our country that bring you hope/despair?
How were you/are you affected by our country's past history?
In what ways does the past still affect people today?
What does the term 'restitution' mean to you?
How do you respond to these two stories (soccer field story and bicycle story)?
How would you label yourself with regards to the past?
What has been done so far to make things right?
How will we know when we've done enough?
What gets in the way of people making restitution?
What do you think will happen if nothing more is done
What ideas do you have for making things right?

---

[1] For a full description, see Peter Berger and Thomas Luckmann (1966) *The social construction of reality: A treatise in the sociology of knowledge.* Garden City, NY: Doubleday.

All interviews were coded by theme and compared to see whether people of varying ages answered in similar or different ways, and whether answers could be grouped by sex, race or level of education. However, the study was qualitative and so while these results cannot be said to represent the views of all South Africans, they do provide a range of views from *different kinds* of South Africans. All names I use in this book are pseudonyms chosen by the respondent. Throughout the book, when a person's name first appears in a chapter, I include their biographical markers (age, race, sex and occupation). Appendix 2 provides a summary of all participants for ease of reference.

Research as intervention

The tradition of emancipatory research[2] is one that seeks to empower the subjects of social inquiry – in this case those who had been dishonoured by Apartheid injustices. It also seeks to persuade or motivate those who are in a position to act on injustice. In the case of this study, my aim was to elicit people's understandings of the effects of the past on the present, and in so doing to help them come to recognise these effects. A further aim was also to invite them to locate themselves with regard to past or current injustices, and to elicit their responses on the subject of 'restitution'. Such an approach is of course deeply political, and one about which I am happy to be transparent. This study is not basic research in which a general question of 'what should be done about the past?' is asked. Instead, my approach is what is increasingly becoming known as 'research as intervention',[3] inquiry that ultimately seeks to offer a framework for education and to guide just action out of its methods of inquiry, as well as through its findings.

In this study, through hour-long conversations (or dialogical interviews[4]), I aimed to shift participants' viewpoints through carefully guided questions, which nonetheless offered them the option not to see and not to be persuaded

---

2   K Lynch (1999) Equality studies, the academy and the role of research in emancipatory social change. *The Economic and Social Review* 30(1): 41–69.

3   Sheila McNamee (1988) Accepting research as social intervention: Implications of a systemic epistemology. *Communication Quarterly* 36(1): 50–68.

4   Franziska Trede, Joy Higgs, and Rodd Rothwell (2009) Critical transformative dialogues: A research method beyond the fusions of horizons. *FQS Forum: Qualitiave Social Research* 10(1), Article 6.

about the need for restitution. The response was much better than I had expected. Most people had not had a conversation about restitution in the South African context; those who knew something of it had generally associated it with government programmes of land restitution, rather than something for individuals and groups to embark upon. Immediately following the interview, and frequently long after in many cases, the conversation continued and expanded.

Heather told me about the ongoing conversation it had started with her father, who I had also interviewed; Cara about ongoing conversations with her parents. I had new conversations with my parents who had also been interview participants. Dylan playfully said at the conclusion of our interview, 'Well if anybody asks me what the word restitution means now, I can tell them, in spades!' Similarly, having Cara, Rebecca, Donovan, Jack, Luke, Sandy, Ted and Peter all come to some new realisation about restitution in South Africa, and what might still be needed, were very gratifying outcomes.

From an educational perspective, this book in general, and the discussion questions in particular, stand in the tradition of Anti-Racist Education which can be described as a 'framework for action … attempting to create a more just world through appropriate standards of behavior and a commitment to activism. … [It comprises a] coherent program for social change, involving the transformation of how the public understands race relations.'[5] A key to anti-racist education is to show 'the economic, structural and historic roots of inequality'[6] and how racism is an organising principle behind 'class and other forms of discrimination that deny human rights.'[7]

Ethical reflections on interviewing intimates

While time and space does not allow for a full ethical reflection of the implications of interviewing people I knew quite well, or my research assistants

---

5 Jack Niemonen (2007) Antiracist education in theory and practice: A critical assessment. *The American Sociologist* 38(2): 167.

6 Paula Morelli and Michael Spencer. (2000) Use and support of multicultural and antiracist education: Research-informed interdisciplinary social work practice. *Social work* 45(2): 168.

7 Morelli and Spencer (2000), p. 168.

knew well, a few notes will be of interest to a scholarly audience. I intentionally sought out people I knew, whose views I thought would be interesting and somewhat diverse, and whose back stories I knew: friends, family members, colleagues from work, students I had taught, and research respondents from my doctoral study with whom I had maintained contact. Knowing people's back stories made it possible for me not to ask long rapport-building questions or detailed biographical questions, although I did ensure each participant completed a brief biographical survey. I also alerted prospective respondents about why I was choosing them, and made sure that they still understood they had the right not to answer questions or to discontinue at any time. I had my research assistants do the same with those they interviewed: to choose people they knew and ensure the same ethical 'outs' were made clear. Of course, because they were 'intimates' people often said yes without a full consideration of the discomfort that might ensue, or said yes to us when they might have refused others. They were also more likely to have been more candid than they might have been with a stranger.

A second outcome of intimate interviewing was the additional caution I have exercised conducting 'member checks'. I did so, not to seek approval for what I wrote about what people told me but, because I know these 'intimates' will be far more easily identifiable, certainly amongst those who know them, and because many know each other. This anonymity remained only thinly veiled despite using pseudonyms, changing some people's job titles, and always providing generic rather than specific names for townships and suburbs. What I aimed at was protecting participants from was unintentionally disclosing hurtful or unwelcome information to a loved one.

For example, when Olivia tells me about how Apartheid had 'belittled' her father and as a result, they grew up with a 'frustrated father' I asked her whether her father knew this. She told me he didn't, but that she would have that conversation with him before he read this book. I didn't want Ted to read for the first time in this book of his son's disappointment, or surprise at his parents' lack of 'anti-Apartheid activism' especially given Ted's self-understanding of what it was he did to oppose Apartheid. Or Sibu's feeling about being judged, even by members of her multi-racial church. I was also concerned that Heather may have been offended by my comment about why she needed *help* to know how to share her inheritance; and that my relationship with Graham would be spoiled by the way I critiqued his responses. These member checks are probably something all researchers should do; often it falls by the wayside because there is no ongoing relationship between researcher and respondent.

A third feature of the kind of interviewing I employed in this study – both its dialogical nature and the intimacy of the relationships I shared with participants – is the ongoing conversations it provoked. It has been difficult to maintain anonymity, and I have had to be intentionally cautious about it at every turn. In many case, I am extremely gratified by people's points of view, or change of heart, or the discovery that no one is ever only one thing – never only racist or only blinded, or even only a social justice warrior. Instead, people have weaknesses, and doubts, and may show enormous compassion on one occasion, and extreme callousness on another. These interviews have opened up dialogue – and there is no reason to believe they won't do the same outside of a research context. My interview with my parents – with whom I have seldom had a serious political conversation except to reprimand them for their racism – is a case in point. I have come to appreciate their views, ambivalence, and historical understandings for the first time. Our subsequent conversations have now taken on a different tone; not completely different, but nonetheless improved.

The theoretical ideas I have drawn on

I have tried to make it clear throughout the book, from where my ideas originate. Here, however, I draw them together and show how each has contributed towards the notion of social restitution. It also serves as a pointer to further reading.

Reconceptualising restitution

Historian Eleazar Barkan[8] set me on a course that helped me to reconceptualise restitution, from a narrow technical concept focused on legal remedies to

---

8 Elazar Barkan (2000a) *The guilt of nations: Restitution and negotiating historical injustices.* London, UK: Johns Hopkins University Press; Elazar Barkan (2000b) Restitution and amending historical injustices in international morality. Claremont: European Union Center of California; Elazar Barkan and Alexander Karn (2006) *Taking wrongs seriously: Apologies and reconciliation.* Stanford, CA: Stanford University Press.

a broader understanding of restitution as a moral pursuit. His views on historical dialogues operating at the level of large-scale conflict are also useful for dialogues about everyday action at community level. Similarly, Todd Calder's and others'[9] distinction between backward- and forward-looking restitution has also been formative. Social restitution is not meant to punish or to send people on a guilt trip. Its purpose is to contribute to a just and thriving country. Discovering the two German words[10] translated as 'restitution': *wiedergutmachung* (making-good-again) and *wiederherstellen* (restoring to as things were, 'making right') further contributed to a renewed understanding of restitution. The goal of social restitution is to make good again – an attainable aim, rather than making right – a near impossibility.

I've also grappled with the relationship between social restitution and structural restitution, and have come to see that they are not directly comparable. The aim of all restitution is structural justice: that is, change permanently embedded in the institutions, laws, practices and circumstances of people's lives, although en route to achieving this state of affairs there may be small wins and local gains. Social restitution relates to *who* does the restitution – individuals and groups of people in civil society and local communities, rather than as programmes of legislated or government-led action. Furthermore, social restitution, by its very nature, is able to focus on both material and symbolic action, and arguably addresses wider aspects of personhood, than is possible in legislation. The results of social restitution may be small, local and experiential but together may have an impact on structural change. Table A1.3 sums up the difference between legal and social restitution as far as I see it.

---

9   William Booth (1999) Communities of memory: On identity, memory, and debt. *American Political Science Review* 93(2): 249–263; Todd Calder (2010) Shared responsibility, global structural injustice, and restitution. *Social Theory & Practice* 36(2): 263–290; Leif Wenar (2006) Reparations for the future. *Journal of Social Philosophy* 37(3): 396–405; Iris Marion Young (2006) Responsibility and global justice: A social connection model. *Social Philosophy and Policy* 23(1): 102–130.

10 Tony Judt (2005) *Postwar: A history of Europe since 1945.* New York, NY: Penguin; Mark Sanders (2007) *Ambiguities of witnessing: Law and literature in the time of a truth commission.* Stanford, CA: Stanford University Press.

Table A1.3 *Comparing social and legal restitution*

	Legal restitution	Social restitution
Basis	Liability	Responsibility
Ultimate aim	Structural change and justice	Structural change and justice
Outcomes	• Restoring to its original condition ('making right') • Compensating or making reparations, satisfying the injured party – whether symbolically or materially • Stripping the perpetrator of unjust benefit • Returning civil, political and property rights • Rehabilitating offenders	• Making good • Restoring personhood, dignity, opportunity, belonging and memory • Redistribution • Representation • Recognition; helping people see
Teleology	Backward-looking; sometimes forward-looking	Forward-looking
Actors	Government/institutions and individuals	Individual and communities
Nature of action	Compulsory	Voluntary
Ideology	Legal obligation	Moral obligation
Temporality	Time bound, sometimes across generations	Across generations
Decided by	Court arbiter	Those who have been wronged in dialogue with perpetrators and beneficiaries

Critical consciousness

Critical consciousness is itself derived from various traditions. I have paid particular attention to Paolo Freire's[11] understanding of critical consciousness as well as the approach advocated by the Black Consciousness Movement. Both argue that those most affected by injustice are able to see the basis of their oppression and must be afforded opportunities to be agents in disrupting it, as Steve Biko writes:

---

11 Paulo Freire (1972) *Pedagogy of the oppressed*. Harmondsworth, UK: Penguin; Paulo Freire (2005) *Education for critical consciousness*. London, UK: Continuum.

The first step therefore is to make the Black man come to himself ... to infuse him with pride and dignity, to remind him of his complicity in the crime of allowing himself to be misused and therefore letting evil reign supreme in the country of his birth. This is what we mean by an inward-looking process. This is the definition of 'Black Consciousness'.[12]

***

What Black Consciousness seeks to do is to produce at the output end of the process real Black people who do not regard themselves as appendages to White society.[13]

The work of German philosopher Jürgen Habermas[14] draws attention to the need for critical self-awareness of all parties involved in transformation. He also suggests that understanding motives and intentions in processes of transformation are important factors to succeeding in justice projects. Critical Race Theory[15] foregrounds the role that power structures maintain in conditions of racial injustice. CRT's analysis has been especially important in making explicit the invisible assumptions of White superiority that almost always disrupt justice projects.

Recognising injustice and symbolic violence

The outcome of such critical consciousness is a *recognition* of injustice,[16] including how it is held in place, and what must be done to dismantle it.

---

12 Steve Biko and Aelred Stubbs (1978) *I write what I like.* London, UK: Bowerdean Press, p. 29.
13 Biko and Stubbs (1978), p. 51.
14 Steve Biko (1977) *Black consciousness and the quest for a true humanity.* London, UK: The Christian Institute Trustees; Jürgen Habermas (1971) *Knowledge and human interests.* Boston, MA: Beacon Press; Jürgen Habermas (1990) *Moral consciousness and communicative action.* Cambridge, MA: MIT Press.
15 Edward Taylor (1998) A primer on critical race theory. *The Journal of Blacks in Higher Education* 19: 123.
16 Nancy Fraser (1998) Social justice in the age of identity politics: Redistribution, recognition, participation. *Social Science Research Center Berlin,* Accessed 11 August 2011 from http://ideas.repec.org/p/zbw/wzboem/fsi98108.html.

Here the work of Nancy Fraser shaped many of my conclusions about dignity and symbolic restitution; how recognition of the dignity of a person and the injustice she faces is as important as the redistribution of resources, although both are necessary, 'neither alone is sufficient.'[17] For Fraser:

> The distribution of material resources must be such as to ensure participants' independence and 'voice' … [while] patterns of interpretation and evaluation express equal respect for all participants and ensure equal opportunity for achieving social esteem.'[18]

> ***

> Only by looking to integrative approaches that unite redistribution and recognition can we meet the requirements of justice for all.'[19]

Giving people the recognition they deserve and recognising injustice is not a simple task. In this study, some refused to see, others saw clearly, yet others saw in distorted ways. Recognition remains a task in itself. Furthermore, this failure to see occurred with both Black and White participants. While this is unsurprising for White participants who have been sheltered, and whose material circumstances do not force introspection or critical evaluation, it is surprising for Black respondents. Here Biko's talk of 'remind[ing the Black man] … of his complicity in the crime of allowing himself to be misused' resonates with Pierre Bourdieu's notion of symbolic violence.

Bourdieu argues that 'symbolic violence, to put it as tersely and simply as possible, is the violence which is exercised upon a social agent with his or her complicity.'[20] Bourdieu's idea of symbolic violence shows how ways of thinking and acting are internalised by groups and social classes frequently resulting in self-blame for failure to achieve or to expect justice. Symbolic violence does 'what political and police violence can do, but more efficiently'[21] without raising a fist or firing a weapon.

---

[17] Fraser (1998), p. 1.
[18] Fraser (1998), p. 5.
[19] Fraser (1998), p. 9.
[20] Pierre Bourdieu and Loïc J. D. Wacquant (1992) *An invitation to reflexive sociology.* Chicago, IL: University of Chicago Press, p. 167.
[21] Bourdieu and Wacquant (1992), p. 166.

Mayaya (Black woman, 34, business executive) and Vukani (Black man, 34, finance executive) sum up viscerally the outworking of such symbolic violence:

> **Mayaya:** Black people understand that there are levels to life and they've stuck themselves right there in the bottom. Everyone that they know in Cape Town is low and everyone that is White or a different race to them there is high. So this is just how life is. Black is not great or good enough, White is the best.

> **Vukani:** The past affects our society. Psychologically we still, as a collective, are subject to that suppression that we were under previously. The sad thing is that we believe it of ourselves ... Some might say the reason the ANC government hasn't done as much to uplift Black people is because they still believe Blacks are worth less than any other racial group in the country. So I think that's the biggest impact that it had on us is our belief in ourselves.

According to Biko, the project of self-emancipation from symbolic violence is one for Black people to work out for themselves. However, there are other ways in which connection and social solidarity can contribute to emancipation.

Connection and social solidarity

For Iris Marion Young[22] social connection has two arms. The first is that injustice in the past is continuous with injustice in the present. Even though initial actors may no longer be around, the effect of the injustice remains along with the unjust gains or privileges conferred on subsequent generations. We are thus socially connected to structural injustice by virtue of our 'cooperation' with 'rules and accepted norms'. Young puts it bluntly:

> Structural injustice occurs as a consequence of many individuals and institutions acting in pursuit of their particular goals and interests ... they are part of the process that causes them.[23]

The second arm is that of social solidarity, where anyone who considers themselves 'a moral agent' accepts a responsibility, an obligation even 'to

---

[22] Iris Marion Young (2003) From guilt to solidarity. *Dissent* 50(2): 39–44; Young (2006).

[23] Young (2006), p. 114.

minimize suffering everywhere, right up to the point where he or she begins to suffer.'[24] Furthermore,

> Persons who benefit relatively from structural injustices have special moral responsibilities to contribute to organized efforts to correct them, not because they are to blame, but because they are able to adapt to changed circumstances without suffering serious deprivation.'[25]

None has said it more clearly than Young: to have benefited from injustices obligates you to correct them.

Disrupting unearned privilege

Young's view on being able 'to adapt to changed circumstances without suffering serious deprivation' is another way to define unearned privilege,[26] specifically 'White privilege' – the concept popularised by Peggy McIntosh. McIntosh's work describes how she came to realise her own 'invisible knapsack' of privilege conferred only by virtue of her Whiteness in relation to the absence of privilege experienced by her Black colleagues in a woman's studies department at a US college. The privilege was invisible precisely because it was unexamined and taken for granted by all. Once examined, and made explicit, we then become morally accountable for it: 'to act both to minimize it personally and transform the social structures that keep it in place.'[27] In post-Apartheid South Africa, 'the overwhelming majority of White South Africans continue to benefit from inherited privileges, while the majority of Black South Africans continue to suffer within Apartheid-created cycles of poverty and oppression.'[28]

---

[24] Young (2006), p. 104.

[25] Young (2006), p. 128.

[26] Peggy McIntosh (1992) White privilege and male privilege: A personal account of coming to see: Correspondences through work in women's studies. In Margeret L. Andersen and Patricia Hill Collins (eds) *Race, class and gender: An anthology.* Belmont, CA: Wadsworth Publishing Company.

[27] Sharlene Swartz, Emma Arogundade, and Danya Davis (2014) Unpacking (white) privilege in a South African university classroom: A neglected element in multicultural educational contexts. *Journal of Moral Education* 43(3): 348.

[28] Swartz et al. (2014), p. 349.

Locating actors

The task of determining who was privileged and who oppressed is relatively easy in the midst of, or soon after, a conflict or injustice has occurred; but more difficult as time passes. For this reason I read a number of texts that located actors, none more thoroughly and influentially than historian and political scientist Raul Hilberg.[29] His victim-perpetrator-bystander triangle of actors was meticulously described in the context of the Holocaust. It proved insufficient for a complex location of actors across generations, including those who were not alive at the time of the injustice but who live with its positive benefits or negative repercussions. Hilberg's triangle therefore omits such labels as an inheritor of benefit, while denying those who resisted injustice – which he includes in the victim category. His benchmark of categories proved useful as a means to question both the names he assigns to particular locations and what he omits.

Rehumanising and restoring personhood

Influenced both by Hilberg and Hannah Arendt's[30] account of the evil perpetrated during the Holocaust, I came to ask what it means to be fully human and how injustice dehumanises, resulting in social ills such as violence, crime, addictions, joblessness, educational failure,[31] and psychic ills such as indifference, the normalization of inequality, and the lack of an ability to connect, listen and empathise.[32] Christian Smith,[33] Francis Nyamnjoh[34]

---

29 Raul Hilberg (1992) *Perpetrators victims bystanders: The Jewish catastrophe, 1933–1945*. New York, NY: Aaron Asher Books.
30 Hannah Arendt (1963) *Eichmann in Jerusalem: A report on the banality of evil*. New York, NY: Viking Press.
31 Swartz et al. (2014).
32 Danya Davis and Melissa Steyn (2012) Teaching social justice: Reframing some common pedagogical assumptions. *Perspectives in education* 30(4): 29–38.
33 Christian Smith (2010) *What is a person: Rethinking humanity, social life, and the moral good from the person up*. Chicago, IL: University of Chicago Press.
34 Francis Nyamnjoh (2004) Reconciling 'the rhetoric of rights' with competing notions of personhood and agency in Botswana. In H Englund and F Nyamnjoh (eds) *Rights and the politics of recognition in Africa*. London, UK: Zed Books.

and Kwame Gyekye's[35] understandings of personhood all reflect notions of people as socially connected and interdependent, and of a sense of humanity as emergent and bestowed in relationship with others. The unjust treatment of human beings by each other therefore results in failed humanity and damaged personhood. Frantz Fanon is particularly helpful here. In describing how we may be 'rehumanised'[36] he describes the constituent elements of our humanity: dignity, equality or sovereignty, and wealth ('bread and land'[37]). These three elements map onto Nancy Fraser's notions of recognition (of dignity), representation (political equality and sovereignty) and the redistribution of wealth and esteem. I have termed them dignity, belonging, and opportunity in my conceptualisation of personhood.

Redistribution of capital and public goods

Redistribution concerns physical and material resources, but also less tangible ones. Here Pierre Bourdieu's[38] forms of capital theory is immensely helpful in expanding Fraser and Fanon's call for redistribution as an integral part of social justice. Bourdieu identifies capitals as economic, social, cultural and symbolic. Economic capital is self-explanatory – it is the physical assets, absence of debt and ability to afford education and the costs associated with accessing the labour market that require redistribution in the aftermath of injustice. However, financial capital is only part of what is needed to overcome the societal exclusion engineered by Apartheid South Africa.

The capital required to access public goods is another. These include health care, good nutrition, clean water and sanitation, housing that provides both shelter and dignity, and a quality education. An additional kind of capital is that of symbolic capital; believing oneself to be worthy of entitlements, as opposed to internalising symbolic violence in which the belief is the opposite. Symbolic capital requires being treated respectfully and being repeatedly

---

35 Kwame Gyekye (1984) The Akan Concept of a Person. In R Wright (ed) *African philosophy: An Introduction*. Lanham, MD: University Press of America, pp. 199–211.

36 Frantz Fanon (1963) *The wretched of the earth*. New York, NY: Grove Press.

37 Fanon (1963), p. 44.

38 Pierre Bourdieu (1997) The forms of capital. In A. Halsey, H Lauder, P Brown, et al. (eds) *Education: Culture, economy, and society*. Oxford, UK: Oxford University Press.

afforded value, even prestige, resulting in a sense of self-esteem that causes one to both feel entitled and confidently ask for these public goods. This knowing and understanding 'the rules of the game' that enables access to goods and services, and that frequently translates into social mobility, Bourdieu terms cultural capital. Finally, Bourdieu describes social capital: the resource that brings access to social networks and connections that translate into opportunities for advancement, employment and further realisation of the privileges and rights of political belonging. Social restitution aims to redistribute all these forms of capital.

Overcoming inaction and everyday action

A final theoretical contribution to this notion of social restitution comes from the very visible gap between knowing and acting, between values and behaviour, between intention and agency. Here Augusto Blasi[39] has helped, if not to solve the problem, at least to locate the timber with which the bridge across the divide can be built. Blasi argues that a sense of personal responsibility is the connecting line between a moral identity and moral action. He shows how not only seeing the need for action, but seeing oneself as a moral agent can motivate people to action. Also important is an emotional connection between agent and subject[40] that can further motivate action. Overcoming inaction is further facilitated when there are scaffolds for action, and when the possibilities for action are attainable. Here Philomena Essed's[41] notion of 'everyday racism' and its response as 'everyday antiracism' is helpful. For this reason I have spoken of 'everyday action' as a response to injustice, and of social restitution as the everyday micro-practices of individuals and groups, rather than only the macro practices of institutional efforts at transformation – although these remain crucial.

---

[39] Augusto Blasi (1980) Bridging moral cognition and moral action: A critical review of the literature. *Psychological Bulletin* 88(1): 1–45.

[40] Augusto Blasi (1999) Emotions and moral motivation. *Journal for the Theory of Social Behaviour* 29(1): 1–9.

[41] Philomena Essed (1991) *Understanding everyday racism: An interdisciplinary theory.* Newbury Park, CA: Sage.

Transferring insights

The ideas I present in this book of critical active social restitution are transferable to other contexts in which injustice has occurred: country contexts such as Rwanda, Bosnia, Chile, Romania and Nigeria in which large-scale conflict, colonial oppression and genocide have, or continue to occur, as well as to other areas of justice. So for example, how might individuals and groups of people go about enacting social restitution to children who have been victims of child pornography and who are now adults? What about in the US, where reparations for slavery remains a topic of discussion, and more recently where lethal police violence against young Black men has been highlighted in the news? What of the many ways in which LGBTI persons have been marginalised, excluded, denied civil rights and even killed in countries like Uganda, Iran and India. Might social restitution be possible in communities where gender-based violence is endemic, or are only legislated remedies possible? What of in cases of bullying, unfair labour practices and corruption, might social restitution be possible, desirable and what might the hoped for results be? These are all questions for a further research agenda concerning how social restitution might be transferable.

Appendix 2
Basic information about participants by pseudonym

Table A2.1 *Participant information*

Pseudonym	Race and sex	Age	Work status
Aloz	Black woman	36	Receptionist
Andiswa	Black woman	25	Customer services
Angela	White woman	37	PhD student
Ann	White woman	74	Retired salaries clerk
Candice	Coloured woman	29	Masters student
Cara	White woman	21	Undergraduate student
Chris	White man	34	Chef
Connie	White woman	71	Non-profit administrator
David	White man	43	Doctor
Donovan	Coloured man	30	Retail sales manager
Dylan	White man	34	PhD student
Fundiswa	Black woman	26	Contract cleaner
Gina	White woman	69	Retired retail manager
Graham	White man	29	Retail marketer
Hayley	Coloured woman	42	Priest
Harry	White man	63	Retired business executive
Heather	White woman	38	Faith-based non-profit
Hillary	White woman	21	Undergraduate student
Jack	White man	71	Retired, government administrator
Jane	White woman	21	Undergraduate student
Johan	White man	48	Peace-building non-profit
Lekho	Black woman	26	Government human resources
Leo	White man	46	Non-profit director
Luke	White man	36	Self-employed businessman
Luxolo	Black woman	29	Unemployed

Pseudonym	Race and sex	Age	Work status
Lwethu	Black woman	24	Retail merchandiser
Lyanda	Black woman	48	Contract cleaner
Manny	Coloured man	48	University administrator
Max	Black man	26	Finance administrator
Mayaya	Black woman	34	Business executive
Mbali	Black woman	28	Finance administrator
Michael	White man	78	Retired architect
Mzwakhe	Black man	29	Government human resources
Naledi	Black woman	21	Unemployed
Noah	White man	21	Undergraduate student
Nobuntu	Black woman	34	Business executive
Nollie	Black woman	32	Help desk assistant
Nontembiso	Black woman	48	Domestic worker
Olivia	Coloured woman	41	Educational non-profit
Palesa	Black woman	22	Finance administrator
Patrice	Black man	60	Teacher
Peter	White man	38	Small business owner
Portia	Black woman	26	Finance administrator
Rebecca	White woman	30	Sales administrator
Ricky	Coloured man	66	Small business owner
Robyn	Coloured woman	33	Administrator
Rose	White woman	36	Part-time lecturer
Sandy	White woman	38	Part-time teacher
Sarah	White woman	37	Teacher
Sibu	Black woman	27	Auxiliary social worker
Sindiswa	Black woman	25	Client services
Sipho	Black man	56	Veteran/Gardener
Siphosethu	Black man	29	Retail floor coordinator
Sizwe	Black man	23	Honours student
Ted	White man	67	Leadership non-profit
Thamsanqa	Black man	32	Masters student
Thomas	White man	23	Recent graduate
Vukani	Black man	34	Finance executive
Welile	Black man	24	Sales representative
Zethu	Black woman	40	Business executive

Appendix 3
10-10-10 restitution dialogues

The following are questions that could be used in implementing a social restitution process. The process revolves around ten people, who are different to each other, meeting together over ten weeks (or a few more), and having ten conversations as set out below. Each heading describes a necessary step in the envisaged process.

Week 1: *Establish a diverse group and have a conversation*

1. Who are we, and why are we here?
2. What are we each going to have to do to make this group work?
3. How will feelings of superiority and inferiority affect our conversation, and what can we do to overcome it in this group?
4. What has been done so far to address the injustices of the past?
5. What do you think will happen to South Africa if nothing more is done about the past?

Week 2: *Discuss how you see South Africa*

1. What are the things in our country that make us despair, and what brings us hope?
2. In the future, what kind of South Africa do we want to be living in?
3. How far away are we from this vision of the future, and why is this so?

Week 3: *Talk about the effects of past injustice on the present*

1. How has each of us been affected by South Africa's past history of injustice?
2. In what ways does the past still affect you today?
3. Why is remembering the past important?

Week 4: *Discuss the meaning of restitution and its potential*

1. What does the term 'restitution' mean to you?

2. How do you respond to the two analogies of a stolen bicycle and an unlevel soccer field that try to describe what has happened in South Africa?

3. What kind of things still need to be done to make restitution for the past?

Week 5: *Discuss the difference between charity and restitution*

1. What is the difference between charity and restitution, and why is this difference important?

2. What examples of restitution could we as a group consider doing?

3. How are these actions different to charity?

Week 6: *Locate all participants in the conversation about injustice*

1. How would you label yourself with regard to the past?

2. How is this exercise helpful or unhelpful, and which labels are easy or difficult to talk about?

3. How should the role of people calling themselves victims, perpetrators, bystanders, resisters and beneficiaries differ in restitution?

4. How should Black and White South Africans' roles in restitution differ?

Week 7: *Discuss ideas for action to restore our damaged humanity*

1. What acts of restitution could we implement in each of the areas of remembering, restoring dignity, offering opportunity, and fostering belonging?

2. What are our practical plans for each of these actions?

3. What happens if we can't agree on what must be done?

Week 8: *Make a plan for implementing and evaluating your ideas*

1. How are we going to implement our plans, and by when?

2. How will we know when we have reached our goals for restitution, in this group, in South Africa?

3. Do we need to take a break in meeting to talk until we have done something concrete in terms of social restitution?

4. When will we next meet?

Week 9: *Discuss attitudes needed for restitution and obstacles that might arise*

1. What attitudes do we need to have, and work on in this group, in order to make progress in restitution?

2. What gets in the way of people making restitution?

3. What lessons are we learning so far when it comes to restitution?

Week 10: *Make plans for an ongoing project*

1. What new stories can we begin to tell about restitution in South Africa?

2. How do we want to continue after this meeting?

Appendix 4
Tables listing selected South African legislation

Table A4.1 *Legislation that entrenched racial discrimination and Apartheid (1856 to 1959)*[1]

1. The Cape Province Masters and Servants Act, No. 15 of 1856, attached criminal liability to breach of employment contracts between unskilled workers (usually Black or Coloured) and White employees in the Cape, and later in all four provinces through subsequent acts.

2. The Natives Land Act, No. 7 of 1913, reserved 93% of all land for White settlers while prohibiting blacks from owning or renting land outside of reserves (7%).

3. The Natives Urban Areas Act, No. 21 of 1923, restricted Black people to certain types of jobs and areas.

4. The Population Registration Act, No. 30 of 1950, grouped people into one of four categories (whose descriptions and labels changed over time): 'White', 'Black', 'Coloured', and 'Indian/Asian'.

5. The Prohibition of Mixed Marriages Act, No. 55 of 1949, and the Immorality Act, No. 21 of 1950 (an expanded version of the 1923 act) prohibited sexual intercourse and marriage between people of all different races.

6. The Group Areas Act, No. 41 of 1950, limited various race groups to particular areas, including removing people from White areas by force and corralling Black people into 'Homelands' or self-governing 'Bantustans' from which they could migrate for work with a *dompas* (Bantu Authorities Act, No. 68 of 1951; Promotion of Bantu Self-Government Act, No. 46 of 1959; Natives Coordination of Documents Act, No. 67 of 1952, respectively).

7. The Suppression of Communism Act, No. 44 of 1950, denied Black people the right to mobilise politically.

8. The Separate Representation of Voters Act, No. 46 of 1951 (amended 1956) had the effect of removing Coloured people off the common voter's roll in the Cape.

9. The Native Labour Act, No. 49 of 1953, effectively reserved certain jobs for Whites only.

10. The Bantu Education Act, No. 47 of 1953, wrote into law the mandate of 'education for servitude' for Black children.

11. The Reservation of Separate Amenities Act, No. 49 of 1953, declared parks, buses, beaches, benches, toilets to be reserved for particular race groups.

---

[1] Truth and Reconciliation Commission (1999a) *Truth and Reconciliation Commission of South Africa Report* (Vol. 1). London: Macmillan, pp. 450–477.

12. Prohibition of Interdicts Act, No. 64 of 1956, denied people the right to appeal against forced removals or participate in labour action.

13. The Extension of University Education Act, No. 34 of 1959, excluded Black people from White universities and created separate universities for various race groups.

Table A4.2 *Selected legislation enacted in South Africa after 1994 to make restitution for Apartheid*

Land redistribution
1. Restitution of Land Rights Act (Act No. 22 of 1994)
2. Provision of Land and Assistance Act (Act No. 67 of 1995)
3. The Development Facilitation Act (Act No. 67 of 1995)
4. Interim Protection of Informal Land Rights Act (Act No. 31 of 1996)
5. Land Reform (Labour Tenants) Act (Act No. 3 of 1996)
6. Communal Property Associations Act (Act No. 28 of 1996)
7. The Land Reform (Labour Tenants) Act (Act No. 3 of 1996)
8. Extension of Security of Tenure Act (Act No. 62 of 1997)
9. Transformation of Certain Rural Areas Act (Act No. 94 of 1998)
10. The Communal Land Rights Act (Act No. 11 of 2004)

Economic opportunities
1. Employment Equity Act (Act No. 55 of 1998)
2. Preferential Procurement Policy Framework Act (Act No. 5 of 2000)
3. Broad-based Black Economic Empowerment Act (Act No. 53 of 2003)

Reconciliation and reparations
1. Promotion of Reconciliation and National Unity Act (Act No. 34 of 1995)
2. Promotion of Equality and Prevention of Unfair Discrimination Act (Act No. 4 of 2000)

Acknowledgements

I have discovered, once again, that one never writes a book alone. I am grateful for the many inspiring companions along the road. Each conversation, comment and cup of coffee provoked, stimulated, deepened and enriched my thinking, and shaped this final product. So a thousand thank yous are due, from a grateful fellow traveller.

To Antjie Krog, not only for writing the foreword, but whose book *Country of My Skull* irrevocably changed my consciousness in 2003, in the month I embarked on my doctoral studies, and whose forthright (and beautifully crafted) words have remained formative ever since. Father Desmond, for being an exemplar of moral courage, humility and good humour, even though I only rarely manage the 7.15am service on a Friday morning at St George's Cathedral in Cape Town.

To colleagues at the University of Cape Town: David Cooper, Francis Nyamnjoh, Viviene Taylor and Xolela Mangcu, for stirring conversations and quiet support. Temba Masilela, Chris Desmond (the economist who helped me calculate the cost of Apartheid for Haley), Benita Moolman and Ben Roberts, at the Human Sciences Research Council, and former colleagues Vasu Reddy and Arvin Bhana for great debates and ongoing encouragement. Enormous thanks to Hlonipha Mokoena at Wits for a close and critical read that went beyond the call of duty and that was invaluable. I am also immensely grateful to the HSRC for the six-month sabbatical that allowed me to get the bulk of the work done for this book and to the Oppenheimer Memorial Trust for their generous funding for my sabbatical and ongoing investment in my work over many years. While on sabbatical, I spent time at the Harvard FXB Centre for Health and Human Rights as a visiting fellow, and am grateful to Jaqueline Bhabha, Jennifer Leaning, Magda Matache and Arlan Fuller, and to Sarah Dryden-Peterson and Helen Haste at the Harvard Graduate School of Education. For the invitations to speak at Princeton, thank you Nicole Basta, and to Dean Borgman at Gordon Conwell Seminary. Each conversation enriched and deepened my thinking. At the University of Cambridge, where I am a visiting fellow in the Faculty of Education and in the

Department of Politics and International Studies, thanks to Madeleine Arnot and Shailaja Fennel.

My research assistants, students and graduate students: Duncan Scott, for the endless hours we spent finding, reading and crafting everything written on restitution and in earnest discussion on the couches and coffee shops of the world; Emma Arogundade, PhD student extraordinaire, I hope I haven't lifted too many of your ideas – thanks for the book title, and for reading, absorbing, critiquing, questioning and challenging my ideas and writing; Nabig Chaudhry, at Harvard, for theoretical notes, help with data analysis and literature searches – glad I could get you hooked on research; Jessica Breakey at UCT, for interviews and long chats about ally-ship and White privilege; Alison Mellon, for applying your legal mind to restitution legislation all over the world, and for summarising it so well for me; Siya Dlokweni: for great interviews conducted on upturned paint tins and for pursuing success against great odds – I'm immensely proud; Babalwa Nyangeni: for conducting interviews in the deep rural Eastern Cape and in the financial institutions of Cape Town – thank you for allowing me to access two diverse and important groups of opinions; Parusha Naidoo and Marlyn Faure: you were both just the gifts I needed to get this book in shape with your smoothing, checking, fixing, shortening; Colleen Blanckenberg, my veteran transcriber: what a marathon and once again impeccably done, along with humorous interludes and hard South African discussions along the way. I have loved learning from you all, *sine qua non*!

My indefatigable colleague and friend Deon Snyman at the Restitution Foundation, where I have the privilege of serving as chair of the board, along with fellow board members – our monthly board meetings have served as a singular inspiration in turning academic thinking into practical reality. My colleagues at the Association for Moral Education and the Trustees of the Journal of Moral Education Trust, for helping me develop my academic career over the past ten years. Thank you for your time, friendship and deep interest, especially to Monica Taylor, Helen Haste, Larry Blum, Jim Conroy, Susannah Frisancho, Neil Ferguson and Angela Bermudez. To Louise Bethlehem from the Hebrew University of Jerusalem who alerted me to the two German words *wiederherstellen and wiedergutmachung* for restitution which marked a conceptual turning point for me at a crucial moment in writing this book.

My friends who cajoled, listened, proof-read, visited, talked, hugged, and generally cheer-led: Caroline Powell, Heidi and Darroch Faught, Rene August, Alison and Gareth Mellon, Robyn Tyler, Annie Ross, Adam Cooper, Richard and Mandy Edwards, Mark and Sam van Deventer, Linda Martindale, Craig Stewart, Ron Begbie, Anthea Klopper, and the inestimable Brian Edwards.

To Jeremy Wightman, Joshua Vernon, Mthunzi Nxawe and Charlotte Imani at the HSRC Press, another great publishing journey, effortlessly done. And of course, to each research participant, who bared their souls on a hard topic and who told truths that have long gone unsaid: thank you for every tear of hope, anger, pain and shame. We are a step closer I think, to another country in our lifetime. God guide us in our efforts.

Sharlene Swartz
Cape Town, Freedom Day 2016

About the author

Sharlene Swartz is a Research Director at the Human Sciences Research Council in South Africa and an Associate Professor of Sociology at the University of Cape Town. She is also a visiting Fellow at Harvard University and at the University of Cambridge, from which institutions she holds Masters and Doctoral degrees respectively. Her undergraduate degrees were obtained from the University of the Witwatersrand and from the University of Zululand in South Africa. Sharlene's expertise and current research centres on social justice for youth in adverse contexts, interpersonal and communal notions of restitution, people-centred national development, the effects of race on educational outcomes, and emancipatory qualitative research methods. Before embarking on graduate studies, Sharlene spent 12 years at a youth NGO where she pioneered life skills and anti-racist programmes for schools. She is the current chair of the Restitution Foundation. Sharlene has published widely in academic journals and has authored or edited numerous books including *Ikasi: The Moral Ecology of South Africa's Township Youth* (2009); *Teenage Tata: Voices of Young Fathers in South Africa* (2009); *Old Enough to Know* (2012); *Moral Education in Sub-Saharan Africa* (2010) and *Youth Citizenship and the Politics of Belonging* (2013).

Select Bibliography

Adichie, CN (2009) The danger of a single story. *TED Talks*. Accessed 10 July 2015, https://www.ted.com/talks/chimamanda_adichie_the_danger_of_a_single_story?language=en

Arendt, H (1963) *Eichmann in Jerusalem: A report on the banality of evil*. New York, NY: Viking Press

Badenhorst, P, Pienaar, J, & Mostert, H (2006) *Silberberg and Schoeman's: The law of property* (5th edition). Durban, South Africa: LexisNexis Butterworths

Baines, G (2014) *South Africa's 'Border war': Contested narratives and conflicting memories*. London, UK: Bloomsbury

Baines, G, & Vale, P (2008) *Beyond the border war: New perspectives on Southern Africa's late-Cold war conflicts*. Pretoria, South Africa: Unisa Press

Ballard, R, Habib, A, & Valodia, I (2006) *Voices of protest: Social movements in post-apartheid South Africa*. Pietermaritzburg, South Africa: University of KwaZulu Natal Press

Barkan, E (2000a) *The guilt of nations: Restitution and negotiating historical injustices*. London, UK: Johns Hopkins University Press

Barkan, E (2000b) *Restitution and amending historical injustices in international morality*. Claremont, CA: European Union Center of California

Barkan, E, & Karn, A (2006) *Taking wrongs seriously: Apologies and reconciliation*. Stanford, CA: Stanford University Press

Bar-On, D (2001) The bystander in relation to the victim and the perpetrator: Today and during the holocaust. *Social Justice Research* 14(2): 125–148

Batley, K (2007) *A secret burden: Memories of the border war by South African soldiers who fought in it*. Johannesburg, South Africa: Jonathan Ball

Bekerman, Z & Zembylas, M (2010) Fearful symmetry: Palestinian and Jewish teachers confront contested narratives in integrated bilingual education. *Teaching and Teacher Education* 26(3): 507–515

Berger, P & Luckmann, T (1966) *The social construction of reality: A treatise in the sociology of knowledge*. Garden City, NY: Doubleday

Bhana, A, Swartz, S, Taylor, S, Scott, D, Dlamini, N & Vawda, M (2011) Education and skills development. In B Magongo & M Motimele (eds) *South African youth context: The young generation*. Midrand, South Africa: National Youth Development Agency

Biko, H (2013) *The great African society: A plan for a nation gone astray.* Johannesburg, South Africa: Jonathan Ball

Biko, S (1977) *Black consciousness and the quest for a true humanity.* London, UK: The Christian Institute Trustees

Biko, S, & Stubbs, A (1978) *I write what I like.* London, UK: Bowerdean Press

Birks, P (1985) *An introduction to the law of restitution.* Oxford, UK: Clarendon Press.

Blasi, A (1980) Bridging moral cognition and moral action: A critical review of the literature. *Psychological Bulletin,* 88(1): 1–45

Blasi, A (1999) Emotions and moral motivation. *Journal for the Theory of Social Behaviour* 29(1): 1–9

Bohler-Muller, N (2012) Apartheid victims group scores symbolic victory against multinationals. *HSRC Review* 10(3): 22–23

Bond, P & Dor, G (2002) *Unsustainable South Africa: Environment, development and social protest.* Pietermaritzburg, South Africa: University of KwaZulu-Natal Press

Booth, W (1999) Communities of memory: On identity, memory, and debt. *American Political Science Review* 93(2): 249–263

Boraine, A (2014) *What's gone wrong? On the brink of a failed state.* Johannesburg, South Africa: Jonathan Ball

Bourdieu, P (1997) The forms of capital. In A Halsey, H Lauder, P Brown & A Stuart Wells (eds) *Education: Culture, economy, and society.* Oxford, UK: Oxford University Press

Bourdieu, P & Wacquant, LJD (1992) *An invitation to reflexive sociology.* Chicago, IL: University of Chicago Press

Braithwaite, J (1999) Restorative justice: Assessing optimistic and pessimistic accounts. *Crime and Justice* 25: 1–127

Brooks, T (2008) A two-tiered reparations theory: A reply to Wenar. *Journal of Social Philosophy* 39(4): 666–669. doi: 10.1111/j.1467-9833.2008.00449.x

Buckley-Zistel, S (2009) Transitional justice in divided societies – potentials and limits. Paper presented at the 5th European Consortium for Political Research General Conference, Potsdam Universität, Germany

Butt, D (2006) Nations, overlapping generations, and historic injustice. *American Philosophical Quarterly* 43(4): 357–367

Butt, D (2009) *Rectifying international injustice: Principles of compensation and restitution between nations.* Oxford, UK: Oxford University Press

Butt, D (2012) Repairing historical wrongs and the end of empire. *Social & Legal Studies* 21(2): 227–242. doi: 10.1177/0964663911435932

Calder, T (2010) Shared responsibility, global structural injustice, and restitution. *Social Theory & Practice* 36(2): 263–290

Carey-Miller, D & Pope, A (2000) South African land reform. *Journal of African Law* 44(2): 167–194

Centre on Housing Rights and Evictions (2005) *The Pinheiro principles: United Nations principles on housing and property restitution for refugees and displaced persons.*

Chapman, G (1992) *The five love languages.* Chicago, IL: Northfield Publishers

Davis, D & Steyn, M (2012) Teaching social justice: Reframing some common pedagogical assumptions. *Perspectives in Education* 30(4): 29–38

Dlamini, J (2014) *Askari: A story of collaboration and betrayal in the anti-apartheid struggle.* Johannesburg, South Africa: Jacana Media

Dlanga, K (2012, 10 June) Why blacks still raise apartheid, Opinion, *Sunday Independent.* Accessed http://goo.gl/eUMTsC

Doyle, S & Wright, D (2001) Restitutionary damages – the unnecessary remedy? *Melbourne University Law Review, 25*(1). Accessed 14 April 2015 http://www.austlii. edu.au/au/journals/MelbULawRw/2001/1.html

Du Preez, M (2013) *A rumour of spring: South Africa after 20 years of democracy.* Cape Town, South Africa: Random House Struik

Du Toit, A (2005) Experiments with truth and justice in South Africa: Stockenström, Gandhi and the TRC. *Journal of Southern African Studies* 31(2): 419–448

Eglash, A (1958) Creative restitution: A broader meaning for an old term. *Journal of Criminal Law, Criminology & Police Science* 48(6): 619–622

Eglash, A (1977) Beyond restitution – Creative restitution. In J Hudson & B Galaway (eds) *Restitution in criminal justice: A critical assessment of sanctions.* Lexington, MA: Lexington Books

Encarnación, O (2007) Pinochet's revenge: Spain revisits its Civil War. *World Policy Journal* 24(4): 39–50

Essed, P (1991) *Understanding everyday racism: An interdisciplinary theory.* Newbury Park, CA: Sage

Fanon, F (1963) *The wretched of the earth.* New York, NY: Grove Press

Fay, D & James, D (eds) (2009) *The rights and wrongs of land restitution: 'Restoring what was ours'.* Abingdon, UK: Routledge

Feinstein, A (2011) *Battle scarred: Hidden costs of the border war.* Cape Town, South Africa: Tafelberg

Ferguson, J (2015) *Give a man a fish: Reflections on the new politics of distribution.* Durham, NC: Duke University Press

Ferguson, N, Burgess, M, & Hollywood, I (2010) Who are the victims? Victimhood experiences in postagreement Northern Ireland. *Political Psychology* 31(6): 857–886

Fields, B (2003) Restitution and restorative justice in juvenile justice and school discipline. *Youth Studies Australia* 22(4): 44–51

Fraser, N (1998) Social justice in the age of identity politics: Redistribution, recognition, participation. *Social Science Research Center Berlin* (WZB Discussion Paper FS I, pp. 98–108). Accessed 7 June 2011, http://ideas.repec.org/p/zbw/wzboem/fsi98108.html

Fraser, N & Honneth, A (2003) *Redistribution or recognition? A political-philosophical exchange.* London, UK: Verso

Freire, P (1972) *Pedagogy of the oppressed.* Harmondsworth, UK: Penguin

Freire, P (2005) *Education for critical consciousness.* London, UK: Continuum

Friedman, S & Erasmus, Z (2004) Counting on 'race': What the surveys say (and do not say). In A Habib & K Bentley (eds) *Racial redress and citizenship.* Cape Town, South Africa: HSRC Press

Geldenhuys, J (2009) *At the front: A general's account of South Africa's border war.* Jeppestown, South Africa: Jonathan Ball

Gobodo-Madikizela, P (2003) *A human being died that night: A story of forgiveness.* Claremont, South Africa: David Philip

Gobodo-Madikizela, P (2014) *Dare we hope? Facing our past to find a new future.* Cape Town, South Africa: Tafelberg

Government Communication and Information Services (2005) *South Africa Yearbook 2005/6.* Pretoria, South Africa: Government Printer

Gqola, PD (2008) Brutal inheritances: Echoes, Negrophobia and masculinist violence. In S Hassim, T Kupe & E Worby (eds) *Go home or die here: Violence, xenophobia and the reinvention of difference in South Africa.* Johannesburg, South Africa: Wits University Press

Gregory, D & Pred, AR (2007) *Violent geographies: Fear, terror, and political violence.* London, UK: Taylor and Francis

Gyekye, K (1984) The Akan concept of a person. In R Wright (ed.) *African philosophy: An introduction.* Lanham, MD: University Press of America

Gyekye, K (1997) *Tradition and modernity: Philosophical reflections on the African experience.* Oxford, UK: Oxford University Press

Habermas, J (1971) *Knowledge and human interests.* Boston, MA: Beacon Press

Habermas, J (1990) *Moral consciousness and communicative action.* Cambridge, MA: MIT Press

Habib, A (2013) *South Africa's suspended revolution: Hopes and prospects.* Johannesburg, South Africa: Wits University Press

Hall, S (2001) The spectacle of the other. In M Wetherell, S Taylor & S Yates (eds) *Discourse theory and practice: A reader.* London, UK: Sage

Hans, J & Stjernstrom, O (2008) Emotional links to forest ownership: Restitution of land and use of a productive resource in Põlva County, Estonia. *Fennia,* 186(2): 95–111

Hilberg, R (1992) *Perpetrators victims bystanders: The Jewish catastrophe, 1933–1945.* New York, NY: Aaron Asher Books

Hill, RA (2002) Compensatory justice: Over time and between groups. *Journal of Political Philosophy* 10(4): 392–415

Iliffe, J (2005) *Honour in African history.* Cambridge, UK: Cambridge University Press

International Law Commission (2001) *Articles on Responsibility of states for internationally wrongful acts*

Jansen, A (2015) *Eugene de Kock: Assassin for the state.* Cape Town, South Africa: Tafelberg

Jong-wook, L (2005) Public health is a social issue. *The Lancet,* 365(9464): 1005–1006

Judt, T (2005) *Postwar: A history of Europe since 1945.* New York, NY: Penguin

Kawachi, I & Kennedy, B (1997) Socioeconomic determinants of health: Health and social cohesion: why care about income inequality? *BMJ,* 314(7086): 1037–1040

King, ML (1968) *Remaining awake through a great revolution.* Accessed 3 August 2015, https://kinginstitute.stanford.edu/king-papers/publications/knock-midnight-inspiration-great-sermons-reverend-martin-luther-king-jr-10

Krog, A (1998) *Country of my skull: Guilt, sorrow, and the limits of forgiveness in the new South Africa.* Johannesburg, South Africa: Random House

Ladson-Billings, G (1998) Just what is critical race theory and what's it doing in a nice field like education? *International Journal of Qualitative Studies in Education* 11(1): 7–24. doi: 10.1080/095183998236863

Langley, W (2007) Fanon: Violence and the search for human dignity. *Human Architecture: Journal of the Sociology of Self-Knowledge* 5(3): 1–3

Lapsley, M, & Karakashian, S (2012) *Redeeming the past: My journey from freedom fighter to healer*. Cape Town, South Africa: Struik Inspirational

Latané, B & Darley, JM (1970) *The unresponsive bystander: Why doesn't he help?* New York, NY: Appleton-Century Crofts

Lerner, M (1975) The justice motive in social behavior: Introduction. *Journal of Social Issues* 31(3): 1–19. doi: 10.1111/j.1540-4560.1975.tb00995.x

Lynch, K (1999) Equality studies, the academy and the role of research in emancipatory social change. *The Economic and Social Review,* 30(1): 41–69

MacIntyre, A (1981) *After virtue: A study in moral theory*. London, UK: Duckworth

Mangcu, X (2014a) *Arrogance of power: Twenty years of disenchantment*. Cape Town, South Africa: Tafelberg

Mangcu, X (2014b) The contemporary relevance of Black consciousness in South Africa: From Black consciousness to consciousness of blackness. In D Pillay, GM Khadiagala, P Naidoo & R Southall (eds) *New South African Review* Johannesburg, South Africa: Wits University Press

Marais, H (2011) *South Africa pushed to the limit*. Cape Town, South Africa: University of Cape Town Press

Marmot, M (2005) Social determinants of health inequalities. *The Lancet* 365(9464): 1099–1104

Marmot, M (2007) Achieving health equity: from root causes to fair outcomes. *The Lancet* 370(9593): 1153–1163. doi: 10.1016/S0140-6736(07)61385-3

Marmot, M, Friel, S, Bell, R, Houweling, T, & Taylor, S (2008). Closing the gap in a generation: health equity through action on the social determinants of health. *The Lancet* 372(9650): 1661–1669

Marmot, M, Ryff, C, Bumpass, L, Shipley, M, & Marks, N (1997) Social inequalities in health: Next questions and converging evidence. *Social Science & Medicine* 44(6): 901–910. doi: http://dx.doi.org/10.1016/S0277-9536(96)00194-3

Matthews, S (2010) Differing interpretations of reconciliation in South Africa: A discussion of the home for all campaign. *Transformation: Critical Perspectives on Southern Africa* 74(1): 1–22

Mbeki, M (2009) *Architects of poverty: Why African capitalism needs changing*. Johannesburg, South Africa: Picador Africa

McIntosh, P (1992) White privilege and male privilege: A personal account of coming to see correspondences through work in Women's studies. In ML Andersen & P Hill Collins (eds) *Race, class and gender: An anthology*. Belmont, CA: Wadsworth Publishing Company

McNamee, S (1988) Accepting research as social intervention: Implications of a systemic epistemology. *Communication Quarterly, 36*(1): 50–68

Merkel, W (2009) Towards a renewed concept of social justice. In O Cramme & P Diamond (eds) *Social justice in the Global Age.* Cambridge, UK: Cambridge University Press

Metz, T, & Gaie, J (2010). The African ethic of ubuntu/botho: Implications for research on morality. *Journal of Moral Education* 39(3): 273–290

Minow, M (1998) *Between vengeance and forgiveness: Facing history after genocide and mass violence.* Boston, MA: Beacon Press

Minow, M (2000) The hope for healing: What can truth commissions do? In RI Rotberg & D Thompson (eds) *Truth v. justice: The morality of truth commissions.* Princeton, NJ: Princeton University Press

Molefe, O (2012) *Black anger and white obliviousness.* Johannesburg: South Africa: Parktown Publishers

Moon, C (2009) Healing past violence: Traumatic assumptions and therapeutic interventions in war and reconciliation. *Journal of Human Rights* 8(1): 71–91. doi: 10.1080/14754830902717726

Morelli, P & Spencer, M (2000) Use and support of multicultural and antiracist education: Research-informed interdisciplinary social work practice. *Social work* 45(2): 166–175

Mullis, I, Martin, M, Foy, P, & Arora, A (2012a) *TIMMS 2011 International results in mathematics.* Chestnut Hill, MA: TIMSS & PIRLS International Study Center, Boston College

Mullis, I, Martin, M, Foy, P, & Drucker, K (2012b) *TIMMS 2011 International results in reading.* Chestnut Hill, MA: TIMSS & PIRLS International Study Center, Boston College

Murali, V & Oyebode, F (2004) Poverty, social inequality and mental health. *Advances in Psychiatric Treatment,* 10(3): 216–224

Niemonen, J (2007) Antiracist education in theory and practice: A critical assessment. *The American Sociologist* 38(2): 159–177

Nyamnjoh, F (2004) Reconciling 'the rhetoric of rights' with competing notions of personhood and agency in Botswana. In H Englund & F Nyamnjoh (eds) *Rights and the politics of recognition in Africa.* London, UK: Zed Books

Parliament of the Republic of South Africa (1996) *The Constitution of the Republic of South Africa.* Pretoria, South Africa: Parliament

Pierre, M, Mahalik, J & Woodland, M (2002) The effects of racism, African self-consciousness and psychological functioning on black masculinity: A historical and social adaptation framework. *Journal of African American Men* 6(2): 19–40

Presidency of the Republic of South Africa (2014) Twenty year South African review, 1994–2014. Pretoria, South Africa: The Presidency of the Republic of South Africa.

Puttergill, C, Bomela, N, Grobbelaar, J, & Moguerane, K (2011) The limits of land restitution: Livelihoods in three rural communities in South Africa. *Development Southern Africa* 28(5): 597–611. doi: 10.1080/0376835x.2011.623921

Ramphele, M (2009) *Laying ghosts to rest: Dilemmas of the transformation in South Africa.* Cape Town, South Africa: Tafelberg

Restitution Foundation (2010) *Restitution toolkit.* Cape Town, South Africa: Restitution Foundation

Reynolds, P (2012) *War in Worcester: Youth and the Apartheid state.* Bronx, NY: Fordham University Press

Roberts, B (2010) Fear factor: Perceptions of safety in South Africa. In B Roberts, M Kivilu & D Davids (eds) *South African social attitudes second report: Reflections on the age of hope.* Cape Town, South Africa: HSRC Press

Roberts, B (2013) Your place or mine? Beliefs about inequality and redress preferences in South Africa. *Social Indicators Research* 118(3): 1167–1190. doi: 10.1007/s11205-013-0458-9

Rosen, M (2012) *Dignity: Its history and meaning.* Cambridge, MA: Harvard University Press

Sanders, M (2007) *Ambiguities of witnessing: Law and literature in the time of a truth commission.* Stanford, CA: Stanford University Press

Schneider, P, Griffith, W, & Schneider, A (1982) Juvenile restitution as a sole sanction or condition of probation: An empirical analysis. *Journal of Research in Crime & Delinquency* 19(1): 47–65

Shonkoff, J, Garner, A, Siegel, B, Dobbins, M, Earls, M, McGuinn, L, et al. (2012) The lifelong effects of early childhood adversity and toxic stress. *Pediatrics* 129(1): 232–246

Smith, C (2010) *What is a person? Rethinking humanity, social life, and the moral good from the person up.* Chicago, IL: University of Chicago Press

Sooka, Y (2000) *South Africa's human spirit: An oral memoir of the truth and reconciliation commission – We should not forget.* Accessed 3 August 2015, http://www.sabc.co.za/SABC/SABCtruth/yasmin.htm

South African Department of Justice (1996) *Truth and reconciliation commission Day 2 – 23 April 1996 – Case No: CT/00100 Christopher Piet (son)* Accessed 3 August 2015, http://www.justice.gov.za/trc/hrvtrans%5Cheide/ct00100.htm

Southern Africa Labour Development Unit (2011) *National income dynamics study*. Cape Town, South Africa: University of Cape Town

Spaull, N (2013) *South Africa's education crisis: The quality of education in South Africa 1994-2011.* Johannesburg, South Africa: Centre for Development and Enterprise

Statistics South Africa (2012) *Census 2011 Statistical release – P0301.4.* Pretoria: Stats SA

Statistics South Africa (2013) *Quarterly labour force survey – Quarter 1. Pretoria:* Stats SA. Accessed 4 January 2014, https://www.statssa.gov.za/publications/P0211/P02111stQuarter2013.pdf

Staub, E (1989) *The roots of evil: The origins of genocide and other group violence.* Cambridge, UK: Cambridge University Press

Staub, E (1996) Activating bystanders, helping victims, and the creation of caring. *Peace and Conflict: Journal of Peace Psychology* 2(3): pp. 189–200. doi: 10.1207/s15327949pac0203_1

Straker, G (2011) Beneficiaries for evermore: Reply to commentaries. *Psychoanalytic Dialogues* 21(6): 670–675. doi: 10.1080/10481885.2011.629564

Swartz, S (2009) *Ikasi: The moral ecology of South Africa's township youth.* Johannesburg, South Africa: Wits University Press

Swartz, S, Arogundade, E, & Davis, D (2014) Unpacking (white) privilege in a South African university classroom: A neglected element in multicultural educational contexts. *Journal of Moral Education* 43(3): 345–361

Swartz, S, Harding, JH, & De Lannoy, A (2012) Ikasi style and the quiet violence of dreams: A critique of youth belonging in post-Apartheid South Africa. *Comparative Education* 48(1): 27–40. doi: 10.1080/03050068.2011.637761

Szymanski, D & Stewart, D (2010) Racism and sexism as correlates of African American women's psychological distress. *Sex Roles* 63(3): 226–238. doi: 10.1007/s11199-010-9788-0

Tangney, J & Dearing, R (2003) *Shame and guilt.* New York, NY: Guilford Press

Taylor, E (1998) A primer on critical race theory. *The Journal of Blacks in Higher Education* 19: 122–124. doi: 10.2307/2998940

Teitel, R (2007) Transitional justice genealogy. *Harvard Human Rights Journal* 16: 69–94

Terreblanche, S (2002) *A history of inequality in South Africa, 1652-2002.* Pietermaritzburg, South Africa: University of Kwazulu-Natal Press

Therborn, G (2013) *The killing fields of inequality*. Cambridge, UK: Polity

Transparency International (2015) Corruption perceptions index 2015. Accessed 15 April 2016, http://www.transparency.org/cpi2015

Trede, F, Higgs, J & Rothwell, R (2009) Critical transformative dialogues: A research method beyond the fusions of horizons. *FQS Forum: Qualitative Social Research* 10(1), Article 6 (online)

Truth and Reconciliation Commission (1999a) *Truth and reconciliation commission of South Africa report* (Vol. 1). London, UK: Macmillan

Truth and Reconciliation Commission (1999b) *Truth and reconciliation commission of South Africa report* (Vol. 5). London, UK: Macmillan

Truth and Reconciliation Commission (2003) *Truth and reconciliation commission of South Africa report* (Vol. 6). Accessed 22 June, 2007, http://www.info.gov.za/otherdocs/2003/trc/

Tutu, D (1999) *No future without forgiveness*. London, UK: Rider

United Nations Development Programme (2015) Human development report. Accessed 14 April, 2016, http://hdr.undp.org/hdr2006/report.cfm

United Nations (1948) *Universal declaration of human rights*. New York, NY: United Nations

Van Vuuren, H (2006) *Apartheid grand corruption: Assessing the scale of crimes of profit from 1976 to 1994*. Cape Town, South Africa: Institute for Security Studies

Wale, K (2013) *Confronting exclusion: Time for radical reconciliation South Africa reconciliation barometer survey: 2013*. Cape Town, South Africa: Institute for Justice and Reconciliation

Walker, C (2005) The limits to land reform: Rethinking 'the land question'. *Journal of Southern African Studies* 31(4): 805–824. doi: 10.1080/03057070500370597

Walker, M (2010) Truth telling as reparations. *Metaphilosophy* 41(4): 525–545. doi: 10.1111/j.1467-9973.2010.01650.x

Weber, M (2002) *The Protestant ethic and the spirit of capitalism: and other writings*. Johannesburg, South Africa: Penguin

Wenar, L (2006) Reparations for the future. *Journal of Social Philosophy* 37(3): 396–405. doi: 10.1111/j.1467-9833.2006.00344.x

Wickham, S, Taylor, P, Shevlin, M & Bentall, R (2014) The impact of social deprivation on paranoia, hallucinations, mania and depression: The role of discrimination, social support, stress and trust. *PLoS ONE* 9(8): e105140. doi: 10.1371/journal.pone.0105140

Williams, D, Neighbors, H & Jackson, J (2003) Racial/ethnic discrimination and health: Findings from community studies. *American Journal of Public Health* 93(2): 200–208. doi: 10.2105/AJPH.93.2.200

Williams, RC (2005) Post-conflict property restitution and refugee return in Bosnia and Herzegovina: Implications for international standard-setting and practice. *New York University Journal of Law and Politics 37*: 441–995

Williams, TM (2009). *Black pain: It just looks like we're not hurting.* New York, NY: Simon and Schuster

World Health Organization (2001) *Mental health: New understanding,new hope.* Geneva, Switzerland: World Health Organization

Young, IM (2003) From guilt to solidarity. *Dissent* 50(2): 39–44

Young, IM (2004) Responsibility and global labor justice. *Journal of Political Philosophy* 12(4): 365–388. doi: 10.1111/j.1467-9760.2004.00205.x

Young, IM (2006) Responsibility and global justice: A social connection model. *Social Philosophy and Policy,* 23(1): 102–130. doi: doi:10.1017/S0265052506060043

Zembylas, M & Bekerman, Z (2008) Education and the dangerous memories of historical trauma: Narratives of pain, narratives of hope. *Curriculum Inquiry* 38(2): 125–154

Index

This subject index is arranged alphabetically in word-by-word order. Figures, tables and illustrations are expressed in italics.